Recent Research in Psychology

Social Change and Personality

Essays in Honor of Nevitt Sanford

Edited by Mervin B. Freedman

Springer-Verlag
Berlin Heidelberg New York London Paris Tokyo

Editor

Mervin B. Freedman
866 Spruce Street
Berkeley, California 94707, USA

ISBN 3-540-96485-1 Springer-Verlag Berlin Heidelberg New York
ISBN 0-387-96485-1 Springer-Verlag New York Berlin Heidelberg

Printed in Germany

Printing and binding: Druckhaus Beltz, Hemsbach/Bergstr.
2817/3140-543210

To Nevitt Sanford this book is dedicated by students and colleagues for whom he has been an inspiration by virtue of his unique ability to grasp the essence of a social problem, to see research issues in the widest theoretical perspective, and to explicate the human relevance of scientific, intellectual, and academic concerns.

Table of Contents

Preface

Nevitt Sanford's career in psychology has spanned the years from the 1930's to the present. The canon of his works is vast--eight books and some 200 chapters, monographs, and articles. The contributions to this book, by students and colleagues, remind us of the great variety and significance of the concerns and interests he has addressed--development over the course of a human life, education (with emphasis upon higher education), personality theory, and political psychology (incorporating the concept of social action).

Arriving upon the scene in psychology when he did, one of Nevitt Sanford's first publications, *Physique, Personality, and Scholarship* (1943), reflected the interest of that time in biology and physiology (a concern of psychology which declined for some time thereafter, to be revived in the 1960's). It was also, however, the decade after psychoanalysis and Marxist ideology had made their dramatic entrance upon the stage of American intellectual life, and these two schools of thought, in many ways contradictory, have profoundly influenced him ever since. Nevitt has never lost his fascination with the power of infancy and childhood to affect development, and with the workings of the unconscious. See his article, "Individual and Social Change in a Community under Pressure: The Oath Controversy" (1953), in which he explicated the manner in which shared unconscious defenses in individuals contributed to a political and organizational crisis. To be sure, he has not reflected the influence of class and economic analysis as dogma, which comes down over the senses like a butterfly net. Rather, he has been ever aware of the significance of political, economic, and social power, culture, language, role, and status in determining the behavior and characteristics of individuals, organizations, and societies.

F. Scott Fitzgerald (1945) wrote that the test of a first-rate intelligence is the ability to hold two opposed ideas in the mind at the same time, and still retain the ability to function. Nevitt Sanford has maintained self and society, internal urges and external constraints and shaping, in a perilous but functional equipoise. In the discipline of psychology, marked as it is today by increasing and often dysfunctional specialization, this capacity to entertain paradox, to forestall premature closing of the boundaries of a system, warrants both close attention and emulation.

One may spend much time explicating the specifics of the contributions Nevitt has made to the psychological sciences. He is in the tradition of the British school of philosophy founded by Jeremy Bentham, known to us as utilitarianism, with its anti-elitist stance, its emphasis on the power of education, and its concern for universal human rights. Bertrand Russell said of it: "As a movement devoted to reform, utilitarianism has certainly achieved more than all the idealist philossphies put together, and it has done this without much fuss "(1959, p. 265). So it is that Nevitt views communities, agencies, institutions, organizations primarily from the perspective of their contribution to the development of their constituent individuals. The fulfilled individual is his measure. For him, for example, the gross national product is not the sole index of national progress; rather, such an index should be based in considerable part on enhancement of the skills, knowledge, and capacities of the people who contribute to economic growth.

Also deeply influenced by John Dewey, who imposed upon the scholar the obligation to put knowledge to work in the solution of social problems, it follows that the Society for the Psychological Study of Social Issues and the International Society of Political Psychology have been dear to Nevitt's heart.

As all who have come to know him cannot fail to be aware, Thomas Jefferson and Sigmund Freud occupy the places of honor in Nevitt Sanford's pantheon of heroes. In many ways, he is a child of The Enlightenment, committed to an Apollonian vision, a world of form and functional structure in which reason, intellect, cognition are to serve to fashion a more just society. His thinking and his work also have been permeated, however, with the cognizance that the Age of Reason produced the Marquis de Sade. Irony, conflict,tragedy perforce are part of his weltanschauung. Bridging the mind and the heart is an Herculean task, but Nevitt has not despaired over the duality and pessimism contained in the psychoanalytic vision. The questions and problems really worth addressing have no easy answers or solutions, and sometime no answers or solutions at all, but it has been a fundamental tenet of Nevitt's professional life to shed what light he could, and to extend a measure of human sympathy along the way.

Through his teaching and his writing Nevitt Sanford has helped many to see more clearly. This festschrift is an occasion to honor him as a scholar, a teacher, an always generous disseminator of the word he shaped so assiduously for so many years. "Proper words in proper places, make the true definition of a style," wrote Jonathan Swift in 1720. And those who have known Nevitt are wont to conjure up images he conveyed to them, social and psychological concerns marked by his signature. Passionate pursuit of the intellectual life needs witnesses. Dr. Nevitt Sanford has been a witness.

REFERENCES

Fitzgerald, F.S. *The Crack-Up*. New York: New Directions, 1975.

Russell, B. *Wisdom of the West*. Garden City, New York: Doubleday, 1959.

Sanford, R.N. "Physique, Personality, and Scholarship." Monographs of *the Society for Research in Child Development*, 1943, *8*, No. 1, whole issue.

Sanford, N. "Individual and Social Change in a Community under Pressure: The Oath Controversy." *Journal of Social Issues*, 1953, *9*, 25-42.

Mervin B. Freedman
Berkeley, 1985

Introduction

Mervin B. Freedman

The essays in this book written by colleagues and former students of Nevitt Sanford are more than encomiums designed to honor him. Because they offer valuable information about and insight into human and social existence in the vein of the spirit and character of this work, they are of interest to social and behavioral scientists. But they are of interest as well to readers who have but little technical background in such fields, for they make human and social life more vivid. The vagaries of sexuality, the professor in the classroom, the foreboding and fear of death, nuclear war and disarmament, anti-Semitism and the American character, the lives of highly educated women are among the topics addressed.

Formally the authors represent the disciplines of psychology, sociology, philosophy, political science, literature, and the humanities. Their thinking unfolds, however, in ways that are truly interdisciplinary and underlying the concept of an interdisciplinary approach are a host of significant considerations. Nevitt Sanford has been ever alert to the limitations of the view from one discipline alone; he has known that to ask a question such as, "What can psychology contribute to an understanding of the nuclear arms race?," is to open the door to a circumscribed vision. The issues involved in nuclear disarmament, for example, are economic, political, psychological, sociological, technological, military, to cite but some, as Christian Bay's chapter, "Hazards of Goliath in the Nuclear Age," explicates.

One is struck by the proliferation in the social and behavioral sciences of books and researches that focus on pushing narrow domains of knowledge ever farther out. Underlying such activity is an implicit assumption that in time such accretions of information will eventuate in a systematic or integrated body of knowledge. That this rarely happens, however, is overlooked. Consider the many, many thousands of researches in psychology devoted to human learning. As Nevitt Sanford has pointed out (1962), if a faculty member in a college or university were to inquire as to which of these researches might be of help to him, the answer would be that except for a relatively small body of research concerned with attitude change none would be relevant to his teaching concerns. Joseph Axelrod's chapter, "The Anatomy of a Paradigm Shift," well illustrates the enormous distance between a sophisticated and complex approach to classroom teaching and most laboratory representations of human learning.

An interdisciplinary approach to issues in the social and behavioral sciences raises the questions as to how and when to define parameters or limits to the system under investigation. The answer for Nevitt Sanford, and hardly a simple answer, begins with the selection of a human or social problem, a problem-centered approach to the generation of human knowledge. The question, which then becomes, "What do I need to know in order to understand this problem?," does not stand alone, but is tied closely to another: "How may I utilize this knowledge or understanding to meliorate this problem?" In the tradition of Henri Bergson, John Dewey, and Giambattista Vico, knowing involves not only perceiving but also doing or making. Bergson emphasizes action in contrast to the application of a static and rigid rationalist approach to scientific inquiry. (Sanford, however, although attuned to Bergson's pragmatism, rejects his more irrational and romantic dispositions.) For John Dewey the role of the scholar should be to put knowledge to work in the solution of social problems. For Vico human beings can best understand what they themselves fabricate. The utilization of knowledge is not only desirable for practical reasons; it is also an avenue for producing more sophisticated knowledge.

Perforce, these issues take one into the realms of values, goals, feelings, and emotions. Much of psychology operates still on the Enlightenment basis that the physical universe is external to observers and is not influenced by their presence. After the fashion of Isaac Newton, Adam Smith, and John Locke, human beings and society could be studied "in the light of the supposed clock-work regularity and predictability of the physical world" (Goldfein, 1974, p. 85). Vico's instrumentalism, Franz Brantano's intentionality, and Edmund Husserl's phenomenology remind observers that they themselves are part of the very thing they have created. Addressing some of these issues in his essay, "Psychology and Humanism," Brewster Smith supports the humanists in psychology and the behavioral sciences who oppose the forcing of human behavior into predetermined patterns. He suggests, for example, that psychology might best be conceived as comprising two systems, one emphasizing understanding, the other understanging plus prediction and control. In promoting a humanistic psychology, Smith does not, however, desert empiricism and realism. He cautions against the subservience of truth to ideology, the choice of hope or wish over experience, the dissolution of the ego or the observer in the quest for wholeness, the triumph of rhetoric over actuality.

To attend to values, goals, feelings, and emotions is to enter into the world of psychoanalysis, which has influenced Nevitt Sanford since his experiences in graduate school at Harvard University and his participation in the life and work of the Psychology Clinic under the direction of Henry A. Murray. Much is the instruction, guidance, and insight provided by psychoanalysis, and many are the cautionary tales it furnishes as well.

"The Anatomy of a Paradigm Shift" by Joseph Axelrod illustrates the educational equivalent of the phenomenon of countertransference in psychoanalysis. The educator, like the researcher and the therapist, has to be ever on guard to prevent imposing his personal metaphorical reality on the world. So Dr. Axelrod's professor engages in a continuous program of self-scrutiny. He is concerned in particular with how, as historical conditions and the terms of life change, the processes of education in the classroom change. The classroom and the relationships between student and faculty member are different in 1985 from what they were in 1965 or even as relatively recently as 1975.

The very mention of the term, psychoanalysis, carries with it an appreciation of the power of the life of impulses and emotions. Nevitt Sanford's writings are suffused with this awareness, as are the contributions to this book. They represent a contrast to the dominant spirit of contemporary psychology as well as to much of the behavioral sciences in general. To behaviorism, with its vision that experience with the world is somehow encoded in one-to-one fashion in the brain, psychoanalysis is, of course, antithetical; and it is antithetical to structuralism as well, with its neglect, if not rejection, of the emotions. The situation of the cognitive emphasis, with its active perceiver, which probably dominates psychology today, is more complex. Emotions are not ruled out, but experience and consciousness are viewed primarily from the perspective of the intellect--Rene Descartes' cogitating I. Consider the chapter, "Changed Sexual Behavior and New Definitions of Gender Role on the College Campus," contributed by Joseph Katz. Dr. Katz does not address sexual development or the impulses as experience formally divorced from the intellectual life of the college. Quite the contrary. He urges rather that the desires of the body not be alienated from intellection, that impulse be placed at the service of thinking and reasoning. In many ways such a suggestion turns the world of higher education upside down. Except for some creative fields, as in the arts, learning is conceived of as a matter of the ego or cognition in the service of responsibility, duty, the conscience or superego. Without ignoring or minimizing intellect or cognition, he argues that in the long run the conscience is not to be coerced, that learning that incorporates desire or Eros is the most complete and fulfilling. Unlike some social critics, however, Ronald Laing or Norman O. Brown, for example, Dr. Katz does not redefine reality in the name of Eros.

The title of this tribute, Personality and Social Change, makes it evident that the emphasis is on the interaction between personality and social processes. Mental life or consciousness is not to be replaced by or translated into social reality--after the fashion of much of contemporary social psychology. Consider the words of Eugene Ionesco: "No society has been able to abolish human sadness, no political system can deliver us from the pain of living, from our fear of death, our thirst for the absolute; it is the human condition that directs the social condition, not vice versa" (1964, p. 91). A human being is not a lifeless shadow of culture patterns. On the other hand, social forces are not translated into feelings and behavior. One may believe with Carl Jung (1971; originally published, 1933) or Charlotte Bühler (1935) that a drive to higher development is inherent in the human psyche. One must also appreciate, however, that there is an historical, cultural, and social side to human destiny--and a biological side as well. So it is that in "Personality Development in Highly Educated Women in the Years Eighteen to Forty-Five," Emily Serkin illustrates the fact of biological necessity that can impinge upon the existential freedom of women--that is, the biological time clock, which dictates that as middle age approaches, the prospects for child bearing diminish. Edwin Shneidman in "Dying, Denying, and Willing the Obligatory" imposes upon the reader an unblinkered look at a tragic truth--the mortal destiny of man. In Mervin Freedman's "American Anti-Semitism Now," past, present, and future reverberate in the person and in the social system. Anti-Semitism waxes and wanes as human character changes, and human character is very much a function of time, and place, and the vagaries of history. So it is that American character differs in 1985 as compared to 1940. German character in 1985 differs from 1933, because of historical, cultural, and social events. Catastrophic social change--for example, the depressions and inflation of the 1920's or the turbulent political climate of the Weimar Republic--is not a prominent feature of the German Federal Republic.

Nevitt Sanford has long propounded that the best way to understand a human phenomenon is to study one or several individuals in depth. When researchers believe that on this basis they really understand the phenomenon under study, this is the time for systematic or quantitative verification. In the absence of such studies emphasizing the complexity of human and social experience, the mythography of the exact sciences can take its toll, resulting in too simple a view of the phantasmagoria of life. Highly refined theories and operations may bring into relief the processes under consideration, but they may obscure other behavior and experience. Vladimir Nabokov wrote, "Caress the details, the divine details." Various of the studies in this book, of educated women, of college presidents, of the professor in the classroom, of the process of a woman coming to grips with her impending death, for example, have the immediacy of authentic life. They are valuable in their own right, and they provide insights that may serve as a scaffold for systematic theory.

The chapters by David Riesman, "The Personal Side of the Presidency," and by Joseph Katz, "Changed Sexual Behavior and New Definitions of Gender Roles on the Campus," address the situation of the college or university and its constituents, students, faculty, administrators. When The American College, edited by Nevitt Sanford, appeared in 1962, this monumental work, to which thirty social and behavioral scientists contributed, represented a unique venture for scholars in these fields. Rare indeed is it for psychologists and other researchers in the psychological sciences to turn their attention to issues in education, particularly in higher education. They may study factories, families, the workings of public bureaucracies and agencies, or stone age tribes in New Guinea, but seldom the very community and institution in which much of their life is embedded. It may be too close to home. These chapters remind us of a considerable unknown, an institutional unconsciousness, that of the workings of colleges and universities.

As the chief architect of The Authoritarian Personality (Adorno and others, 1950) Nevitt Sanford helped to establish a new paradigm in the psychological and behavioral sciences, that of research on a consequential social issue (in that case authoritarianism and prejudice) utilizing empirical, quantitative techniques. The chapters in Personality and Social Change concerned with anti-Semitism and with sexual behavior and gender roles among college students further this tradition. Information from interviews and observation is integrated with results of scores on tests and scales and with survey research findings.

It can be said of great artists and social critics--Fyodor Dostoievski, Leo Tolstoi, Marcel Proust, Sigmund Freud, for example--that they read the mind of an age. Something much more modest, of course, applies to the contents of this book, but nonetheless, some of the most significant issues of our times are addressed: among them the educational mission of the university; the situation of students, faculty, and administration; sexual development in young people; the estate of educated women; dying in an age in which faith is not transcendent. Perhaps the most pressing concerns are the subjects of "American Anti-Semitism Now" and "Hazards of Goliath in the Nuclear Age." For here the stakes are high--

the survival of humankind. Germany, Russia, and Cambodia in this century remind us that the state has become the greatest killer in history, and that nuclear warfare has the potential for making such past events insignificant by comparison.

If there is a message in this volume, it is a commitment to the power of self-knowledge and personal responsibility as exemplified by Brewster Smith's contribution, "Psychology and Humanism." Moral exhortation is a poor substitute for awareness based on sound empirical research and critical analysis. Normative science, on the other hand, cannot serve as the ultimate source of values. Someone once described his own work as a tour of perplexities and unfortunately not as a guide to the perplexed. One may challenge the sphinx and kill the stranger at the crossroads only to find that the enemy is within. One must struggle with society and with the self as well, in the spirit of the poets, novelists, and dramatists, and contrary to Jean Jacques Rousseau's vision. One cannot resort to history or romantic trust in some mystical instumentality to do what only people can do acting through politics. Awareness of this hard fact, however, is no excuse for tumbrel resignation and lassitude of the heart. "Things may be hopeless but not serious," as Europeans who have long lived on the fringes of disaster are wont to say. An enlightened and pragmatic approach to resolving human and social problems is our best hope for surviving in a world worth living in, and the authors of this book, who have contributed their work to honor Nevitt Sanford, a pioneer on this path, hope that they have furthered this end.

REFERENCES

Bühler, C. "The Curve of Life as Studied in Biographies." Journal of Applied Psychology, 1935, 19, 405-409.

Goldfein, A. "The End?" Commentary, 1974, 57, 84-85.

Ionesco, E."The London Controversy." Notes and Counternotes. New York: Grove, 1964.

Jung, C. "The Stages of Life." In J. Campbell (Ed.), The Portable Jung. New York: Viking, 1971 (originally published, 1933).

Sanford, N. "Higher Education as a Social Problem." The American College. New York: Wiley, 1962.

Joseph Axelrod

Joseph Axelrod is professor of humanities and comparative literature at San Francisco State University and the director of liberal arts at the Academy of Art in San Francisco. He has served on commissions and steering committees for the American Council on Education, the American Association for Higher Education, and the Modern Language Association and is the author of three MLA reports and two ACE publications; he also for a time served as Associate Editor of the AAHE yearbook. He is the author of The University Teacher As Artist and has co-authored writings in higher education with Mervin Freedman, Paul Heist, Joseph Katz, and Nevitt Sanford.

Christian Bay

Christian Bay is a professor of political science at the University of Toronto. He earned his degree in law (1943) and his Ph.D. in political science (1959) at the University of Oslo in Oslo, Norway. He has taught in the University of Oslo, Michigan State University, University of California in Berkeley, Stanford University, and the University of Alberta, where he also served as Chair of the Department of Political Science. His books include The Structure of Freedom (1958, 1970) and Strategies of Political Emancipation (1981).

Mervin B. Freedman

Mervin B. Freedman is Professor of Psychology at San Francisco State University. He received a B.S. degree from the City College of New York in 1940 and a Ph.D. in psychology from the University of California in 1950. He has held teaching, research, and administrative positions at the University of California, Berkeley, the University of California, San Francisco, Vassar College, and Stanford Universities, and has been a Fulbright Research Fellow at the University of Oslo and a fellow at the Center for Advanced Study in the Behavioral Sciences. His reaserch and writing have been centered on studies of higher education and in recent years on political psychology, studies of racial, ethnic, and religious relationships in the United States in particular.

Joseph Katz

Joseph Katz is Professor of Human Development and Director of Research for Human Development and Educational Policy at the State University of New York at Stony Brook. He has engaged in many studies of the intellectual and emotional development of undergraduate and graduate students, including extensive studies of the changing relations between male and female undergraduates. His association with Nevitt Sanford began at Vassar College in 1952.

David Riesman

David Riesman is Henry Ford II Professor of the Social Sciences, Emeritus, at Harvard University. He received the B.A. degree (1931) from Harvard University, and the J.D. (1934) from Harvard Law School. With Nathan Glazer and Reuel Denny, he is the author of *The Lonely Crowd* (1950) and *Faces in the Crowd* (1952). Additional works include *Constraint and Variety in American Education* (1956) (with Evelyn Thompson Riesman), *Conversations in Japan* (1967) (with Gerald Grant), *The Perpetual Dream: Reform and Experiment in the American College* (1978), and *On Higher Education* (1980). Three of Mr. Riesman's books on higher education have been given the Award of the American Council on Education; in 1980, he received the Award of Merit for Contributions to sociology of the Eastern Sociological Society; in 1983, the Distinguished Contributions to Teaching Award of the American Sociological Association.

Emily Serkin

Emily Serkin is an administrative assistant at The Jewish Community Federation in San Francisco. She received her B.A. degree (1970) from Radcliffe College in social relations and her Ph.D. (1980) from The Wright Institute Graduate School in social-clinical psychology. Before joining the staff of the Jewish Community Federation she worked as an editorial assistant at Jossey-Bass Inc., Publishers.

Edwin Shneidman

Edwin Shneidman, Ph.D., is Professor of Thanatology and Director of the Laboratory for the Study of Life-Threatening Behavior at UCLA. He was co-director and co-founder of the Los Angeles Suicide Prevention Center and was the charter chief of the Center for the Study of Suicide Prevention at the National Institute of Mental Health in Bethesda. He has been a Visiting Professor at Harvard and at the Ben Gurion University of the Negev (in Beersheva); Clinical Associate at the Massachusetts General Hospital and at the Karolinska Hospital (in Stockholm); and a Fellow at the Center for Advanced Study in the Behavioral Sciences (Stanford). He has been president of two divisions (Clinical and Public Service) of the American Psychological Association (and has won their Distinguished Awards) and was Founder-President of the American Association of Suicidology. He has edited or co-edited twelve books. He is author of *Deaths of Man* (nominated for the 1973 National Book Award in Science), *Voices of Death* (1980) and *Definition of Suicide* (1985), as well as over 150 articles and chapters on suicide and death in various publications, including the *Encyclopaedia Britannica*, *Comprehensive Textbook of Psychiatry*, and the *Encyclopaedia of Psychology*. He is an active member of the Melville Society and has published on Melville and Moby Dick.

M. Brewster Smith

M. Brewster Smith has been professor of psychology at the University of California at Santa Cruz since 1970. Previously he has taught and administered at Chicago, Berkeley, New York University, Vassar, and Harvard, where he received his Ph.D. in 1947. He is past president of the American Psychological Association (1978) and of three of its divisions: the Society for the Psychological Study of Social Issues (1958-59), Theoretical and Philosophical Psychology (1983-84), and Humanistic Psychology (1984-85). In 1985-86, he was president of the Western Psychological Association. In 1986 he received SPSSI's Kurt Lewin Memorial Award for bringing scientific psychology to bear upon important social issues.

Many, many thanks are due Mrs. Harriet Renaud for her editorial contributions to this volume. Dr. Joseph Katz helped the editor in various ways, and Dr. Martin Levine contributed useful criticisms for several of the chapters. Mrs. Clarisse Severy did all the typing, exercising great care, patience, and skill.

The Anatomy of a Paradigm Shift: Toward a theory of learning, With exhibits from the Humanities and other disciplines

Joseph Axelrod

The year is 1980. Ricky Smith, a freshman at Lone Mountain College, is sitting in his humanities class--one of his general education courses--listening to a lecture about the Holocaust. He hears about the six million Jews, and the many others as well, who had met their deaths during the Hitler years in Germany. "How could such a horrible thing have happened?," the lecturer asks. "What were its causes? Was it a particular combination of causes or was there one significant underlying cause?" Then, after a pause, he says, "Well, let's look first at some important historical facts."

Ricky settles back in his seat, prepared to half-listen. It isn't that he's inattentive or disrespectful. Quite the contrary. It's simply that he knows that there *was* one significant underlying cause and he knows *exactly* what it was.

He knows that God created the Jewish people in the first place so that His Son might be born among them. That was their mission, their entire function on earth. Once that function had been fulfilled, it was God's plan that the Jewish people should go out of existence. But by insisting on survival, they had violated God's plan. What is the price such a stiff-necked people must pay? Nineteen-hundred years of suffering, climaxed by the Holocaust of the Twentieth Century--with more of the same to come. Why is the professor going on and on when the picture is so clear? As he walks out of the lecture hall at the end of the class hour, Ricky tells himself that the *real* explanation is as simple as it is profound.

The year is 1984. His four years at college have changed Ricky profoundly. The belief system that he had held when he entered college is now an antique piece of intellectual baggage that he still recognizes as having been his own at that time; but it is now a foreign object to him. A great paradigm shift (or rather, in the terms used later in this paper, a great metaparadigm shift) has taken place.

How did this shift occur? What sorts of complex learning experiences did Ricky Smith undergo during the years from 1980 to 1984 that caused such a radical transformation in his entire belief system? And what role did his college teachers play in bringing about that transformation?

The Starting Point

I cannot resonstruct in detail what happened in Ricky Smith's case, though I will presently report more about his development during the college years. As concerns the general process of paradigm shift, however, I believe I now do understand what happened. I have recently come to understand better some of the mysteries of this complex process because I myself have, during recent years, gone through such a "shift" about the nature of learning itself--a paradigm shift that has resulted in a new theory of learning and the implications of this theory for the job a college teacher faces.

If experiences of this sort can be said to have a beginning date, my own adventure began sometime in 1979 when Nevitt Sanford and I were editing the new edition of _College and Character_ (1980). We had received a manuscript from Wilbert McKeachie, consisting of his rewritten chapter for the book. As I read the manuscript, I came across a passage that, on the surface, sounded innocuous enough--even perhaps obvious. But as I looked into it more deeply, it set my mind whirling.

The passage consisted of a single sentence: "The teacher can be effective in helping students learn only if he or she first makes the effort to learn from the students the structures through which they perceive the problems the teacher places before them (1980, p.212)." I should perhaps explain that at that particular time--or shortly before--a group of faculty colleagues team-teaching in NEXA, the Humanities-Science Convergence Program at San Francisco State University (Gregory, 1979, 1980), had systematically examined Thomas Kuhn's essay on the structure of scientific revolutions (1962, 1970), and I had been introduced to the concepts Kuhn labeled "paradigms" and "paradigm shifts." (Readers who need definitions of these terms should, at this point, quickly read through "Exhibit B," the last section of this paper.) Already these words had taken on a broader meaning than Kuhn had originally intended and had entered the general vocabulary of academic and intellectual discussions. As a consequence, those concepts were at the center of my thoughts as I reflected about that passage in the McKeachie chapter.

A second faculty forum, as it happened, took place shortly afterwards--this time with colleagues in the Humanities Department--at which we discussed curriculum changes in our general education Humanities courses. At that faculty forum, I posed a theory about the relationship between (a) certain curricular reforms in general education courses and

(b) certain views about the nature of learning. As a result, our group was led to focus on the paradigm shifts that have occurred among American Humanities professors during the last half century or so, as curricula for general education courses were being developed in the humanities. Those discussions with my Humanities Department colleagues constituted an important stage in my adventure, and readers will find some conclusions about that segment of the history of American higher education formulated as "Exhibit A."

Then events took a new turn. While I continued discussions of the nature of teaching and learning with colleagues, I also brought up the same subject in a discussion with a group of bright and articulate students. I was working at the time on a research project that included as subjects four able and cooperative students just completing their freshman year at two Bay Area campuses. They were describing in some depth the nature of the learning experience they were then undergoing in their courses. They had, all four of them, done their secondary school education at high schools they considered excellent. The picture they gave of their freshman-year experience in college showed me that in the case of these particular students, and many others like them, the assumptions college professors seem most frequently to hold about the high-school-to-college-transition happen to be invalid.

These students felt strongly about what they called "a discrepancy" between their last semester in high school and their first semester in college. A word of explanation is needed here to convey adequately both the content and the force of their reaction. It is commonly assumed by college faculty members that when high school students enter the university, they meet a new set of intellectual challenges that are far more rigorous than those they encountered in high school; and, therefore, in order to survive the freshman year in college, students must greatly enlarge their repertoire of learning responses. If growth occurs--at the level of either intellectual development or of the nonintellective aspects of personality--then there must take place, to state the point in Chickering's language (1980), recurrent cycles of challenge and response, differentiation and integration, disequilibrium and equilibrium.

No researcher in the field fundamentally disagrees with that conception of "growth" (though it is true that not everyone might like Chickering's specific language). The basis on which this now commonly accepted view of "growth" rests was built through a remarkable series of research findings in the 1950's and 1960's that described in some detail the changes that take place during the college years. This body of research began with the projects, done in the 1950's and earlier, reported in <u>The American College</u> (Sanford, 1962), and culminated a decade or so later with such studies as those by Freedman (1967), Trent and Medsker (1968), and Feldman and Newcomb (1969). That significant changes did take place as a result of the college experience, there was no doubt; the evidence was clear. What, however, was not clear from the data was the cause-and-effect relationship. How much of that growth in students resulted from their interaction with professors and how much from other experiences accompanying college courses?

In the case of Ricky Smith, the experiences that affected his belief system (and eventually brought about a transformation in it) were so varied, so numerous, and so subtle as to defy classification or analysis. It happened gradually. There was no sudden "realization;" there was only minimal "conflict." Ricky would be the first to admit that his professors had had a great influence, but he also stated that he strongly felt the influences of myriad contacts with other students and with co-workers at his various jobs. For Ricky, the college years were years of great change. He insisted doggedly on exploring his own spiritual beliefs and those of others, and he was active in various facets of institutionalized religion; and during this process, he found himself moving from conservative religious beliefs, with an emphasis on theological questions, toward more liberal religious views, with an emphasis on ethics and social action. As for faculty influence, he said he could not determine whether indeed it was pivotal in his development; but (he told us) he rather thought it was.

Whatever the answer might be for Ricky (or for the four college freshman), the rank and file of the professoriate believe that faculty activity is the central "cause" of learning among college students--that as a result of work done under the guidance of professors, student learning strategies increase markedly in scope and depth, as students move from high school and work their way through the college experience. For my four freshman students, however, nothing could have been further from the truth--judging, at least, by their experience in the first year of college study.

First of all, this experience convinced them that the range of learning strategies they had acquired by the time they completed their high school education--and the subtlety with which these responses were being applied to learning situations--was much wider than their college instructors believed them to be. Second, those responses were, as a consequence (they claimed), not being fully utilized in their freshman-year courses. Third, the students voiced a fear that they felt increasingly as the freshman year moved to its close. Translated into technical language, what they feared was that their repertoire of learning responses would probably become smaller, with less flexibility and subtlety, than it had been at the time of their high school graduation--unless, of course, they were to engage in more "challenging" learning than they were experiencing in their courses. They did not, apparently, feel that in their experiences on campus outside of their courses, they were being challenged in any unusual way. It is interesting to note that in the case of Ricky Smith, on the contrary, serious challenges were already taking place during his freshman year, initiated both in his courses and in activities not related to his courses.

A brief commentary on the word "challenge" is necessary. I am using the word here in a strictly technical sense, even though the students and I, during our discussions, articulated these same notions entirely in lay language. In the technical meaning of the term, a situation "challenges" learners _only_ when their repertoire of responses is not capable of coping with the situation satisfactorily and new responses must be sought. Although Ricky and the other students used no such technical language, it was clear to me even from their roundabout and imprecise lay language that we were talking about the same processes.

Surface Levels and Deeper Levels of Learning

At a certain point in my thinking, then, four influences came together: my study of the McKeachie chapter in _College and Character_, the faculty seminars in NEXA (the Humanities-Science Convergence Program), the faculty forum discussions with my humanities colleagues, and the intensive work I did with my four college freshmen. And this combination of events forced upon me a re-examination of the nature of learning. Suddenly, one day, I was able to articulate the following slowly growing realizations:

- that in every teaching-learning transaction there are, without exception, _many_ interlocking levels of learning activity;
- that it is possible, almost immediately, to analyze out _four_ levels of such activity; and
- that we can be virtually certain there are many more levels, perhaps dozens or hundreds.

Of course the reader will understand that as these insights took shape, I also realized that words like "levels" and phrases like "numbers of levels," which I found myself using, are simply metaphoric ways of expressing the concept. It is quite obvious that there are no levels or layers here and that all the crisscrossings and connections are not literally crisscrossings and connections. Such imagery is in fact deceptive; but metaphor is the only pathway open to us if we want to formulate these insights.

Of the four "levels" (I shall not use quotation marks henceforth) that became obvious to me, the first is clearly visible at the surface of things; three others, too, are there, at successively deeper strata. All of them, I realized, are always involved in every learning experience. That was my new (and startling) insight. Learners acquire "knowledge"--that is, learn or mislearn something--not only at the particular level on which they or their mentors are consciously focussing but also at all the other levels as well.

I became convinced that these four or more levels of learning response are stimulated simultaneously in every learning transaction, and it is the interrelationship among these levels of activity that gives each learning experience its peculiar nature. It is this interrelationship that determines, in effect (I wrote in my notes at the time), what is learned, how much learning takes place, and how that learning occurs.

The first level of learning activity. On Level One, the learning level closest to the surface, the student masters (more or less adequately) the subject-matter content of a course. The emphasis, in this context, is on the word content. This is significant for a reason that will emerge directly; for there are two major dimensions to a given subject-matter, its content and its form. The first of these is the crucial dimension at Level One; the second is the crucial dimension at Level Two. As we have already implied, the elements that enter the student's learning activity at Level One are relatively visible to an observer and quite explicit for the instructor. Students are motivated to acquire facts and principles, concepts, theoretical frameworks, and the like, and also to master certain tools and perform certain skills. All of these, taken together, constitute the "content" of the course. It falls into what, many years ago, Bloom (1956) and his coworkers called the cognitive domain of knowledge. Relevant theories and paradigms (for example, the theory of evolution in a general education biology course) must be--it goes without saying--part of the "content" of certain courses, and these intellectual structures must be taught (and, hopefully, acquired) at the first level of learning activity.

The second level of learning activity. Level Two lies much less close to the surface. It is a two-layered entity of extreme complexity. I will describe first the layer most immediately related to Level One. While the first level of learning deals with subject-matter content, on Level Two the student learns the intellectual structures by means of which the content of the course (including its paradigms) is perceived by the teacher. I label these intellectual structure "metaparadigms;" they supply the framework that provides the principles of selection for seeing new "relevant" paradigms and other cognitive items that, as the learning process moves forward, become significant at Level One.

And it is that same conceptual framework, of course, which governs the selection and organization of the entire subject matter of the course. As the first level of learning focuses on subject-matter content, the second level of learning focuses on subject-matter _form_. That is, while the material being transmitted on the first level consists of facts, principles, theoretical frameworks, and the like, it is the intellectual structures found at Level Two which ultimately give "sense" to those facts, principles, theories, and so forth; it is those structures which serve to connect all the discrete data and explanations of those data that students gather together as they master the course material at Level One. And while the activity at the first level is relatively visible (and certainly explicit for the instructor and student), only at rare moments do the metaparadigms that exist on the second level of the teaching-learning process become explicit, _qua_ paradigms, during the process of instruction.

Only rarely are those concepts or intellectual frameworks discussed _per se_. Often, however, many instructors find themselves facing clear evidence to show that some (or many) of their students are looking at the subject-matter through a different (and from the faculty members' point of view, incorrect) framework. Until these learners can look at the material through the "correct" framework, their instructors may be aware that something is amiss but may not be able to identify what it is. Clues are given, of course, when distortions and omissions begin to characterize their students' knowledge of the subject-matter. When this happens, conscientious professors may make attempts to transmit the "correct" way of organizing the subject-matter content; but not many faculty members are sufficiently self-aware, as teachers and learners, to realize the nature of this task. Hence most of the teaching that goes on at Level Two is not self-conscious. And, as we shall see, in any case, even the most self-aware professor cannot teach a metaparadigm _per se_. The way teachers communicate metaparadigms--that is, the subject-matter _forms_--is by the very way they teach the subject-matter _content_ of the course.

The most significant observation to be made about Level Two is that teaching can truly be said to take place successfully at that level only when a metaparadigm _change_ is internalized for the student. A paradigm--and this observation applies to the simplest as well as the most complex (including also metaparadigms)--can change in three ways. It can, while retaining its essential nature, become more complex. Or it can change in its nature; and this is when a "paradigm shift" takes place. There are two varieties of paradigm shift. When a particular paradigm or metaparadigm goes through this kind of change gradually, then a whole new set of insights _eventually_ leads the student to replace the old framework with an entirely new one. But it is possible (we are told by those who have undergone mystical and other sudden learning experiences) for a paradigm to shift not gradually but suddenly; in such cases of sudden flashes of illumination, a whole new set of insights instantaneously replaces the old framework with an entirely new one.

In my over thirty years of college teaching, I have never been aware of this last instance of paradigmatic change taking place in a student as a result of activity in one of my classes. But many teachers must be aware of many instances where they have played a key role in the other type of change, the gradual paradigm shift.

Examples of Level Two Learning Activity: _Illustration 1_. In her general education Humanities course, Professor Adams makes elaborate arrangements so that her students may be directly "exposed" to works of art. Professor Adams strongly believes that a certain kind of direct experience with art is indispensible in her course. She has, however, barely formulated her view in any systematic way. She is not, as it happens, very much of a philospher and, while she talks well about specific artworks, in general she mistrusts aesthetic analysis and "talk _about_ art." To Professor Adams, there is no substitute for a group experience with a work of art during which she "points" to details she wants her students to notice, saying to them, "Did you see this?" and "Doesn't this make better sense when you look at it this-and-that way?"

Now suppose certain of her students do not share with Professor Adams her particular in-the-mind structure (or, if you like, read "metaparadigm") about the nature of a "desirable" art experience. We can assume that they are not, in all probability, even aware of the nature of this mismatch. They may well be aware of "difficulties" they are having in this course. They may even, in describing those difficulties to a counselor, ascribe them to "personality differences." But clearly that is not the underlying cause. If the students become aware that their expectations differ from their professor's expectations about the role that contact with artworks should (or could) play in their lives in that particular course, they may suspect that it is not just a "personality difference." But the probability is that students will hardly possess the sophistication to know what is wrong. If Professor Adams, however, knows what is happening, then as the course proceeds, she will help the students understand, and then internalize, the metaparadigm through which she sees the role of art experiences, and to accept it, even if only for the time being, as "correct."

Illustration 2. A certain view of the way language "works"-- one's central concept about the very nature of language--inevitably serves to organize an individual's insights about, and attitude toward, the way students should learn a foreign language. Our colleagues in the field of linguistics tell us that there are radically different views among them about the way languages "work." Moreover, the particular metaparadigm an individual holds will determine how that person (if a teacher) believes one should go about teaching a foreign language, or (if a student) how one should go about learning that language. Here too, a student's learning in a particular foreign language class will be ineffective if the metaparadigms in the foreign language professor's head and in the student's head do not match--especially when, if they do not match, the instructor is unaware of the fact.

The experience may actually become unpleasant for the student (or for both the student and the teacher), if it turns into a kind of struggle between them about the importance of certain kinds of learning tasks --say, the memorization of grammar rules. This "difference in opinion about the homework assignment" may actually arouse resentments and hostilities which will further interfere with learning. But with this observation, we have now crossed the line between Levels Two and Three; and we are discussing some affective aspects of this language-learning illusration. We are therefore already anticipating the activities that reside at Level Three. The experiences in the affective domain take place simultaneously with the acquisition of the metaparadigms of Level Two and the subject-matter content of Level One.

Illustration 3. We move now to a third illustration that shows sharply the complex relationship among facts, principles, paradigms, and metaparadigms. Helen Longino and Ruth Doell point out in a recent article (1983) that in past years, according to theories of human evolution, the turn to hunting by males early in human history is seen as a crucial step in the development of tools and in the evolution of our upright posture. Evidential data for this man-the-hunter paradigm, lying in the environs where hominid remains have been discovered,are the chipped stones which, it is theorized, were used as tools for killing the animals and preparing them for eating. To translate the matter into the language we have introduced in this paper, the data are interpreted in this particular way because they fit so well the paradigm of man-the-hunter and his significance in human evolution.

And why should that paradigm govern the interpretation of the data? Because any scientist whose world is androcentric (and certainly that description covered virtually all scientists until recent years) will be drawn by that very metaparadigm (that is, androcentrism) to the man-the-hunter theory in the first place, since that theory fits so well into the androcentric metaparadigm.

But Longino and Doell point out that an entirely different interpretation arises if the gynecentric framework is the starting point--that is, in the language used here, if it is the gynecentric metaparadigm that supplies the framework by which we "make sense" of the world we are exploring, then it is quite possible that the investigator would come up with another theory: that pregnancy and breast-feeding created a syndrome of needs in women that led them to use organic tools--sticks and reeds--to gather food. This woman-the-gatherer theory (in our language, "paradigm") would clearly fit better into the perspective based on a gynecentric framework.

Longino and Doell believe, it should be said, that eventually a theory will evolve that is not gender-based (their word) at all, one that (in our language) will fit a metaparadigm that is neither andro- nor gynecentric. When such a structure comes into being, a significant metaparadigm shift will have taken place. Clearly, this shift has already begun; it _is_ taking place--but we are witnessing only its very beginning stages.

Here again, as in foreign language examples, there are simultaneous learning activities--often of a highly emotional nature--taking place in the affective domain which lies at Level Three as well as in the paradigmatic domain of Level Two. Exhibit A, dealing with metaparadigm shifts among Humanities professors that have affected the organization of general education Humanities courses, will supply additional examples of Level Two activity, showing the role metaparadigms can play as Humanities courses themselves are conceived and organized.

The second layer of Level Two. We have been discussing what happens at the first layer of Level Two. Let us now turn to the second layer. We are still in the universe of metaparadigms, and a special category of metaparadigms resides at this second layer; these are the conceptual frameworks that professor and student hold about the nature of learning and, especially, about the appropriate roles and the expected behavior of professor and student in the teaching-learning transaction.

Professors communicate to their students the metaparadigms that organize the subject matter of the course (the constructs that lie in the first layer of Level Two) in invisible ways; in the same way exactly do professors communicate the metaparadigms they hold about the roles they themselves intend to play, and the roles they expect their students to play, in the teaching-learning process. Examples of Level Two activity at this second layer will be given presently.

Transmitting the metaparadigms in the classroom or lecture hall. How are the metaparadigms that reside at both layers of the second level transmitted from teacher to student? Teachers communicate these forms by the way they teach the course content. There is no other way to transmit them. These myriad and gigantic frameworks--these intricate and complex structures that illuminate the connections between phenomena--cannot be taught directly, as one teaches a piece of information or a theory. If a metaparadigm is taught directly, through words, and if that is the only way it is learned--through words--it will simply be mouthed back as a string of words, much as a piece of information or a concept is memorized by students not yet ready to "internalize" this knowledge but who can faithfully repeat it on a paper-and-pencil test.

But if metaparadigms cannot be taught directly, how do students "learn" them? How do new metaparadigms come into being? When do metaparadigm shifts take place? Under what conditions? How do these insights come about? Above all, what, precisely, are the interrelationships between the learning activities at Level One (course content) and the learning activities at Level Two (the metaparadigmatic structures) in a student's college experience?

One wishes a detailed record were available showing the steps that led to the transformation in Ricky Smith's mind between the time he entered Lone Mountain as a freshman--and had absolute knowledge of "God's plan" for Jews (and other human beings as well)--and the time, three or four years later, when this view was replaced by an entirely different metaparadigm. It would be especially interesting to know the details of the relationships between the acquisition of course content in his various courses and that metaparadigm shift.

Even though we do not have those data, all of us who work in the classroom setting can confirm the significance of the relationships between learning activities at Level One and Level Two. We know that learning at Level One will be haphazard and chaotic, if it is not accompanied by the learning activity at Level Two that "fits" the requirements of the course content. Knowledge of form and content--as students learn what we teach--proceed apace, each supporting the other in a single, experiential process. But the precise nature of that interaction remains to be discovered. The interaction that must be studied is not a simple one to analyze, however, for two reasons. First, it is a constantly changing, dynamic interaction. Second, the levels we have labeled "Three" and "Four and Beyond" also play their roles as elements in that single process.

The third level of learning activity. At Level Three, we are in the realm of attitudinal knowledge and the other kinds of knowledge in the "affective" domain. Let us start our explanation of it with an explanation. Karla, a first-year college student, tells me in an interview that she had never known what "browsing" in a bookstore or a library was like, until she was required to "do it" for a high school English class and had to be taught how. And now, she says, "I just *love* doing it."

How did Karla learn to "love" such an activity? ("Loving" to browse in a library is, after all, a learned behavior.) What is the relationship between the birth and development of that "love" and other specific elements in Karla's experiences--like her English teacher's behavior in (and out of) the classroom, Karla's experiences at school prior to the time she was "taught" to browse, the environmental factors present in her English class, the course content, the character of the first browsing assignment, and the like?

Learnings in the affective domain are often called "emotional"--even McKeachie uses that term in his *College and Character* chapter--but a word of warning, it seems to me, must be issued by those who use this label. In the affective domain of learning, it is true, there lie certain *non*intellectual processes to which the label "emotional" might well apply--such as the growth of likes and dislikes, interests and enthusiasms, involvements and commitments, guilts and shames. But also present in the affective domain of learning are such *intellectual* habits and attitudes as, for example,"open-mindedness" or "curiosity." Indeed, the center of the whole complex habit we call critical thinking --where curiosity and open-mindedness are among the many components--lies at this third level of learning activity.

The fourth level and beyond. What are factors that are called into play during the years when people learn to perform "behaviors" such as these?

- to act increasingly as autonomous individuals;
- to tolerate ambiguity and complexity in the ever more intricate world that surrounds us; or
- to express their impulses in controlled ways.

A great deal of research has been done, especially since the mid-1950's, on college student change at these deep levels. The data supplied by this body of research, excellently summarized by Knefelkamp (1980), give a surprisingly complete picture of changes that take place during the college years.

Those data, however, do not explain how or why those changes take place; the data do not enable us to determine what *processes* trigger those changes--what factors "cause" those gradual transformations that the Ricky Smiths in our college classrooms undergo. Once we come to understand these processes better, we will be able to achieve greater insight into two complex issues. The first involves the interrelationships and connections between the activities at each of the learning levels we have described here. There is no question, as I have already indicated, that _every_ learning experience involves activity of some kind at _every_ level we have described. Some of the examples we have already given illustrate this point. The second issue is the relationship between behaviors the professor carries on in the classroom and the learning activity of students.

The next section of this paper deals with the second of these issues.

Metaparadigms in the Other Layer of Level Two

Earlier we characterized the transmission of metaparadigms to learners (Level Two) as taking place in two layers. The metaparadigms in one of these layers--the structures through which the facts, principles, and other subject-matter elements are perceived by the teacher--have already been described and exemplified. The other category of metaparadigms that exists on Level Two consists of those that the teacher holds about his or her role in the teaching-learning process. Such metaparadigms govern a professor's behaviors in the class session and determine his or her expectations of the roles that students will play. Even more important, they determine the learning "levels" that the professor believes most germane to a college instructor's function in the classroom.

An investigation I carried on about a dozen years ago at the Center for Research and Development in Higher Education, University of California (Axelrod, 1973), and more recent follow-ups of that project (1980) suggest that the metaparadigms that faculty members hold about teaching "styles" are formed in large part by the relative importance that college professors attribute to each of the three component elements of the teaching-learning process, that is, the subject-matter, the professor, and the student--or, to describe these elements somewhat more accurately (a) the facts, principles, theories, skills, and so forth explicitly covered in the course being taught (b) the teacher as the "model" for students and (c) the learners and their unique needs. Each of these elements has its own requirements and makes its own demands in the teaching process. Typically, we discovered, professors give one of these elements top priority and expect the other two elements to accommodate themselves to its requirements and demands. Differences in priorities that faculty members hold about these elements result in four distinct and "prototypical" teaching styles; these are described in detail in the University of California study and can only be summarized here.

To the faculty member who gives highest priority to the facts, principles, skills,theories, and the like to be covered, neither the needs of the students nor the particular strengths or predilections of the professor are permitted to reshape the course--except in quite minor ways. Professors who hold this paradign of what a class section ought to be like usually view with alarm any suggestion that the content or organization of a course be changed in order to "facilitate" the learning process. When they are induced to change subject matter to accommodate to the special needs of their students, such professors fear they are tampering with academic standards and, in the long run, they believe that they are doing something detrimental to those very students who are being "accommodated." Such professors follow a "principles and facts" prototype (let us call it Metaparadigm A), and it is this structure which governs the way they play their roles in the classroom and the expectations they have of the way students will play theirs.

HYPOTHESIS: PART A. We can expect that professors who follow Metaparadigm A--whether self-consciously or not--would tend to emphasize learnings that reside at Level One; at the same time they would not be aware--not even wish to be aware--of learnings at Levels Three or Four or beyond. Awareness at Activity Level Two would probably depend on their conceptual sophistication and the degree of their awareness of the philosphic foundations of their disciplines.

Metaparadigms B, C, and D are held by those professors who emphasize one of the other two components in the teaching-learning process. They contend that adherence to this principles-and-facts metaparadigm is based largely on academic myth. What, they ask, is so sacred about subject-matter anyway? They hold that the conventional perimeters and standard content of each field of knowledge are determined by historical accident and preserved (generally with only minor revisions and updating) by scholars in good standing with the "establishment"--represented typically by the "wheelers-dealers" at the learned societies and by the publishers of textbooks and the editors of learned journals. Not holding subject-matter coverage sacrosanct, such professors tend to emphasize one of the other two elements of the teaching-learning process--the "human" elements, that is, the teacher or the learner.

The professor who follows Metaparadigm B focusses on the second element in the teaching-learning transaction--the teacher--and believes that the other two elements must be modified to accommodate themselves to the particular strengths of each professor. Those who hold Metaparadigm B argue that if professors are to be pushed into shapes that are not their own, their humanity and individuality will be lost. It is the task of every professor, the argument runs, to function as a _model inquirer_ or--if inquiry is not the activity to be modelled--as a _model master_ at synthesizing the knowledge or at exercising the skills students are expected to acquire.

Not nearly as concerned as their principles-and-facts colleagues with the systematic coverage of subject-matter, professors who hold Metaparadigm B are satisfied to use _samples_ of subject-matter in demonstrating for their students the way experts (namely, they themselves) deal with the problems presented by the material. Students and their needs are crucial in this relationship, and subject-matter, of course, remains important for such professors, but the instructors place themselves at the center of every learning experience they offer their students.

HYPOTHESIS: PART B. Professors who hold Metaparadigm B emphasize what we have been calling Level One of learning activity (though to a lesser extent than those of their colleagues who hold Metaparadigm A); but because of the more personal nature of their teaching roles, they tend also to emphasize aspects of Level Three (the affective domain) as well. Most important, because such professors often reject "established" ways of organizing subject-matter, they are more aware of the metaparadigms that lie at the first layer of Level Two, and the likelihood is that they will teach those frameworks with greater self-consciousness.

Metaparadigms C and D place the student at the center of the teaching-learning transaction. Professors who hold these metaparadigms argue that the teaching process will not be effective if conditions require the element we identify as "learner" to be vastly reshaped before the process can get started. Their view is that if students are expected to accommodate themselves to the elements we identify as "teacher" and as "subject-matter" --if students are to be pushed into a shape that is not their own--the whole educational enterprise is endangered. The students' requirements, the steps needed for _their_ development, are what is crucial. For professors who hold Metaparadigms C and D, a college exists not simply as an institution training students to qualify for "jobs" in the society but primarily to meet its students' educational needs as growing human beings.

It became apparent during our Berkeley investigation that student-centered professors were of two kinds and that the distinction between these was of great significance. Professors who hold Metaparadigm C emphasize student "development" but limit efforts in that direction to _intellectual_ development. The class sections of such faculty members, we found, were typically organized around their desire to help students acquire the cognitive knowledge they need (the facts and principles--to be sure--but, beyond that, the intellectual skills and abilities) and _also_ the intellectual attitudes, in the affective domain, that would enable the cognitive knowledge to come alive. It became clear in our observations of faculty members who hold Metaparadigm C that verbal skills and reasoning played primary roles in their classrooms; they encouraged students to develop ease in a variety of intellectual skills--analytic, rational, "scientific"--and to move freely from formulating problems to analyzing data, testing hypotheses, and drawing up tentative solutions. They emphasized much less than professors holding Metaparadigm A the mere acquisition of facts and principles.

HYPOTHESIS: _PART C_. _Professors who hold Metaparadigm C would emphasize the intellectual skills and abilities that reside at what we have identified as Level One of learning activity; more important, they would be particularly sensitive to intellectual attitudes that reside at Level Three and to related developmental processes at Level Four. In addition, the likelihood is that--given their emphasis on analytic skills--they would be aware of the metaparadigms operating at Level Two and that this awareness would be reflected in their teaching._

Professors who hold Metaparadigm D also focus on the learner, but with a difference. They stand in sharp contrast to their colleagues who hold Metaparadigm C. Those who hold Metaparadigm D treat the student not only as a "mind" but as a total individual whose intellectual, emotional, aesthetic, and other needs are inseparable.

HYPOTHESIS: _PART D_. _Professors holding Metaparadigm D would be especially concerned with changes occurring at what we have identified, in the learning process, as Levels Four and Beyond. But they would be concerned with the cognitive knowledge of Level One, as well, and certainly with the whole range of affective learning at Level Three. Their attention to activities at Level Two, first layer, would depend on their degree of sophistication. But they would clearly be sensitive to learnings at Level Two, second layer._

Summary of the hypotheses: Metaparadigm A is the prototype held by the "principles-and-facts" faculty members--those who have mastered the standard cognitive knowledge in their fields and who teach _what they know_. They watch and supervise carefully the learning activity of their students at what we have identified as Level One.

Professors who hold Metaparadigm B are "instructor-centered." They also emphasize cognitive knowledge but their unique point of view and powerful personality help to organize the material in a special way.

They teach <u>what they are</u>. Like their colleagues who follow metaparadigm A, their emphasis on Level One activity is strong; but they tend to be more self-conscious about the subject-matter metaparadigms that lie in the first layer of Level Two; and, concomitantly, they cater less to the "established" ways of organizing knowledge in their fields. Moreover, because they add a personal element to their teaching, they feel some--or even great--concern (though they may not necessarily externalize that concern) with the encouragement of activity at Level Three.

Of the two student-centered prototypes, Metaparadigm C focusses on the development of intellectual skills. Professors who hold this metaparadigm see their function as training minds. Their concern is with facts and principles only as starting points. They are concerned as well with the metaparadigms that lie in the first layer of Level Two, with the intellectual growth that develops from activity at Level Three, and with related developmental changes in personality at Level Four. They <u>train intellects</u>.

Those who hold Metaparadigm D work with students as "people." They are concerned with cognitive knowledge at Level One, metaparadigmatic patterns in both layers of Level Two, and the affective knowledge--the <u>whole</u> range of it--at Level Three. But above all, their teaching style is influenced (even governed) by their concern with activity that will stimulate growth in their students at Levels Four and beyond. They work with students as <u>whole, growing, changing human beings</u>.

EXHIBIT A: Metaparadigmatic Patterns in General Education Humanities Courses (1920-1980)

In our discussion of Level Two, we spoke of the metaparadigms through which professors organize their materials and structure their courses. Exhibit A presents an extended example of this process, covering the whole sweep of development in the twentieth century of general education courses in the Humanities.

General education "Humanities" courses are generally thought to have begun with John Erskine's courses at Columbia University during the years following World War I. The development of general education humanities courses from that time to the present can be most fruitfully traced, I believe, through four cycles, each roughly fifteen years long. In each cycle--as the reader might expect--a <u>different</u> metaparadigm dominated curriculum development.

<u>The 1920-1935 cycle</u>. In the first of the four cycles, the domi-

nant curricular structure was an historical "survey" of the human race. The course was invariably a kind of history of Western Civilization, with emphasis on the progress of mankind. It began with cave societies and ended with Einsteinian physics, Stravinsky, Pirandello, Picasso, and--above all--with the European and American democracies. This metaparadigm, with its frank and obvious ideology, proved an excellent framework by means of which humanists could tie together in a single course the diverse products and processes of the Western humanities.

The appeal of this kind of historically organized survey course continued long beyond the year this cycle came to a close as a curricular "movement." Indeed, the most noteworthy example of its most recent popular manifestation--some forty years later--is Bronowski's *The Ascent of Man* (1973). Students in a NEXA course at San Francisco State University (our Humanities-Science Convergence Program mentioned earlier), where *The Ascent of Man* is used, have reacted fiercely to its Western, male biases and to its sometimes almost naive optimism, even as those same students have come to recognize and respect the genius of Bronowski. Anyone who analyzes the Brownowski television series or scrutinizes closely the Bronowski text must conclude that the course exhibits a peculiar quality of "datedness." But the content of the course is anything but dated. It is the metaparadigms that have served to organize the course materials and not the substantive content that makes it sound like a course out of the Thirties. For by the mid-Thirties, at the prestigious schools, a new metaparadigm was beginning to replace the older Humanities "survey" course.

The era from 1935 to 1950. The roots of the metaparadigm that was beginning to emerge in the mid-1930's lay in the school of "new criticism" that was just then becoming popular among humanists. The "new criticism" placed the emphasis on study of artworks themselves. In the earlier "historical approach," the artwork was often experienced (usually only in an excerpt) in order to illustrate its period of history; in the newer courses, knowledge of the artwork's historical period was significant mainly because it helped the apprehender understand aspects of the work better; but it was the unique universe of the work that was to be experienced and historical knowledge took on importance (when it did) only as a kind of handmaiden to that deeper goal.

By the end of World War II, innovative general education humanities courses had joined the new movement. And this shift was taking place at many different kinds of campuses. Certainly the most prestigious schools were leading the way--schools as different as Stephens College in Missouri, with its stylish, student-centered image, and the College of the University of Chicago, with its intellectually rigorous program and fiercely analytic and self-conscious methodology. The innovative courses at such schools usually organized themselves around genres, emphasizing the study of original works (and invariably in wholes) both as unique pieces in themselves and as "representative" of their genres. This metaparadigm dominated innovative humanities courses from about 1935 to about 1950, and courses on more traditional campuses followed suit later on.

The third epoch: _1950-1965_. As the 1940's came to an end, a new era in higher education began. The rapid social change of the war period and the early post-war years had brought new pressures to curriculum makers. When these pressures were verbalized and justified, the word _values_ began to make its appearance in titles of humanities courses and of textbooks written for those courses.

Around 1950, the notion became popular in higher education literature that values were at the center of the humanities and that was what differentiated them from the sciences. It so happens that, precisely in 1950, San Francisco State College (as the University was then known) launched its newly designed general education sequence in humanities--a sequence of two courses required of all students. Its title was "A Study of Life Values" and descriptions of it appear in the higher education literature of the 1950's. (see, for example, Axelrod, 1953; Thomas, 1962.)

But by the late Fifties--and certainly by the beginning of the Sixties--those courses had already become dated in a world that was no longer the domain of the genteel tradition. To the social activists among the students and the faculty, such courses seemed almost absurdly academic--especially to the students from Berkeley, Stanford, and San Francisco State in the late Fifties who were washed down the steps of the San Francisco City Hall by policemen wielding fire hoses. (The occasion was a demonstration protesting the appearance of the House Un-American Committee in San Francisco.) And in 1958, the first statement of "student concerns" was delivered to the administration at Berkeley. The 1960's were on their way, but the old metaparadigm remained dominant on most campuses until about the middle of the new decade. At San Francisco State, the title of the required Humanities course was changed from "A Study of Values"--the word "Life" had been dropped some years earlier--to "Masterworks in the Humanities."

The years 1965 to 1980. While the great reforms of the 1960s could also be said to have had a "values" emphasis, the metaparadigm took a different shape. For activist students and faculty members, "relevance" was the criterion by which value was judged, and the word relevance--vague as its meaning might now appear to be--had quite specific meanings in the rhetoric of that period. No one at that time--that is, no one who understood what was happening--asked "Relevant to what?" The 15-year cycle in general education that covered, roughly, the years 1965 to 1980 produced course structures in the humanities that tied together the older material of the humanities with current concerns that were as dramatic as they were powerful : the tragedy of Viet Nam, civil rights and student power, corruption in high places, and the ecosystem of the faltering spaceship Earth.

The new mataparadigm--on the basis of which general education courses in the humanities were structured during the late 1960's on many campuses--responded to those concerns. The courses seemed to work, more or less. But during the last years of the 1970's, those very courses began to serve as a sourse of dissatisfaction and irritation for many faculty members. There was good reason. The times had changed. Suddenly, during the Seventies, there began a nationwide reform movement in general education programs.

The 1980's. The reform movement that started in the late Seventies was part of a groundswell affecting all of education--from kindergarten through graduate school. Its slogan: Back to Basics. The announcements of new, more rigorous degree requirements at Harvard, Berkeley, and Stanford were given enormous attention in the public press. Soon, almost every campus was following their example. By 1980, under the influence of this new conservatism in education, a new cycle also began in the history we are tracing here. What contribution the new era will make to the improvement of a humanistic education remains to be seen.

The metaparadigms into which the back-to-basics movement "fits"--and by which it is justified--vary enormously. For some faculty members at Lone Mountain, the metaparadigm is a kind of sophisticated but traditional medievalism, exciting and energetic. For others, the metaparadigm by which the new movement is justified consists of a rigorous framework of intellectual skills of a high order. But for many individuals the metaparadigm that accommodates the back-to-basics movement so sympathetically is based on a social doctrine antagonistic to the gains made by the "ethnic" populations of America. Unfortunately, in the eyes of many members of the general public, the governing metaparadigm rests on a one-to-one relationship between "real" education and such behaviors as skill in spelling, neatness of handwriting, and proper dinner-table behavior. In general, the Back-to-Basics concept, as it is being applied both inside and outside of the educational establishment, appears to be dated and woefully inadequate in today's world, and one can only hope that it will not persist for too many years as a strong force in American education.

EXHIBIT B: Paradigm and Metaparadigm Defined and Illustrated; and a Final Note about Ricky Smith

When Thomas S. Kuhn wrote his 1962 essay on the structure of scientific revolutions to which we referred earlier, he introduced the word paradigm in a new context, but intended that its meaning remain highly restrictive. He borrowed the word from the field of linguistics; words change shapes in different contexts according to certain patterns that all members of that speech community have "in their heads" (without necessarily being able to formulate that pattern or even being aware that it exists), and the grammarians among them (or from the outside) come forward to describe the paradigms and to identify which sets of words "follow" this or that paradigm. The significant point is that language paradigms are in-the-mind structures which all members of a given speech community share and of which, in the main, they are unaware. Yet those paradigms <u>determine</u> their language behavior. For Kuhn, in a given scientific community, precisely such paradigms determine how scientific problems are conceived, formulated, solved.

In spite of Kuhn's original intention to restrict the use of the term, it took on a host of other, broader meanings. Actually, some of those broader meanings can be found in his 1962 essay. An analysis of the meanings of "paradigm" in the Kuhn essay, done by Mastermann (cited by Kuhn, 1977, p.294) reveals that Kuhn actually used the word in 22 different meanings there. Kuhn himself, though somewhat astonished to learn what he had wrought, later recognized the need for this broadening of meaning for "paradigm," and, 15 years after the original essay appeared, in the preface of a collection of later essays (1977), he wrote: "Proponents of different theories (or different paradigms, in the broader sense of the term) speak different languages--languages expressing different cognitive commitments, suitable for different worlds." (pp. xxii-xxiii)

In its broad meaning, then, a paradigm is an intellectual framework through which we order a segment of our universe, through which we "make sense" of it: of how things are and how, as time passes, they will be or ought to become. Examples of such frameworks:

- the theory of evolution, including its implications about the "creation" of human beings;
- the view of human nature that posits as basic elements superego, ego, and id <u>versus</u> a view that posits mind, body, and soul;
- the model we hold in our heads of our solar system and the relationship of our planet to the rest of the universe;

- the way we picture bacteria "attacking" the body and how we marshal our "defenses" against them;
- the way we see "female" as the antithesis of "male" and vice versa.

The metaparadigm. The context of the present paper requires, for clarity, the introduction of a new term by which an unusually complex paradigm--one that is, in fact, a superstructure of many interrelated, smaller paradigms--can be identified. I arbitrarily use the term "metaparadigm" for such a superstructure.

A paradigm never stands alone, in isolation. Paradigms are always connected to other paradigms in larger entities. And it is these larger entities which I am calling metaparadigms. But the two terms are meant to be relative in their meanings. A given intellectual structure can be identified as a metaparadigm if, in its context, it stands in contrast to a simpler structure. The same paradigm would not, however, be identified as a metaparadigm when, in another context, it stands in contrast to a more complex intellectual structure--of which, in fact, it may be a part.

The distinction, though relative, plays an important role in our illustrations in this paper; and it also correlates to two quite different levels on which paradigms "make sense" of the universe we experience. As we have already seen, they make sense because a given set of observations seems to fit nicely as a "set" within one of these in-the-mind structures; and it, in turn, leads to our observation of other "facts" as members or nonmembers of that set. But on another level, we find that same paradigm fitting in nicely with its neighbor paradigms within one of the superstructures we identify as a metaparadigm. The metaparadigm stands in contrast to an individual paradigm, which, while it has great power, governs only a fairly limited piece of our universe. The following four examples illustrate this principle.

Illustration 1. A common view of human nature "sees" human beings as entities that combine three elements: body, mind, soul. The metaparadigm of which this paradigm is a part would have greater power in that it is more encompassing and permeates daily or even hourly decisions and behaviors taking place in our professional-personal lives. Such a metaparadigm could, for example, constitute one's whole view of health and illness at each of those three levels, physical, mental, spiritual.

Illustration 2. When Professor Zelig sets forth to her class the penalty she will impose on students who turn papers in late, her policy is based on a principle about rewards and punishments. That principle makes sense for her (and hopefully for her students also) within a complex paradigmatic pattern of thought that covers an important facet of college life--and life in general--dealing with justice and injustice. In all likelihood Professor Zelig would be able to formulate that principle for her students if she were called upon to do so, or if she were to find she needs to justify to herself or her classes why she punishes students who turn in late papers. There is, of course, a good chance that she may not be able to formulate the paradigm and may not even wish to. It is certainly the case, nonetheless, that whether she has this ability or not (or whether she would wish to excercise it if she did have it), the power that resides in the paradigm for influencing Professor Zelig's decisions and behavior is considerable.

In any case, as Professor Zelig goes about the grading of her late papers, she may not be aware that, in turn, her "justice:injustice" paradigm is itself a piece of a much larger and more complex structure in her head--the metaparadigm we call the Protestant Work Ethic. And these connections between paradigms and metaparadigms are what Illustration 2 is intended to illustrate.

Illustration 3. A given paradigm may have precisely such connections (the ones exemplified in Illustration 2) with several or even with many metaparadigms. For example, as we saw in Illustration 1, the model in a person's head of the human being as some sort of "body-mind-soul" combination can, for certain individuals, function as part of a larger medical paradigm that focusses on the definition of health and disease; and at the same time, the same paradigmatic model may also have a whole set of entirely different connections with a theological-philosophical metaparadigm (held by the same individual) that asserts the primacy of "spirit" over "matter."

Illustration 4. With this illustration, we return to Ricky Smith. For one brief period toward the end of his freshman year in college, Rick struggled with a problem in logic that signalled to him something was seriously amiss. If the Holocaust (he reasoned) was really part of God's punishment of the stiff-necked Jewish people, then how can anyone place blame on Hitler and his henchmen--for were they not serving as the Lord's instruments? Some larger voice within him told him this could not be so, that Hitler could in no sense be held blameless, even for a passing, speculative moment. At one point during the struggle, however, he allowed himself to be persuaded, by a fanatically religious neo-Fascist classmate, that Hitler could not be all bad since he had saved Germany, Western Europe, and perhaps, eventually, even the whole world from the scourge of Communist atheism. For a brief period in Ricky's life, then, all those concepts worked together for him in one gigantic metaparadigm, each substructure supporting and reinforcing the others. The superstructure began to fall apart as he gained additional cognitive knowledge through his university studies and applied logical reasoning more consistently and firmly to his thinking--Level One activity in the learning theory presented earlier in this paper. Other conceptual frameworks began to make better "sense" out of those facts and principles--Level Two activity. An increasing sense of responsibility for social action began to pervade the affective realm as his religious concepts changed--Level Three activity. And all kinds of changes were taking place at deeper levels--certainly a growing sense of autonomy and independence of mind and a sense of intellectual freedom that was almost overwhelming. What was going on inside of Ricky Smith at Levels Four and beyond can hardly be described in the language of science.

REFERENCES

Axelrod, J. "Teaching Values in a Humanities General Education Course." In S.J. French (ed.), _Accent on Teaching_. New York: Harper and Row, 1953.

Axelrod, J. _The University Teacher as Artist_. San Francisco: Jossey-Bass, 1973.

Axelrod, J. "From Counterculture to Counterrevolution: A Teaching Career, 1959-1984." _New Directions for Teaching and Learning_, 1980, No. 1, 7-20.

Bloom, B.S., et al. _Taxonomy of Educational Objectives. Handbook I: Cognitive Domain_. New York: McKay, 1956.

Bronowski, J. _The Ascent of Man_. Boston: Little, Brown, 1973.

Chickering, A.W. _The Modern American College_. San Francisco: Jossey-Bass, 1981.

Feldman, K. & Newcomb, T.M. _The Impact of College on Students_. San Francisco: Jossey-Bass, 1969.

Freedman, M. _The College Experience_. San Francisco: Jossey-Bass, 1969.

Gregory, M.S. "NEXA: The Science Humanities Convergence Program at San Francisco State University." _Liberal Education_, 1979, _6_, 66-91.

Gregory, M.S. "The Science-Humanities Program (NEXA) at San Francisco State University: The 'Two Cultures' Reconsidered." _Leonardo_, 1980, _13_, 295-302.

Knefelkamp, L.L. "Faculty and Student Development in the 80s" _Current Issues in Higher Education_. Washington, D.C.: American Association for Higher Education, 1980.

Kuhn, T.S. _The Structure of Scientific Revolutions_. Chicago: University of Chicago Press, 1962 (Revised edition, 1970).

Kuhn, T.S. The Essential Tension: Selected Studies in Scientific Tradition and Change. Chicago: University of Chicago Press, 1977.

Longino, H. & Doell, R. "Body, Bias, and Behavior: A Comparative Analysis of Reasoning in Two Areas of Biological Science." Signs: Journal of Women in Culture and Society, 1983, 9 (2), 206-227.

McKeachie, W.J. "Approaches to Teaching." In N. Sanford & J. Axelrod (Eds.), College and Character. Berkeley, Montaigne, 1980.

Sanford, N. The American College. New York, Wiley, 1962.

Sanford, N. & Axelrod, J. (Eds.). College and Character. Berkeley: Montaigne, 1980.

Thomas, R. The Search for Common Learning: General Education, 1800-1960. New York: McGraw-Hill, 1962.

Trent, J.W. & Medsker, L. Beyond High School. San Francisco: Jossey-Bass, 1968.

Hazards of Goliath in the Nuclear Age: The need for rational priorities in American peace and defense policies

Christian Bay

The growing peace movement in the United States must reach out and communicate more effectively with those among their compatriots who want a strong military defense. This is the first of the main themes in this paper; for good and for ill, the fate of the whole world depends on what is happening politically within the world's leading superpower. On the one hand, we must assume that the pro-peace people and most pro-defense people equally want to avoid nuclear war; that, to this extent, both sides share the same highest-priority aim. But, on the other hand, I have some real difficulties with seeing Dr. Strangelove as sane. And Dr. Strangelove remains alive and well, and apparently is still influential in parts of the pro-defense community in the United States. In fact, I encountered his reincarnation in Washington not long ago: an academic who claimed expertise in questions of military strategy and said he is kept very busy by consultation assignments for the Department of Defense. I heard him speak, to an academic gathering, about his doomsday scenarios and his misgivings about the dangers of democracy in general and of broad peace movements in particular, at least within the United States. He referred to displays of photos of Hiroshima after the atom bomb as intellectual terrorism, and he briskly assured his listeners that with an effective, though admittedly expensive, civil defense program 90 million American might survive even a big nuclear war.

Yet, I think of most of the pro-military defense community as committed to a peaceful accommodation between the superpowers, and open to rational dialogue. I have to.

The second main theme in the paper is that the nuclear arms race and the on-again-off-again, and now on-again, cold war is mainly an American responsibility, and that it is primarily up to this country

----

A contribution prepared for the Fifth Annual Meeting of the International Society of Political Psychology, Washington, D.C., June 1982. I am grateful for critical suggestions from my colleague, Joseph E. Fletcher. A different version of this paper has been published in Alternatives.

to lead us out of the deadly nuclear power game that it has forced upon the Russians, and now proposes, if Reagan and Weinberger have their way, to escalate further. Up through the 1960's, the U.S. has been overwhelmingly more powerful than the U.S.S.R. (to which Mr. Kissinger and many other notables have testified). Abuses of U.S. power in Viet Nam, Guatemala, Chile, and so on, up through the Bay of Pigs and the Missile Crisis, go a long way toward explaining the massive Soviet arms efforts of the 1970's; and now the firm Soviet resolve to preserve their hard-won rough parity with the U.S. in military strength, even if this may make for continuing deprivation and oppression for the Soviet peoples.

The third main theme in my paper is that a nationalistic perspective on defense is today utterly obsolete and very dangerous. The U.S. and the U.S.S.R. now share the same objective interest in stabilizing the present balance of terror; in freezing the military technology and arms deployments at present levels, with a universal nuclear test ban instituted not next year but now; and in urgently seeking rational formulae for multilateral reductions in the nuclear arsenals. Defense is an international problem, and an ecological, economic, and political as well as military problem. It is a problem that requires very close, mutual trust-building agenda of collaboration between Moscow and Washington as well as other capitals, along with communications and exchanges that include military and other professionals, civil servants, and academics. Building peace is too important a task to be left to the leading statesmen and politicians.

Dr. Strangelove's reincarnation, to whom I have referred, told us in his presentation that it is impossible to build peace in today's world since, while the United States is dedicated to the cause of freedom, the leaders in the Kremlin want to make the world safe only for policemen. We may never know, of course, unless we try to find out. George F. Kennan is a much wiser man. He said many years ago that we will never know whether the Russians will want to go through an open door until we stop trying to push them through a closed door.

Peace and war issues are charged with emotions. We would be less than human if this were not so. The one thing that all cold warriors and all peace marchers appear to agree on is that the issues that divide them are of great urgency.

No wonder, then, that of all continuing political controversies, the issues of peace and defense have suffered probably the most from obfuscation, misrepresentation, sloganeering, and other kinds of flagrant irrationality. But this occurs because of contending interests as well as emotions. To compound the problem of achieving rational discourse in this area, where rationality is so badly needed, enormous economic and political interest-coalitions have a great stake in influencing the assumptions that most people make, or that powerful individuals make, about what is the right way to preserve or defend the peace. Our emotional involvement with these issues may for some of us reflect primarily our fear of modern war and its horrors, and for others primarily the fear of enemies abroad and at home, enemies believed to have great power and evil intentions; or both kinds of fears may coalesce as equally salient.

When a nation is deeply split, as the U.S. was over the war in Viet Nam, and is today over our leadership in the arms race, there is a tendency for fears to multiply and reinforce each other, until many people come to think of fellow citizens who disagree with them as enemies of all the values that they cherish.

My own position is not one of neutrality between the cold warriors and the peace marchers, but I propose in this paper to start with what the antagonists have in common, objectively and subjectively; then I discuss what I take to be the principal _general_ obstacles to achieving a rational resolution of their differences. This will lead to my principal concern: to attempt to formulate for discussion some _general_ priorities among peace and defense issues, with attention first to how we must _talk_ about them, and then to how we must attempt to _act_.

Common Interests and Concerns

Objectively speaking, all members of the human race have a lot in common--a lot of interests, sentiments, and other proclivities. The most pressing interest that we all share today must be to find protection against the peril of universal destruction by way of a nuclear holocaust. All or most animals, too, share our dependency on preserving the eco-system on which most, perhaps all, animal life depends.

Jonathan Schell's _The Fate of the Earth_ (1982) examines, as he puts it, "the physical extent, the human significance, and the practical dimensions" (p. 219) of the nuclear danger which today threatens all of mankind and most other vertebrates with extinction. He thinks about the unthinkable but, unlike Herman Kahn (1962), Schell searches for a way to achieve human survival, not for a way to make American interests prevail. He appeals to the good sense and the humanity of supporters as well as opponents of the arms race.

Speaking softly but carrying the weight of a passionate concern for the whole human race, Schell conveys, as no other writer has conveyed so sharply and concretely, the nature of the catastrophes confronting us, and how very near we may be to the final curtain of the "second death," the death of all hope and all future generations by way of universal human extinction, with the earth either stone-dead or reduced to a "republic of insects and grass" (1982, pp. 115, 168-169, 175). If the outcome he describes is awful to contemplate, so are the final hours of higher life, or final days and weeks and months, in the event that the nuclear holocaust leaves some areas more or less intact but is sufficient to destroy the layer of ozone that shields us from the ultraviolet rays of the sun. Blinded animals and men without adequate life support systems will hobble around for a short time only, as desperate predators or as lunatics. The least horrible fate would be suffered at Ground Zero or within a few miles from there: instant incineration.

Subjectively speaking, both supporters and opponents of the arms race in this country have a natural reluctance to face up to and to try to comprehend these probable scenarios. We feel so helpless anyway. Many of us probably feel like expendable pawns on a giant chessboard played by the White House against the Kremlin.

We worry about our own immediate families and friends, without taking on the heavier burden of worrying about all of humanity. "We deny the truth that is all around us," writes Schell. It is easier, less uncomfortable, to look the other way, and to follow our leaders, who in turn follow their own instincts or the conventional wisdom of a pre-nuclear age. As Schell continues: "Indifferent to the future of our kind (Here he means human kind, not his own nation, to which few claim to be indifferent.), we grow indifferent to one another. We drift apart. We grow cold. We drowse our way toward the end of the world" (1982, p. 30).

There is a sense in which many peace marchers as well as most cold warriors are avoiding the insights that Schell reports to us, not as a scientist with privileged information but as a reporter who investigates boldy and writes lucidly about generally available information. Many people on both sides tend to oversimplify the issues, and are too quick to assume bad faith or stupidity if not lunacy on the part of their opponents. Proponents of the arms race tend to denigrate not only most Russians and most communists, but also most resisters and opponents or even critics of the arms race. Many opponents of America's role in leading the arms race are correspondingly quick to attribute bad faith, special interests, or even fascist proclivities to those who push for heavier investments in armaments.

They may be right, of course, on either side. The point is that they are often much too quick to make such judgments, too sure about their unqualified validity, and not open enough to contrary evidence. On both sides, people too often lose sight of the humanity of people on the other side, and of their potential ability to question some of their own premises. Beliefs harden; potential converts are lost; and the horizon may get narrower than it has to be, on both sides.

To opponents of American armaments I shall say: If there is a human right to peace, there is a right to defense as well; a right to take appropriate defense measures, and to resist major unilateral disarmament measures, unless reciprocation is assured. To the proponents of American arms I shall say: The other side has exactly the same right to peace as we have, and exactly the same duty as we have to refrain from defense measures that undermine the security of other nations.

Objectively speaking, I would want both proponents and opponents of present U.S. arms policies to agree that peace must be the first human right (Bay, 1979, 1980a), prior in importance to any other political objective; and secondly, that a right to peace in principle must entail a right to defense, that is, to defensive preparations calculated to deter or resist attack, _within the restriction_ that such preparations must not include measures that in turn augment the real or plausibly perceived threat against other states. Peace is the first human right for people in all countries.

More concretely, I shall argue that it is in America's best interest to maintain for now some of its present defense capabilities, just as it is also the case that energetic multilateral disarmament efforts are essential if Americans want to improve their objective prospects for enhanced national security. The point to be stressed later on in this paper is that defense in our time must be seen as an _international_ task that requires close and continuing international consultation and cooperation, and must be carried out in ways designed to develop and maintain mutual trust between the powers (Bay, 1981a).

To the extent that this is done well, the prospects will be brighter for eventual achievement of what must be humanity's overriding goal: an international system of complete disarmament, nuclear and conventional, save for local, national, and international police forces.

Obstacles to Resolution of Differences

On the question of general obstacles to achieving a rational resolution of the sharp differences between supporters and opponents of the arms race in this country, let me first of all point out that this is not the same issue as the resolution of the sharp differences between the great powers or power-blocks. Pragmatically speaking, it is a prior issue, important not in its own right but in its bearing on the political feasibility of bringing about more constructive defense policies in the U.S., and, in consequence, in the U.S.S.R. and other countries.

The long and bloody history of nationalism and international antagonisms suggests that a stable world order cannot be established quickly. What we can aspire to in the short run is not to abolish nationalism or the symbols and prerogatives of national sovereignty. The immediate task is to increase our odds for survival in the dangerously divided world of nations in which we now live, until the time comes, we must hope, when a federal world system becomes either possible or unnecessary.

The immediate question I am addressing is not, of course, how to achieve national unity in the U.S. over defense and foreign policy issues. To resolve such issues irrationally is what politics is about, much of the time. Consensual backing for aggressive foreign policies and military postures has been easy to achieve for many regimes. A reckless regime usually has the option of provoking potential enemy states and thereby increasing international tension. In the past, war scares have been effective means of creating national unity--not to mention actual wars on a modest scale, like the recent war over the Falklands, or the Malvinas. That kind of unity is the unity of sheep or, more accurately, the unity of lemmings.

What is at issue here is how to achieve in this country a rational consensus on at least a few of the most basic war- and peace-related questions, as a prelude to an eventual world consensus on rational international defense policies, and also as a way to resist the dangerous jingoist tendencies in high places in the present period. More precisely, I address the issue of general obstacles to the achievement of such rationality in the U.S.

First, let us dispose quickly of the argument that all humans are (irrationally) aggressive by permanent instinctual endowment, "like other animals." Few animals other than humans kill their own kind; in some species it happens, but mainly in courtship rivalry between contending males. Protection of offspring or of territory may involve attack on other animals of the same species but, unless escape is barred, the weaker animal will run away and the stronger animal will not, except among some humans, pursue in order to kill. "The human enjoyment of death for its own sake, as seen in the ritualistic spectacle of the bullfight or in hunting for 'sport,' is certainly unmatched elsewhere in the animal kingdom" (Lazarus, 1974, p. 269).

Some, not all, humans enjoy hunting animals; relatively few enjoy hurting or killing other humans, or engage in such activities unless they are under orders to do so, in times of crisis or war. There is no evidence for assuming the existence of a universal aggressive instinct as a general obstacle to rational efforts to end war; psychologists have found it more fruitful to study human aggressive behaviors in the contexts of prior suffering of various kinds, in combination with learning processes which in turn are culturally influenced (Berkowitz, 1969). Moreover, even if there were universal aggressive instincts, or if aggressive urges are common in the U.S. and some other nations, many outlets other than war or preparations for war appear to be available for gratification of such urges. Indeed, modern nuclear warfare is so impersonal, so hypothetical until it actually happens, and so immediately lethal for aggressors as well as victims that it is difficult to see any prospects for instinctual gratification in planning for it, even if the macho-rhetoric accompanying such planning can perhaps be gratifying. Even the shouting of crazy slogans like "Nuke the Ayatollah" could perhaps give emotional gratification to some, but such slogans are hardly seriously intended, and are probably not repeated by people in the vicinity of nuclear triggers. Not yet, anyway, we must devoutly hope.

In short, "human nature," whatever it might conjecturally be like in the raw, beyond man's and woman's culturally, historically, and experientially conditioned patterns of behavior, is surely not a weighty obstacle to human rationality in the sense and in the context that here concerns us.

The context is, let us be reminded, a situation in which enormous risks are confronting Americans and all other peoples, whether we want to confront them or not. And the sense of rationality that we should be concerned to push for, within the U.S. public, is first of all a capacity and an inclination not only to worry about but to assess these risks and all their aspects realistically and, secondly, a capacity and an inclination to think about and discuss alternative stratagies to reduce and eventually to remove these risks and hazards (the greatest hazards first). The greatest hazards are those that threaten the most extensive damage or destruction to human lives and health, multiplied by the probabilities that they will in fact materialize. In all assessments of risks and risk-reducing aims and strategies there are large elements of uncertainty, which to the rational mind will suggest the urgent necessity of erring on the side of caution.

In this context I shall briefly consider only four broad categories of general obstacles to a rational discussion of security issues in the U.S.: sociological factors, having to do with great concentrations of power; historical factors, having to do with nationalism, private enterprise, and liberal acquisitive individualism; semantical factors, having to do with implicitly persuasive definitions of key words; and psychological factors, having to do with the continuing reinforcement of hostility and fear and capabilities of committing enormous atrocities.

Sociological Factors

The main obstacle to rationality in public discourse and policies on defense in this country is in the concentration of economic and political power in relatively few hands. It is an elementary insight in the sociology of organizations that organization entails oligarchy, and that oligarchical tendencies are apt to be more extreme, and less inhibited by considerations of reason and justice, the larger and more powerful the organizations become. Modern states control enormous amounts of wealth and power, as do many multinational private corporations. Most powerful of all corporations (for states, too, are corporations) are the two superpowers, the U.S. and the U.S.S.R. We must recognize that in both states there are small elites that have giant stakes in protecting the security of their own domestic control of power; for rulers and power elites in all or most countries, this is likely to be a very salient kind of "defense issue."

In the U.S. one often hears that America is an "open" society while the U.S.S.R. is "closed." For some purposes this assessment has a degree of validity, but as a ground for complacency about how American military and economic power is used in today's world, this assessment is profoundly irrational and dangerous. Sadly, there is little rational discussion in the U.S. regarding defense policy postures or their premises, in part because powerful vested interests, both private and public, insist on pushing for a heavily armed nation, a nation in a position to dictate to other countries when persuasion is insufficient; preferably to all other countries, to the extent that U.S. "vital interests" are concerned (Etheridge, 1978). And the latter concept is flexible: U.S. "vital interests" tend to expand when U.S. military and economic capabilities expand. Like other leading powers in the past, in the name of peace this country seeks preponderance of military and economic strength; even more blatantly than previous regimes, the Reagan administration pursues not peace and security in the abstract but peace and security on terms that to the government appear optimally beneficial to American private and associated public interests.

While the hazards of a nuclear holocaust are not ignored, their salience in and around the White House and the other centers of power in the U.S. appears to be lower than the salience of various other kinds of risks--like risks of declining poll ratings for the President, risks of less friendly regimes coming to power in other countries, or risks of losing propaganda points in the continuing confrontation with the U.S.S.R. Similar priorities have been evident in the treatment of defense-related issues in most of the mass media, although at this time there appear to be tendencies toward a more serious concern with the dangers of nuclear war in some of the media, in response to a growing public concern.

Historical Factors

Now let us consider the issues of historical obstacles to rationality in these matters. In the past the U.S. was very safe from external enemies. "God's country" was blessed with great natural wealth and also with geographical distance from other powerful nations. Today the natural wealth no longer appears boundless, and the geographical distance from Europe and Asia, and from the U.S.S.R., no longer offers protection from war.

Ironically, the prevailing liberal ideology of free enterprise, free speech, and free political choice has nourished as well as justified an actual system of private enterprise dominated by corporate giants: a system of mass media largely controlled by powerful economic interests, and a system of biennial political choice between rather similar candidates and parties, much as the supermarkets offer choice between similar products that we have been told we need. The crowning achievement of this ideological development, in this as in many other countries, is the *democratic makebelieve*: the profound popular conviction that the U.S. is a democratic and therefore also a righteous country, in which, all appearences to the contrary, the many control the few; there the citizen is obligated to obey the laws, and has only himself/herself to blame if, occasionally, the public interest fails to prevail over selfish private interests (Bay, 1971, 1981b).

Writers as diverse as Karl Marx, Leo Strauss, and Hannah Arendt have charged liberalism with diverting the attention of philosophers as well as citizens from the requisites of the public realm, or the common good. Man is a political animal. People have a real stake in the well-being of their community and society, and therefore in one another's well-being as well. The liberal is a political cripple, each of these writers in effect charges, in that the liberal pursues self-interest in his or her private life while neglecting to give prior attention, or even equal attention, to issues of social justice, or the commonweal. In Jefferson's rustic America, a system of underdeveloped politics could work, but not in a world of giant corporations and lethal technology, a world with avarice as well as dangers and fears magnified beyond the scale of individual human jealousies.

We need to understand how certain basic premises of liberal ideology make it difficult for so many Americans to be rational on peace and defense issues: in their daily lives they compete, in many zero-sum contests; if they win, their gain is visible and valued, more so than the loss to others is regretted, or the loss to the community in case their gain is unjust; their nation is their "team;" if thanks to their wealth, they can equip themselves adequately to outgun other nations, their gain is visible and valued, not their loss, nor the decreasing stability or justice that may result. And they tend to think of nations much as they think of competing private firms. They feel good when their nation appears to make headway at the expense of other nations, and do not even raise,and much less weigh, the issue of what is just, or in the international public interest.

In Jefferson's time, U.S. nationalism was in many ways a constructive force, which helped build the new, for its time, progressive nation. But in today's powderkeg nuclear world, it surely is a fact that the stakes of Americans in the <u>international</u> common interest in building a world of peace are vastly heavier than are their stakes in the prosperity or the military edge that the United States, Inc., may gain by way of supposedly shrewd nationalist foreign and defense policies. After two centuries of liberal heritage, many Americans appear less than ready to grasp that their national interest now urgently requires an internationalist perspective, at least on issues of peace and security: They need to demonstrate the same active concern for the security of nations with which they have been in conflict as they exhibit for the security of the U.S. It must become clear to Americans that the competing nations will either be living together or will be incinerated together.

Semantic Concerns

Semantic obstacles to rationality are common in every politically relevant context. Languages are political as well as social institutions. They develop in interaction with human cooperative <u>and</u> communicative needs, while also reflecting the structures of political control and domination. Languages shape our identities, not only as members of ethnic communities with their roots in the past, but as members of powerful or subordinate social classes. Paulo Freire (1974) has argued that a necessary beginning in the emancipatory struggle of the oppressed is to achieve mastery over their own political words; in further elaboration, Jürgen Habermas (1979) has developed the argument that the crucial aspect of the struggle for freedom under late capitalism is to struggle for approximations to undistorted communications.

Every language serves legitimate purposes; every system of authority has its semantic lines of defenses. Mass media, schools, and common usage attach positive and negative connotations to common words, and also over time expand or contract initial cognitive meanings, which in turn suggest and encourage stability-preserving patterns of thought and behavior. This is not due to any complicated conspiracy but to the outcome of innumerable word-transactions by which individuals pursue their perceived interests and values, including parents, teachers, editors, and political and economic leaders.

Words, for example, like "nation," "democracy," "liberalism," "freedom," "security," and "defense" are positive words, in contrast with negative words like "subversion," "dictatorship," "communism," "oppression," "vulnerability," and "surrender." This is obvious; it reflects social realities rather than semantical convention. The point I want to stress is that strongly positive and negative words acquire restrictive meanings with stability- or loyalty-promoting implications for thought and behavior. "Democracy," for example, nowadays firmly denotes the kind of political system we have in the U.S., regardless of any amounts of data we may have to show that popular participation on important political decisions is minimal (Bay, 1971, 1981b). The very idea of a struggle for (more) democracy in the U.S. comes to be seen by many as redundant.

"Violence" is generally understood to refer to what criminals and revolutionaries are doing; inflicting unauthorized harm or damage to persons or property; not to what police forces or armies or agencies like the CIA (in friendly countries) may be doing, and still less to what a traditional or imposed political and economic system may do to destroy and harm human lives (Galtung, 1980).

More germane to the concern of this paper is the common use of words like "defense," "security," and "deterrence." "Defense" has come to mean, not preparedness-efforts to reduce risks and hazards of all kinds against our lives and all that we value the most. Instead, at least in the context of "national defense," the word has come to refer to military efforts to deter armed attack against national or allied territories, and to preparedness to fight a war if deterrence fails. This is precisely the kind of semantic restriction that I shall be most concerned to break through in this paper. This cognitive restriction tends to rule out the importance or even the good sense of evaluating alternative kinds of defense measures, and of assessing the relative weight of the various values that we want to defend, or the estimated weight of the various categories of risks, including but going beyond the risks of military action. To argue, as I do along with many others, that we must be prepared to defend our peace is one thing. To take it for granted that we must do this by military means, only or mainly, is quite a different matter. To the extent that we continue to assume this in part because governments and departments of defense always define "defense" that way, we are palpably irrational.

Exactly the same points can and should be made (but will be omitted in this paper) about the uses and abuses of the term "security." "Deterrence" is cognitively clearer and less subject to semantic slanting, compared to terms like "violence" and "defense" and "security." But whole theories about human nature and behavior tend to be assumed even in otherwise professional discussions of deterrence. For example, deterrence theorists occasionally exclude the possibility that there might be other, both in the short run and in the long run, more reliable inducements than deterrence to refrain from military threats of attack, in the U.S. government's encounters with less than friendly foreign governments. "Those people understand only the language of force" is a statement too readily accepted at face value when applied to the Soviet rulers; I doubt that this is true of many national leaders in any country, but it is probably most nearly accurate as a description of the restricted outlook of those who make such statements. The problem with deterrence as the principal defense posture is psychological as well as semantic, to be sure. Deterrence requires that each government claims, and very insistently, in order to be believed, that it is ready to commit monstrously inhuman acts if its "vital interests" are directly menaced or attacked--a posture hardly conducive to building a sense of mutual trust between the regimes of the world's superpowers.

Another problem with the rationality of the semantics of "deterrence" in the U.S. is the implicit assumption that it is a one-way process. I have yet to see in American deterrence literature pertaining to the NATO-Warsaw Pact confrontation any suggestion that its side, too, must be deterred from exploiting relative weaknesses, or "windows of vulnerability," on the other side. And I recall that most Americans appeared to approve of President Kennedy's preparedness to go to war in the Cuban missile crisis, over the issue of denying the U.S.S.R. the option of deploying the same kind of nuclear deterrent in Cuba as the U.S. insisted on maintaining in Turkey.

Psychological Factors

Semantic restrictions on the rationality of discussions of defense issues lead into the range of psychological obstacles, which are even more pervasive. Only a few can be touched on here.

"There is no way to peace," the late American pacifist, A.J. Muste, is reported to have said: "Peace is the way." You cannot achieve conciliation, as Gandhi knew so well, unless you act in a consistently conciliatory manner, as far as circumstances permit.

By way of contrast, let us see what Mr. Ronald Reagan had to say in his first press conference as President, about the leaders of the nation on which, along with his own, the fate of the world nowadays depends. The Soviet leaders, he said, claim "the right to commit any crime, to lie, to cheat . . ."(Gwertzman, 1981, p. 1). Two days earlier, Mr. Alexander Haig, the new Secretary of State, had accused the Kremlin leaders of being "involved in conscious policies, in programs, if you will, which foster, support and expand" international terrorism in many parts of the world (Gwertzman, 1981, p. 3). Months later, a front page article in the *International Herald Tribune* reported on prolonged State Department staff efforts to find evidence with which to support Mr. Haig's purportedly fact-based charge. The search has been in vain so far (Taubman, 1981). Had Mr. Haig chosen "to lie, to cheat" as a way of launching the new administration's dialogue with Moscow?

In considering the problem of psychological obstacles to rationality on defense issues on the governmental level these matters are on the surface, I believe, but they affect the climate of discussion in the U.S. The Soviet leaders, as we all should know, are likely to see such rhetoric in the context of American domestic politics. But as domestic input such charges increase the difficulties Mr. Reagan would have with a large section of U.S. public opinion, in the event that at some point he should desire better relations with the Moscow regime.

Psychologically far more dangerous, I think, is the continuing discussion, within the Pentagon and in the mass media, of the actual possibility of nuclear warfare, in terms that would make us believe that American generals, and President Reagan, are prepared under some foreseeable circumstances to unleash an actual holocaust on Russian cities, or that attribute to the Russian leaders a corresponding readiness to inflict the same category of horrors on American cities. In their strategic planning exercises, our appointed experts no doubt have to think about and make programs for worst-case scenarios: *suppose* the Russians saw an opportunity to win a quick war against the United States or one of its allies without themselves suffering unacceptable losses, and suppose they were callous enough to act accordingly. Suppose they thought they could launch a first strike that would cripple the American first and second strike capabilities, and tried to actually do so. What then?

A continuing professional preoccupation with such scenarios easily leads one to take the small but psychologically momentous further step of assuming that the Russians would possibly launch a war if the perceived advantages were supposed to outweigh the costs; such an assumption comes all the more easily to people who suppose communists to be more callous about losing human lives than Americans, and who often tend to forget the enormous sufferings of warfare on Russian soil in their past and recent history, a sobering experience unmatched in recent U.S. history.

The next assumption is that Americans must be just as ready to unleash a holocaust as the Soviets are supposed to be, and that indeed they are, or their deterrent posture would be less than credible. Over time, a dangerous folie a deux develops: Each side, and in the U.S. this includes the media and public opinion, tends to become progressively more brutalized by mutually reinforcing attribution processes, based on what was initially merely hypothetical war games with worst-case scenarios. (Does the Pentagon ever take an interest in pursuing peace-building games based on best-case scenarios?)

Perhaps the Soviet leaders are in fact capable of such monstrous acts. I do not know for sure, and therefore I am not a unilateralist, at least not a radical one. But neither do I know, and I am sure the Russians don't know, whether President Reagan and his generals would launch a nuclear to take advantage of perceived Soviet "windows of vulnerability," which will become considerable if his administration's plans for large additional investments in the arms race are not curtailed. In psychological terms what worries me most, therefore, is the kind of climate of opinion that Mr. Reagan and his administration have been encouraging, along with many rightwingers and liberal anticommunists throughout the country. The combination can be lethal, when (1) fast-growing, enormous nuclear arsenals for deterrence and defense and (2) thinking about worst-case scenarios (pegged to now precarious assumptions about arms-parity and mutual assured destruction of both a first-striking and a second-striking power) are combined with (3) profoundly irrational climates of opinion. In some of our mass media, and possibly in some influential minds in and around the Pentagon, the Soviet leaders tend to be portrayed as Hitler-like desperadoes, out to destroy American freedom and civilization; communism is said to equal fascism. Conceivably, these compliments are returned by some of the hardliners in Moscow, whose influences may be enhanced by the Reagan administration's belligerent posture; although at this time the posture may undergo some modification, whether it be real or just a public-relations effort to undercut the apparently growing peace movement in the U.S.

In her discussion of the Eichmann trial, Hannah Arendt communicates with inspired clarity her sense of the enormity of the crimes that can be perpetrated as a result of *lack of thought*, lack of thought about public matters of justice and the requirements of a civilized political order (Arendt, 1980). In an important sense Adolf Eichmann was an archetypical *liberal*, I would say, because he thought about his private life and his career only. In a different country he might have lived out his days as a respected member of his community; had he, for example, been English, or Russian, or American.

In the U.S. today a Hitler could hardly be tolerated. Yet the developing psychological climate makes atrocities beyond a Hitler's wildest imagination increasingly possible, perhaps probable. For one thing, very different standards are already being used to judge Soviet and U.S. conduct in world affairs. This reflects and in turn provides additional fuel for the accumulating antagonism. For example, the Soviet military support of a puppet regime in Afghanistan is seen to be monstrous, and rightly so. The recent American conduct in Vietnam, on the other hand, is by many thought of as a costly mistake originating in good intentions, while others, who appear to be closer to the Reagan administration, assert that we were wrong in having been too humane to go for all-out victory. The U.S.S.R.'s pressure on Poland is said to be intolerable, while our bailing out of El Salvador's far bloodier regime is said to be pro-democratic and responsible. And so on.

The upshot of these and other similar applications of double-standards over many years is a psychological climate that induces many leading Americans to be no more restrained in what they *say* they would like to see inflicted on the Russians than the German Nazis turned out to actually *do* to Europe's Jews. I do not for a moment suggest any analogies between a Reagan and a Hitler, but I *do* suggest that many Reagan supporters seem to resemble Adolf Eichmann in their complacency about plans for future atrocities and their lack of personal apparent concern about issues of justice and humanity. And this posture is not limited to people who support President Reagan on domestic policies. Many Russians, I suspect, may be just as guilty of not objecting to obvious preparations for mass murder in foreign countries, but in general they have less opportunity than most Americans have to acquire critical information and to protest.

Two well-known Soviet dissidents, who are humanists first and critics of the U.S.S.R. (*and* U.S.) regime second, suggest that the psychological readiness to commit vast atrocities in the event of war may be more advanced today in Western Europe than in Russia. I fear this is true, and that Western Europeans nonetheless by a considerable margin take second place to many Americans, including many who presume to call themselves members of the "Moral Majority." The brothers Roy and Zhores Medvedev (1982, p. 40) express their conviction that "Everyone in Russia would feel it as a personal tragedy if any war or accident led to the destruction of Paris, London, Rome, Amsterdam or Madrid." Then they ask whether West Europeans would feel the same depth of sorrow if Moscow or Leningrad were destroyed. Would most Americans? I would like to believe that Mr. Reagan would, but he has so far provided little evidence to support this belief. It seems disturbingly apparent that many leading U.S. strategists might consider a hypothetical loss of Moscow or Leningrad an "acceptable" price to pay for assured American world hegemony, in the name of freedom and democracy; perhaps it would be thought of as a modest price to pay.

The seeds of universal death are in our lack of active concern in the West with the whole international community's shared defense needs, I believe; defense in the broadest sense of protecting our existence and all that we value the most as human beings.

Let us now turn to the more constructive and more difficult task of proposing some rational priorities in our attention to and discussion of peace and defense issues; it is simpler to demonstrate sources of irrationality than it is to be constructively rational. In conclusion I shall be bolder still and try to derive from these general points some tentative implications for policy and political action relative to peace and defense.

Priorities in Peace and Defense Issues

The general points that I want to make are fairly straightforward, in my view, but I think some of them will be quite contentious. For one thing, I shall take issue with some beliefs that are widely held among Pentagon officials and their supporters and also with some that are widely held among peace movement people: I disagree with the view that the U.S.S.R. is principally to blame for the present arms race, and also with the view that both superpowers are about equally responsible for it. There are very good reasons, as I shall argue, for the growing peace movements in many countries to focus on the U.S. or its administration as the main target of their protests, as well as the main focus for our hopes for changes that can reduce some of the worst hazards that

confront all of us.
Let me begin with some premises about the nature of peace and defense issues.

Connotations of Peace and Defense

Peace must be broadly understood, as encompassing not only "law and order" among states, but as well the absence of severe oppression by way of structural violence (Galtung, 1980). Infliction of severe violence on human beings is the most basic of evil actions; nuclear war will inflict this evil with extreme ferocity at an enormously large scale and is therefore the supreme evil. But a rational peace movement must aim for positive as well as negative peace; an international or transnational order that brings about an end to imperialism and other structural as well as deliberate oppression that destroys human lives and basic human rights (Galtung, 1975). The peace that we seek must first of all bar nuclear war, and secondly all war, but it must also facilitate the continuing struggle for protecting the most basic human rights of people everywhere. Major hazards that we need to defend against, defend our peoples as well as those without means to defend themselves, are natural catastrophes like floods and earthquakes; major epidemics; famines and droughts; radioactive and other poisonous pollution that can harm present and future generations and make the earth less healthy or less inhabitable. Military preparedness is only one kind of defense policy, which is today necessary in some contexts but which in a more rational world needs to be supplemented with many other kinds of resources and strategies; and military personnel will in a more rational world prepare for many kinds of rescue operations and other tasks that do not involve infliction of violence. To save human lives, and then to protect conditions that make the struggle for optimally _human_ lives possible, are the two most basic tasks of defense policies. They are what justifies investments in defense.

Like all other human and social issues, peace and defense issues must be studied empirically as well as in their normative or value contexts. Empirical peace research is nowadays flourishing in a number of universities and independent research institutes, and its results are in the public domain. Defense research is also flourishing, especially in the U.S. and the U.S.S.R., but it is to a large extent oriented to concerns of military hardware and software and to strategies of international confrontations; it is amply funded, and its results are to a considerable extent classified, at least temporarily. Neither peace researchers nor defense researchers by and large appear to recognize that in a more rational world they would be pooling their research efforts, for they should be concerned with studying how to protect exactly the same values, the same priorities: human lives, meaning first of all physical survival, with protection from major illnesses and permament injury; but meaning also, next in importance, protection *for* dignity and personal freedom, or protection *from* conditions of alienation and repression. Defense is a universal political need if peace is a universal political need. The term defense should be taken to mean preparedness to ensure the lives and well-being of all in a just order. For humanity and for national collectives, "peace" refers to what must be defended; for each individual, "human rights" refers to what must be defended, with the right to life coming first. In every good hospital, this is understood; not yet in most states.

Peace as Preservation of Human Rights

Let me elaborate on my conception of human rights as the substance of positive peace and as the objective of governments. I contend that to build a just order of human rights is what governments are *for*. Let us call *values* whatever we want or need to achieve, preserve, and defend, as human beings in a social order that coexists with other social orders on our small planet. From my humanist perspective, the root of my values is in my sense of solidarity, not only with some human beings (who, inevitably, tend to remain uppermost in my attention), but with all human beings. The legitimate task of governments, from the same humanist perspective, must be to establish the *most basic human rights* for all. More precisely, as I have argued elsewhere, it is to establish and protect the universal right to life, to health, to social solidarity or dignity, and to personal freedom, in that order or priorities (Bay, 1980b, 1981b). Morally rather than legally speaking, a government is legitimate and in a position to claim loyalty and support *only* to the extent that it protects these basic human rights for all, better than no government, and better than could any alternative kind of government (Bay, 1968, p.241).

All human rights cannot be equal, if all humans are to be entitled to the dignity of treatment as equals. Torturing someone is an even worse violation of human right, if compared to silencing someone, or refusing someone an exit visa. Destruction of an indigenous people, whether by malice or neglect (for example, by failure to protect its habitat), is an even worse violation than the arrest of a writer. The *ultimate* violation of human right in our time, and in all time, would be a nuclear holocaust, as I have argued at the outset, drawing on Jonathan Schell's account.

A nuclear holocaust, if it comes, begins with a first-use of a nuclear weapon. An imaginary post-human chronicler, perhaps from another planet, might come to decide that the termination of our human civilization was initiated over Hiroshima on August 6, 1945, when a U.S. President proved psychologically capable of giving the order to drop a nuclear bomb over a defenseless city; in fact, over two cities, when Nagasaki was also struck, three days later. It was evident that American and allied public opinion in some countries at the time welcomed these acts, as it was assumed that they had speeded up the ending of World War II.

For the next three or four decades, to be sure, no more nuclear bombs have been dropped for the purpose of killing people, and we must keep hoping that none ever will be. But it is profoundly disturbing to some of us that every U.S. President since Truman, with the possible exception of Ford, has, according to Daniel Ellsberg's well-documented account, "felt compelled to consider or direct serious preparations for possible U.S. initiation of tactical or strategic nuclear warfare, in the midst of an ongoing, intense, non-nuclear conflict or crisis" (Ellsberg, 1981, pp. 4-5). Moreover, the U.S. government has so far, under each successive administration, in sharp contrast to the U.S.S.R.'s posture, consistently refused to enter into any negotiations toward a treaty that would commit each nuclear power to refrain from being the first to use a nuclear weapon, in any future conflict. On the contrary, in addition to the various specific threats discussed by Ellsberg, the highest U.S. military authorities have time and again explicitly claimed that they wish to preserve the option of first use, even in theaters of war not directly involved in a military conflict. No other nuclear power has ever claimed the prerogative of using nuclear arms except for purposes of defense against nuclear arms. During the current U.N. Special Session on Disarmament the Soviet Foreign Minister presented a statement from President Brezhnev to the effect that the U.S.S.R. now unilaterally takes on "an obligaiton not to be the first to use nuclear weapons;" predictably, according to the New York Times, State Department officials promptly dismissed the Soviet initiative as "old hat" and "a clever public relations gimmick" (Miller, 1982, p. 9).

Some authoritative U.S. military experts believe that protracted nuclear wars can be fought without escalations leading to the final holocaust. On May 29, 1982, the leading policy-makers of the U.S. Department of Defense, "in a new five-year defense plan, have accepted the premise that nuclear conflict with the Soviet Union could be protracted and have drawn up their first strategy for fighting such a war," according to the New York Times (Halloran, 1982, pp. 1,6). Virtually every authoritative independent specialist in warfare strategies, along with the leading Soviet authorities, have discussed the practical possibility of a nuclear war that would remain limited in scope. More recently the Palme Commission has in its report characterized such an idea as an illusion; to entertain it at all one would have to "make incredible assumptions about the rationality of decision makers under intense pressure, about the resilience of the people and machinery in command and control systems, about social coherence in the face of unprecedented devastation and suffering . . ." (Lewis, 1982).

I think it is necessary at this point to challenge the dogmatic assumption held by so many in the U.S., and much in evidence in all the mass-circulation media, that those who struggle for peace and disarmament must denounce U.S. and Soviet armaments with equal vigor, once they choose to attack American arms race efforts. This assumption does violence to the sorry record of continuing U.S.leadership, over the last four decades, in the design, development, production, and deployment of virtually every kind of weapon and delivery system; the single exception being the Intercontinental Ballistic Missiles (ICBM), based on Sputnik technology. The list of U.S. military first includes: the atomic bomb, the intercontinental bomber, the hydrogen bomb, the submarine-launched ballistic missile (SLBM), the multiple warhead (MRV), the anti-ballistic missile (ABM), and the multiple independently-targeted warhead (MIRV).

Now being deployed, also in Europe, are cruise and Pershing missiles. And Washington now appears to insist on opening up an arms race in space as well, over strenuous Soviet protests. No doubt the U.S.S.R. will keep on responding in kind, unless the Reagan administration at long last can be induced to cease and desist from pushing the world's luck still further.

My political point is that the Kremlin has been given no realistic choice but to keep struggling, at great cost, to catch up with the U.S. strategic lead, since 1945. Only during the 1970s was a rough balance, an approximate over-all parity in strategic nuclear weapons, achieved; while the U.S.S.R. remains behind in the total number of nuclear warheads, and more U.S.S.R. than U.S. warheads are vulnerable to first strikes, there is today a sufficient deterrent power on both sides in terms of global strategy. If any one side still has a "window of vulnerability," as Hans Bethe (1982) testified to the Senate Foreign Relations Committee in May of 1982, it is the Soviet Union; yet it is the Soviet leadership, not the U.S. administration, that consistently in recent months and years has insisted on the principle of parity, and now keeps calling for preserving the present approximate strategic balance. At this time, as before, any further boost in the arms race is mainly a U.S. responsibility.

Over the long term, only multilateral disarmament can reduce our shared danger of a nuclear holocaust. In the short run nuclear deterrence must remain mutually effective, based on rough parity between the weapons systems deployed by the superpowers; and what must be avoided first of all is the prospect of new, possibly de-stabilizing weapons systems. The most urgent task in the U.N. Special Session on Disarmamant must be to press for a comprehensive ban on all further nuclear weapons testing; paradoxically, for the present we must defend the *balance* in the balance of terror, until we get more rational leaders, who appreciate that de-escalation, not further escalation, of the superpowers' arms race is now the most urgent defense need, for both sides.

The Need for Human Solidarity

Psychologically speaking, public support for peace between nations requires that most people sense that what they have in common as human beings, across the frontiers, outweighs what separates them. Understandably, World War II made many Americans consider the Germans, at least the German Nazis, less than human, and the Japanese also. The Nazis had been known to slaughter Jews and Slavs in large numbers, claiming that *their* racial stock was inferior to that of the Germans (Kelman, 1973; Sanford and Comstock, 1971).

What is the psychological situation of dehumanizing perceptions versus human solidarity across dividing frontiers today? As the Medvedev brothers fear, decades of cold war may have dulled the awareness in western countries of the humanity and the civilization that the Germans, the French, and the North Americans share with the Russians. Whatever crimes have been committed in the name of communism, and there have been many, there is a basic humanistic appeal in Marxism, to man as a species-being craving brotherhood and solidarity, which is less pronounced in individualist liberalism, with its stress on freedom and acquisitive values (Bay, 1981b). Even indoctrinated communists claim to feel fraternal concern for the working class in capitalist countries. On the other hand, even zealous cold warriors in this country claim to be in solidarity with the long-suffering Russian and Soviet and East European peoples.

With racist states and movements now largely a thing of the past, there is probably not much *dehumanizing* hatred across the East-West divide, either among political decision-makers or ordinary people; least of all in its immediate vicinity, in Germany. But there is much thoughtlessness, I fear, on the Eichmann model, in the Pentagon as well as the Kremlin and in the military-defense think-tanks on both sides, where zero-sum strategy games deal with hypothetical millions of deaths on a daily basis, with none of the participants, it appears, getting sick to their stomachs.

With respect to the broader public orientations in our part of the world, recent empirical studies show that capitalistic social welfare policies along with times of relative affluence have enabled many young people in various liberal countries to "outgrow" their possessive individualism and privatism, and to develop apparently life-long commitments to postmaterialist values, including concern with more democracy and freedom of speech (Inglehart, 1977, 1981). Other empirical work has demonstrated that a sense of fair play is deeply rooted in many young Americans, and can be brought actively to bear on public issues by way of very modest informational stimuli to make them question the sense of their value profiles and priorities (Rokeach, 1973).

The 1960's as well as the current apparent groundswell of concern with peace issues and anger with the Reagan administration, show that Americans are a people capable of changing their political posture. In that sense at least, for good and for ill, Americans are a free people, as capable of waging peace as they are of applauding plans to incinerate other nations, depending on their most salient anxieties at each time, and on their effective access to political knowledge.

Prerequisites of Peace

Peace requires defense, in at least three meanings of the term:

- military defense by way of deterrence;
- psychological defense by way of a sense of shared values and tasks;
- political defense by way of activating shared aims, priorities, and strategies.

Military Defense

In the past, wars could be won. Today, between hostile superpowers, they must be deterred. That means that neither the U.S. nor the U.S.S.R. can prudently take any <u>large</u> or sudden unilateral steps toward disarmament

(What the powers can do will be discussed below).

But to achieve and maintain stable mutual deterrence must come to be seen, also in the highest places in Washington, as an international problem that requires a close collaboration with allegedly hostile powers, not as a U.S. problem or a U.S.S.R. problem that can be unilaterally resolved. The beginning of rational thinking about deterrence is to be as concerned, in public and in private, with protecting the other side's margin of safety as with protecting one's own side's margin of safety. Yet such a concern appears to have been totally absent so far from the Reagan's administration's authoritative statements on defense policies. On the contrary, there have been many indications of hopes of achieving strategic superiority (Beilenson and Cohen, 1982), with little awareness in evidence of the possible hazards of trying to back the U.S.S.R. into a corner of desperation. There has been frequent talk, also by President Reagan himself, about alleged "windows of vulnerability;" but these are never Russian, they are always American windows.

Shared Value and Tasks

In psychological terms it is clear that a sense of shared values is nurtured by way of active cooperation between different kinds of people on joint tasks that are deemed important by all. As modern attribution psychologists know so well, what we do profoundly influences how we perceive ourselves as well as others. What we do together, constructively, makes us sense the importance of the values that we share (Harvey and Smith, 1972).

To be sure, the Russians have in the past been excessively remote and secretive, in many contexts. This must be understood in its historical context, however. The Russians, and especially the U.S.S.R., have a history of suffering invasions by hostile powers; at least from 1917 into the 1960's, they have been the strategically weaker power in a hostile world (Kissinger, 1977). It may have been necessary, to make up by way of secrecy and massive domestic repression what was deemed an otherwise dangerously vulnerable deterrent posture (there were the wars of intervention, the rise of Hitler, the temporary U.S. monopoly of nuclear bombs and the demonstrated readiness to use them, and then the cold war). After the 1960's, on the other hand, the Russians have seemed more ready than the Americans to initiate joint, constructive international or bilateral projects.

What is the situation today? Take cooperation in space as an example. A program of space cooperation was launched in 1972 and renewed for another five-year period in 1977. But, while the U.S.S.R.'s space program has sent a French and a Soviet astronaut into space together, the Reagan administration last May 24 decided not to renew the U.S.-U.S.S.R. joint space program: "Accordingly, American space officials had to break off discussions . . . on new cooperative arrangements in planetary exploration. Working groups established under the 1972 agreement to arrange cooperative ventures in space meteorology, environmental studies, lunar and planetary exploration, and space biology and medicine have been disbanded"(Wilford, 1982, p.11).

Political defense issues will be discussed below: Here I want to make only two general points:

Rational Defense. First, rational postures require the recognition of the necessity of international defense arrangements and institutions that gradually come to complement and eventually to substitute for the present system of "Mutual Assured Destruction" on which our peace now probably to a large extent depends. Beyond worst-case scenarios to ensure that retaliatory ("second-strike") capabilities against ("first-strike") surprise attack are up-to-date, we need confidence-building scenarios that focus on the gradual removal of, on a bilateral basis, first of all the most destabilizing weapons systems (Fischer, 1981). At the same time we must initiate extensive collaborative ventures that utilize the armed forces with their command staffs on both sides for joint constructive tasks, like, for example, famine relief, peace keeping in troubled areas, and environmental tasks like reforestation and cleanups.

Secondly, rational defense postures require that we insist on American leadership in initiating a gradual reversion in the U.S.-U.S.S.R. arms race, to launch a downward spiral. The compelling reason for this is that the U.S. has during the last decades been the leader in the arms race, every step of the way, until the 1970's. Since 1962, the U.S.S.R., smarting under their humiliation in the Cuban Missile Crisis, has pulled out all the stops to try to catch up, to earn a position of parity with the U.S. as a superpower. While the Russians have achieved almost parity in the most essential strategic nuclear weapons systems (and superiority in some conventional weaponries like tanks, while remaining inferior in anti-tank weapons), the U.S. keeps on leading in crucial areas like accuracy of delivery systems, explosive power by weight, and in advanced weapons technology more generally; they also have more warheads, but such numbers are of limited over-all strategic importance, for there is such a thing as "enoughness" in deterrence postures, so long as an ample second-strike capability is maintained on both sides.

De-Stabilizing Breakthroughs in Research. The greatest danger for all of us in the next decade or two is that the U.S. weapons technology laboratories may come up with new, de-stabilizing breakthroughs in military research. The most dangerous arms race now moves ahead within the U.S. between the huge corporations competing for lucrative defense contracts, with immense potential earnings at stake. For the rest of mankind, however, also in America, it is vitally important that "the genie be kept in the bottle." What we need very badly are treaties to ban all further military research, or at least a comprehensive universal test ban treaty with adequate safeguards, since new weapons systems can hardly be deployed without advance testing; a test ban, unlike a ban on all military research, can readily be monitored (Myrdal, 1980).

That the danger of nuclear war comes chiefly from the U.S. is not a moral but a factual judgement. It is easy to understand why the Reagan administration, given the beliefs and the rhetoric that led to Mr. Reagan's election victory, is reluctant to forego U.S. "advantages" in the race for still more quick and deadly weapons systems. But I hope to have made it clear, too, why it is of the utmost importance for the defense of this country and all countries to induce the current administration to stop in its tracks, which now points straight toward a likely ultimate holocaust. This is a political task of vastly greater urgency than the also commendable tasks of expressing our solidarity with the Afghan freedom fighters, or with trade unionists in Poland, or Turkey, or Brazil, or even in the U.S.

Restraining the Pentagon

A final note, before I turn to the issues of political action, about the inevitable charge of anti-Americanism, every time someone accuses a U.S. government of conducting reckless or unjust foreign or military policies.

As the late Norwegian writer Sigurd Evensmo wrote in a newspaper editorial many years ago, during the early stages of the cold war, nobody in one's right mind can be anti-American, anymore than it would make sense to be an enemy of the Missouri or the Tennessee river. But a rational person may well be desperately worried about destructive powers of great force running wild, whether in a river or, more so, in a great power's military establishment (1953, p. 3).

Speaking for myself, just as in retrospect I see the need for a Tennessee Valley Authority to tame a mighty, once destructive river, so I see today a desperate need for taming the monstrous powers of destruction of the Pentagon, in collusion with powerful U.S. arms industries and associated interests in Washington and across the country; an unholy alliance today cheered on by a sizable, well financed, and ably directed so-called Moral Majority. What I think we can and must try to do about this is for my concluding discussion. Let me just emphasize that I consider my own basic political aims and commitment profoundly pro-American, as well as pro-Russian and pro-humanity.

Peace and Defense Indivisible

In an understatement I said at the outset that I am not neutral between the peace activists and the proponents of a stronger military defense for the U.S. On most issues I side with the peace activists. Yet I resist the notion held by many peace activists that most defense activists are not concerned to achieve peace, and the notion that one must either be for total nuclear disarmament in the immediate future or for continuing to maintain and expand our present military defense preparations. Seeking a middle ground, I have argued that because we need peace we need defense, including nuclear military defenses for the immediate future; what we do not need, and must learn to resist more effectively, are "defense" policies that demonstrably serve to increase the danger of a nuclear holocaust.

I think I have shown, first, that for many non-rational reasons of various kinds, American leaders remain imprisoned in obsolete ways of thinking about defense. Instead of preparing to defend us against the whole range of deadly hazards to our civilization, including massive nuclear military and industrial accidents, the killing of life in our lakes and rivers, violations of basic human rights in the Americas and elsewhere, American authorities appear fixated on the notion that a forever hostile U.S.S.R. poses the only large threat against the U.S., and that it can be met only with military weaponry in immense quantities and associated confrontational economic policies. Secondly, I have tried to show that this posture of the U.S. and its NATO partners feeds historical Russian and Soviet fears, and has probably forced the Soviet authorities into far more energetic militarist and repressive policies than would have been likely in a less threatening environment.

If we insist on peace, as rational persons must, then the first premise must be that world peace nowadays is indivisible, in the exacting sense that all national military defense measures must be worked out *in cooperation with potential enemy states* and be geared to serving the security needs of both sides. International defense collaboration requires openness and the gradual development of considerable mutual trust. One important challenge is to develop ways of negotiating and interacting calculated to strengthen a sense of mutual trust, in cautious stages, while experience is gained.

It is most important that American generals and other officials and influential citizens become involved with Soviet counterparts in trust-developing ways. In this country, peace activists must learn to deal with cold warriors, and vice versa, in ways that will strengthen their sense of what they have in common as human beings, even while they differ, perhaps radically, on peace and defense policy priorities.

There are short run and long run tasks to be addressed jointly, across both front lines. Between the U.S. and the U.S.S.R. leaders the short run peace and defense objective must be a safer, more stable nuclear and conventional military balance, while the longer run tasks include bilateral arms reductions as well as constructive positive-peace ventures of many kinds. Among short run objectives to be shared between U.S. peace activists and military defense supporters is support for the principle of minimum adequate deterrence coupled with the right to peaceful demonstrations against militarism and to concientious objection to military service; among longer run tasks to be shared might be ventures to protect the environment and to assist endangered populations, of humans or of animals, within the U.S. or elsewhere.

To stretch a hand across a hardened front line is always difficult, but I think we have to try to do so within the United States, in joint recognition of the ultimate disaster that threatens all of us. More openness to discussion is required, if we are to build the kinds of coalitions that can induce, even coerce, our leaders in Washington to communicate in more constructive, friendlier ways with their Soviet counterparts, whose suspiciousness the Carter and Reagan administrations, and a succession of anti-Soviet foreign policy makers, from Acheson and Dulles to Brzezinski and Haig, have done so much to feed.

Action Alternatives

I should like now to present a few conclusions about specific action alternatives, drawing on my arguments thus far. Speaking as a humanist and a political psychologist, I will very briefly address three levels of peace and defense efforts: What can be achieved by citizens' involvement in nonviolent peace movements? What are some promising options among ways of negotiating between the superpowers? What kind of role can the United Nations play in developing institutions for building negative and positive international peace?

Overcoming Apathy

The political institutions in the U.S., as in most countries, breed political apathy most of the time. A sense of powerlessness is widespread, for reasons well understood in terms of attribution psychology. We are taught and constantly reminded that we live in a democracy, where the people are the boss. When we look around and see how bad things are and how impotent we are to do anything about it, our sense of powerlessness is reinforced. While Americans by and large express cynicism and gripe about many things, few question the legitimacy of the economic or the political system (Lane, 1979). Most of the time we are ideologically confined, as it were, within a very stable system, even though its rewards are very unequally distributed, and even if we know that it places all of our lives in jeopardy.

Yet the U.S. remains an open system in some important ways, and at times it becomes politically possible to work outside and against its stabilizing rules, or against some of them. At such times powerful personal resources of many individuals are set free. In the 1960's a powerful resistance movement against an unjust war (and against racism and sexism) emerged that was profoundly liberating for many young people, in particular, and eventually forced a U.S. President out of office. In the 1980's a similar movement may be on its way, this time against militarism and blind anti-Sovietism, or <u>for</u> a safer, less incendiary world. It may come to sweep another President out of office, with his rightwing entourage--or the more amiable President Reagan may in the end become the figure head for a more rational and humane administration. As John Kenneth Galbraith (1982) recently remarked, President Reagan deserves some of the credit for having kindled, with his many belligerent and anti-detente statements, the now broadbased peace movement in this country.

It is a pluralist movement with many components, and some of them have priorities in conflict with those of others. That is no cause for worry, for all or most components have deepened people's sense of their humanity and potential political power; as in the 1960's these are activist groups with broad interests, united first of all in their determination to prevent nuclear war, though many are also concerned with human rights and on that basis oppose U.S. policies that preserve oppressive third world regimes.

<u>The Freeze Campaign</u>. This movement contributed to the Kennedy-Hatfield Resolution in the U.S. Senate of March 10, 1982, which asked for "a complete halt to the nuclear arms race," and for a negotiated "mutual and verifiable freeze on the testing, production, and future deployment of nuclear warheads, missiles, and other delivery systems." Within the first

month, 24 U.S. Senators and 166 Representatives had endorsed this freeze proposal.

A Nuclear Weapons Freeze Campaign Clearing House has been established to coordinate local freeze movements across the country, and people have been encouraged to go to work to publicize and perhaps place on local ballots similar kinds of resolutions. Ground Zero is another focus for hundreds of local action groups that seek to make people aware of the hazards of nuclear war in <u>their</u> communities, and spur them to try to do something about it. Meanwhile, many professional groups, and here physicians have been particularly important, have organized for the purpose of insisting that the drift toward nuclear war be halted.

It was hardly a coincidence that on May 9, 1982, in a major address, President Reagan for the first time advanced proposals to Moscow for nuclear arms reduction negotiations to begin <u>and</u> dropped all reference to "linkage"--the previous demand that Moscow demonstrate "good behavior," as judged by Washington, as a requirement for negotiations (Gwertzman, 1982). President Reagan also not long ago commented on the Freeze movement: "Many have been attracted to the idea of a nuclear freeze. Well that would be fine if we were equal in strategic capability. We're not. We cannot accept an agreement which perpetuates current disparities" (Newhouse, 1982, p. 44). This is a crucial premise that underlies his hardline posture but it is a singularly unconvincing one. The lack of credibility of this premise supports a "newly fashionable view in Washington" to the effect that Mr. Reagan may be on his way back to the policies of detente of recent Republican administrations (Newhouse, 1982, p. 104).

This may or may not happen. The crucial value of the Freeze Movement and related peace activities is in the participatory processes that strengthen the political awareness and the personal sense of power of many hundreds of thousands of individuals, reduced to passivity before because they did not think there was anything that they could do that could have a political impact. This activated multitude of individuals in turn may give most Americans a more effective access to critical political knowledge, with which to build more democratic communities that are bold enough to insist that resistence to nuclear war is a local as well as a national, and an international issue. When, for example, Toronto's City Council not long decided to support a ballot on which the voters could express their views on the arms race, the Councillors appeared impressed with testimony from the City's health officials to the effect that a nuclear attack would gravely affect the public health situation in the city, and public health is acknowledged to be a municipal concern.

Deficiencies in Negotiations

In peace negotiations between the two superpowers one might speculate that the best results could be achieved if the most anti-militarist specialists on both sides did the negotiating. That would, of course, be a political impossibility in the U.S. and probably in the U.S.S.R. as well. The least beneficial results could be expected if one side were represented by hard-line militarists and the other by anti-militarists. Within existing historical constraints the pragmatically sensible course presumably is to have "centrist" representatives do the negotiating for the U.S. government, so that agreements are feasible on the basis also of equity, not only on the basis of relative power, and so that agreements are likely to be honored, being supportable by the mainstream of U.S. opinion and by the U.S. Senate. But official negotiations should be supplemented, as I shall argue in a moment, with unofficial experiments or exercises in negotiation.

The importance of such supplements is augmented, as we shall see, by the fact that President Reagan's most relevant senior appointments have been of hard-liners who in the past had expressed their belief that preponderance of arms, not negotiations to achieve parity, should be the American strategy. Thus, the chief START negotiator, General Edward Rowny, said in 1980, "We have (in the SALT II negotiations) put too much emphasis on the control of arms and not enough on the provision of arms." And the first Reagan-appointed head of the U.S. Arms Control and Disarmament Agency, Dr. Eugene D. Rostow, one of the leading hawks in the Vietnam war and a founder of the rightwing Committee on the Present Danger, since 1976 the most anti-Soviet pressure group on defense policy issues in Washington, has been replaced by an even harder-liner (Brownstein and Easton, 1982).

The point to stress, more important than personalities of people, whose options, views, and behavior can change, is that negotiations never succeed unless there is a political will that they should, on both sides. To the extent that Washington remains determined to seek to regain its past superiority and would be unsatisfied with a mere strategic balance with the U.S.S.R., negotiations will be a smokescreen behind which to continue forging ahead with the arms race. That is why it is so important to press for a Freeze now, instead of some time in the future.

As I indicated earlier, many leading Americans appear to think of negotiations betweens nations much as businessmen think of negotiations between private firms. Each side is out to maximize its own immediate advantage at the other side's expense. As J.W. Burton has argued so convincingly, in the world of nations, rational negotiators would look not so much for ways of resolving confrontations by way of compromise (although at times there may be no other peaceful resolution immediately possible), as they look for creative solutions that would leave both sides better off than before (by attending to underlying needs on both sides), and perhaps disposed to engage in mutually beneficent cooperation as a way of implementing or following up the agreement reached (Burton, 1979).

Military superpower negotiations are said to require much secrecy because military secrets must be protected. Yet the SALT I and II negotiations yielded breakthroughs in mutual revelations of data on present military arsenals and deployment--a development no doubt facilitated by satellites and related new technologies that make it harder to keep military preparations secret. New verification possibilities make mutually advantageous, safe arms accords more feasible than in the past, if there is a political will on both sides. They make it more possible for outsiders to exert intelligent influence and pressure to make sure that there is going to be a serious commitment on the part of American political leadership, a will to engage in serious negotiations in search of reasonable agreements rather than a desire to engage in mere Presidential image-serving rituals.

Active Role of Citizens

This is where <u>we</u> come in. As concerned citizens with some access to critical political knowledge and/or relevant technical expertise of one sort or another, we can push politically for more openness about negotiating positions, and for more reasonableness or fairness, or for more attention to our international interest in reaching equitable solutions on specific contentious issues. Perhaps even more important, we can press for a freeze on all further weapons testing and deployment while negotiations continue.

Teachers and academics can do more. We can organize negotiations of our own, in mock sessions involving role playing with designated persons to represent the two powers, or the several powers. In his simulation research, Harold Guetzkow (1971) contributed much useful insight on systematic factors affecting the course of negotiations. Even more ambitiously as political experimenters we can try to involve Soviet colleagues in joint research programs on the practice of international arms control negotiations, drawing on the results of the pioneering efforts of Herbert C. Kelman and associates with particular reference to the very complex Middle East and Indian Sub-Continent conflicts. There the emphasis has been on studying how alternative kinds of group processes can facilitate or impede a meeting of minds, and secondly on how social psychologists as impartial, yet deeply concerned intermediaries, can contribute to this meeting of minds, or to the prospects for agreements. Thirdly, if carefully selected (assuming that this applies to the team of intermediaries, which must also be fairly balanced politically) knowledgeable academics, defense officials, and other civil servants and professionals participate, on both or on all sides, and all negotiations are kept strictly off the record, then it is also possible that useful new ideas may emerge. If this is acceptable to all participants, these ideas can be publicized and/or communicated to the respective governments (Kelman and Cohen, 1979).

Kelman appears to have taken some of his cues from the well-known Pugwash Conferences, which for many years have brought leading scientists together, from the U.S.S.R., the U.S., and other countries, for the purpose of seeking mutual understanding on contentious peace-related issues; particularly in times of crisis, these continuing discussions may have exerted some modifying influence in Washington as well as in Moscow and other capitals.

The chief drawback to superpower negotiations may well that they tend to be so time-consuming. Unless we achieve an effective freeze agreement on all testing and deployment of new weapons while negotiations continue, the world may not have time to await the outcome of further arms-reduction negotiations.

There is an alternative to formal negotiations, however, which has been developed initially by Charles E. Osgood. It involves carefully planned unilateral initiatives that invite reciprocation from the other side. Osgood used the acronym GRIT, for Graduated and Reciprocated Initiatives in Tension-Reduction. "In brief," writes Svenn Lindskold, "one takes deescalatory steps without requiring prior commitment and assumes that these deescalatory actions will eventually be reciprocated. Osgood terms it an arms race in reverse" (1979, p. 276). After stressing the straight self-interest motive on both sides, Lindskold suggests further psychological dividends as a likely outcome: "With each rewarding the other by taking deescalatory steps, mutual attraction is fostered in place of hostility . . . , and trust is promoted through benevolent action and through open and truthful patterns of behavior . . ." (1979, p. 276).

Has GRIT been tried? Amitai Etzioni makes a pretty good case that an approximation to GRIT has been tried, and with considerable success. It can be said to have been initiated by President John F. Kennedy in his "Strategy for Peace" address of June 10, 1963, some eight months after the Cuban Missile Crisis when he, for one thing, announced a unilateral halt to all atmospheric nuclear tests, in the context of asking Americans to reexamine their attitudes toward the Cold War. The Russians responded with printing the full Kennedy text in the two principal daily newspapers, and among other conciliatory gestures Mr. Khrushchev, too, agreed to end all atmospheric nuclear tests and also announced a halt to the production of strategic bombers. However, late in 1963, prior to the assassination of President Kennedy, Washington discontinued the peace offensive for reasons of domestic politics. The President's political advisors became increasingly worried, on the eve of a Presidential election year, that Kennedy was becoming too vulnerable to charges of being "soft on communism" (Etzioni, 1967).

In the political climate of today, thanks to the Freeze campaign and many related movements, I think U.S. public opinion is ready not only to tolerate but to demand serious arms control negotiations with the U.S.S.R.; and that it would also welcome a reasonably bold, if carefully planned and explained, to American opinion as well as to world opinion, GRIT-type experimental peace offensive.

The most important role of social scientists who worry about nuclear war at the present time is, I think, to serve as "impartial, yet deeply concerned intermediaries" between the U.S. and the U.S.S.R. negotiation postures, to the extent that the substance of these positions can be forced into the public domain. We should be capable of mobilizing considerable pressures toward this end.

I hope the day is now past, when American academics expect of themselves or each other that they must side with the U.S. in every negotiating confrontation with foreign powers. Perhaps it will be said, and I think this is true, though with many exceptions, Roy E. Medvedev, for example, that Soviet academics can be expected to side with U.S.S.R. postures. So what? This in no way negates the crucial interest we all have in seeking to reverse the arms race, in ways so rational and equitable that they will stick. We must be equally concerned with closing dangerous "windows of vulnerability" on both sides, and we must strenuously oppose all indications, and there have been many, that the Reagan administration keeps pushing for new advances in military technology with which to again tilt the balance against the U.S.S.R. (Aldridge, 1981).

As concerned academics we must endeavour to follow closely the American government's negotiating strategies and tactics, and examine the kind of peaceful world it seeks to achieve. We must transcend the traditionally narrow conceptions of patriotism that in effect have given governments blank checks every time they get themselves into difficulties with foreign powers. We must learn to enhance our effectiveness as advocates of peace in general and of freeze in particular, with a reversal of the arms race as our most pressing goal.

The Role of the United Nations

International organizations are no panacea. Like all other organizations they tend to become top-heavy, insensitive to needs for change, and committed to their own welfare as organizations, especially when they become large. The United Nations is a large organization, with many problems of bureaucratic rigidity and inefficiency. However, there are few today who would deny that the world badly needs the U.N. even with its shortcomings. Its most crucial value surely is that it provides a permanent forum that gives to every government and every political movemant <u>some</u> incentive to formulate and advocate its positions with restraint and reason, in terms that aspire to be understood and perhaps approved by the real or perceived "world opinion," or the nearest thing to its visible maifestation, the U.N. General Assembly.

It is not yet widely understood that the major problems of peace and defense today are international in scope and require continuing international, multilateral, and bilateral efforts in behalf of the nation-transcending international interest. This is least understood, it appears, in the Pentagon, with its recently reaffirmed posture of preparing to fight a protracted nuclear war. It appears to be far better understood in the broad peace movements that have developed in the last years, first in Western Europe and then in North America as well. Also, it seems to be better understood in Moscow than in Washington (Russian losses of life in two world wars have been stupendous compared to American losses); many U.S. leaders understandably are reluctant today to give up the hope of regaining its recent stance of superiority, up to the Cuban Missile Crisis at least, "when the United States was overwhelmingly more powerful than any other nation," to quote Henry Kissinger (1977, p. 98). It is Moscow, not Washington, which consistently has called for full implementation of the SALT II agreement and for further efforts to freeze the arms race, as a first priority, on the basis of the principle of parity between the two superpowers. And the U.S.S.R., not the U.S., has repeatedly sought agreement on the principle of no first use of nuclear weapons.

There is hardly anything the U.N. can do to exert political pressure directly on either superpower. But it can work on strengthening its own relevancy and importance as a sounding board for broad international peace movements. Yet I think that there are promising opportunities for the U.N. to take on a more active, independent role in improving the prospects for a lasting peace; opportunities provided by rapid recent advances in computer technologies and in satellite-related technologies for observing in minute detail most kinds of military deployments in all countries. Most national claims and accusations regarding military deployments can now be assessed and disputed or verified by every government that has acquired the appropriate intelligence technologies (Myrdal, 1980). It is time for the U.N. to go to work to develop its own, entirely public, intelligence-gathering, -assessing, and -publicizing apparatus. The wider its scope and the more effectively and authoritatively it can perform this task, the less possibility for duplicity on the part of national governments, including superpower governments; and, what is more important, for I doubt that there is much duplicity now, the stronger the incentives to moderation on all sides, to avoid needless confrontations with increasingly well-informed peace movements and pro-defense movements in support of international security.

Proposals of this kind have already been advanced. The French government during the 1978 U.N. Special Session on Disarmament proposed the establishment of a U.N. International Satellite Monitoring Agency (ISMA). This agency would seek data from the member states but would also build a satellite-based intelligence-gathering apparatus of its own. The reception of the proposal was mixed at that time. The U.S. rejected it, the U.S.S.R. was non-committal, and most West and East European governments welcomed it. The issue was referred for study to a U.N. Group of Experts, which in October the following year in its preliminary reports stated that the plan is technically feasible and in a subsequent, more definitive report, dated August, 1981, concluded that even in its most developed and expensive phase, "an ISMA would cost the international community each year well under one per cent of the total annual expenditure on armaments" (United Nations Documents A/34/540 and A/AC. 206/14, 1981).

Also other aspects of world security could well be studied by authoritative transnational agencies. Johan Galtung has proposed, and not necessarily for U.N. sponsorship, an International Storehouse of Disarmament Ideas which would do more than gather facts: "What is needed, besides excellent descriptions of the current state of affairs, are predictions of what will happen if the system is left unchecked, and some theory as to why the world is as it is. Simply stated, two things: (1) some vision of <u>the goal</u>, a 'disarmed world,' a 'world without the bomb' --but in detail, with specifications--and (2) a vision of <u>how to get there</u>, with some very concrete ideas as to the first steps" (Galtung, 1980, pp. 225-226).

In my own view the U.N. should prepare to launch in the near future an initially small new agency that would have big ambitions: an International Defense Agency, whose primary task would be didactic, perhaps more so than Galtung's proposed agency, which seems to assume a primary emphasis on dispensing and applying available theory, also, to be sure, a most important task (Bay, 1981a). As the most crucial cognitive task of peace education I see bringing about in the public consciousness a conceptual divorce between "defense" and "national," and between "defense" and "military." This is not to deny that there are real and important problems of national military defense, but it is essential to induce people, and especially people in the pro-military camps, to come to see their traditional concerns as parochial and irrational until they are placed in the wider context of international defense problems, and of problems of all kinds of threats, man-made and natural, that endanger or destroy large numbers of human lives today, or the lives or health of people of future generations.

Other proposed international defense agencies like the ISMA ought to be kept separate from the proposed IDA: ISMA would have an essentially technical task to do, which requires a considerable budget, even if modest compared to current national arms expenditure. Organizations are less likely to become rigid and deflected from their initial objectives, the smaller they are and the more strictly defined and unambiguous their tasks.

From this perspective the proposed IDA might not seem a sound idea at all. The IDA is envisaged as in a sense a dialectically developing agency. Initially it would do no more than sponsor seminars and study groups that draw on data from ISMA and from the leading peace and defense research institutes. Its further branching out would depend on how well, to the satisfaction of important movements as well as national governments, it would perform its initial task as a representative of a budding international consciousness of shared ideas and interests related to peace and defense issues. Perhaps it would eventually be enabled to become engaged in peace action projects, to defuse brewing hostilities, to protect endangered populations, to restore damaged nature, or whatever.

As political psychologists we recognize that our consciousness and values in large measure are shaped by what we do, especially along with others. Many good people today develop semi-paranoid views of alleged enemy nations and political systems while pursuing careers related to weapons research or manufacture. The mere existence of highly visible agencies like the proposed IDA, or ISMA, would give many people welcome ideas of what they would rather do with their lives. There would be no dearth of people, in the U.S. and in other countries, wanting to enlist in international peace and defense studies or action projects. Participants probably would acquire a new consciousness of how good it feels to work for peace and international defense purposes. Like returning Peace Corps participants, many would return to their own countries with a commitment to public service rather than to narrow private interest (Ezekiel, 1968; Smith, 1969).

New organizations are temporary expedients; it takes great and continuing efforts to keep them approximately on course. Organizations are means to ends, initially, but all have a tendency to become ends in themselves and to make self-serving use of talk about purposes. The struggle for a fuller awareness of what is at stake in our time must continue; it requires inspired books like Jonathan Schell's, it requires access to critical knowledge and discussion in the media, and it requires broad participation in active peace movements, movements inspired by and in turn strengthening a new internationalist consciousness, resistant to every traditional nationalism.

Experiments with new international agencies are a further necessity, in continuing interaction with emerging ideas and fresh experience. But the most crucial immediate requirement for all these openended possibilities, surely, is a Freeze now, on all further arms production, testing, and deployment, to lend us some time for cautious experimentation with many new approaches to solving our enduring problems of international defense. A Freeze could safely be initiated by the U.S. tomorrow, by way of a unilateral moratorium that invites multilateral Freeze negotiations, as Jerome Wiesner has argued (1982). Washington has led the world into the nuclear arms race, and now must be asked to lead us out of it. It is our task, as people concerned with peace and defense, to work hard to make such a political change of course possible for the U.S. President, and necessary.

REFERENCES

Aldridge, R.C. The Counterforce Syndrome: A Guide to U.S. Nuclear Weapons and Strategic Doctrine. Washington: Institute of Policy Studies, 1981.

Arendt, H. Eichmann in Jerusalem: A Report on the Banality of Evil. New York: Penguin, 1980.

Bay, C. "Needs, Wants and Political Legitimacy." Canadian Journal of Political Science, 1968, 1, 241-260.

Bay, C. "Foundations of the Liberal Make-Believe." Inquiry, 1971, 14, 213-243.

Bay, C. "Positive Peace and Rational Human Rights Priorities." Bulletin of Peace Proposals, 1979, 10, 160-171.

Bay, C. "Peace and Critical Political Knowledge as Human Rights." Political Theory, 1980a, 8, 293-318.

Bay, C. "Human Needs, Wants, and Politics: Abraham Maslow, Meet Karl Marx." Social Praxis, 1980b, 7, 233-252.

Bay, C. "To Secure the Right to Peace: A Modest Proposal to Defense Planners." Bulletin of Peace Proposals, 1981a, 12, 339-348.

Bay, C. Strategies of Political Emancipation. Notre Dame, Indiana: University of Notre Dame Press, 1981b.

Beilenson, L.W. & Cohen, S.T. "A New Nuclear Strategy." New York Times Magazine, January 24, 1982, 34-44.

Berkowitz, L. (Ed.). The Roots of Aggression:A Re-Examination of the Frustration-Aggression Hypothesis. New York: Atherton, 1969.

Bethe, H. "The Inferiority Complex." New York Review of Books, June 10, 1982, 30, 3.

Brownstein, R. & Easton, N. "Why Are These Men Negotiating for Us?" Village Voice, June 15, 1982, 8-15.

Burton, R. Deviance, Terrorism and War: The Process of Solving Unsolved Social and Political Problems. Oxford: Martin Robertson, 1979.

Ellsberg, D. "Call to Meeting." Monthly Review, 1981, 33, 1-26.

Etheridge, L.S. A World of Men: The Private Sources of American Foreign Policy. Cambridge, Massachusetts: Massachusetts Institute of Technology Press, 1978.

Etzioni, A. "The Kennedy Experiment." Western Political Quarterly, 1967, 20, 361-380.

Evensmo, S. "Et annet Amerika." Orienteering, September 11, 1953, 3.

Ezekiel, R.S. "The Personal Future and Peace Corps Competence." Journal of Personality and Social Psychology, 1968, 8, Monograph Supplement, Part 2.

Fischer, D. "Invulnerability without Threat: The Swiss Concept of General Defense." New York: Starr Center for Applied Economics, New York University, 1981.

Freire, P. Pedagogy of the Oppressed. New York: Seabury, 1974.

Galbraith, J.K. "The Waste of the Arms Race." Lecture, University of Toronto, May 13, 1982.

Galtung, J. Peace: Essays in Peace Research. Copenhagen: Christian Ejlers, 1975.

Galtung, J. The True Worlds: A Transnational Perspective. New York: Free Press, 1980.

Guetzkow, H. "A Decade of Life with the Inter-Nation Simulation." In R.G. Stodgill (Ed.), The Process of Model-Building in the Behavioral

Sciences. Columbus, Ohio: Ohio State University Press, 1971.

Gwertzman, B. "Reagan Attacks Kremlin." International Herald Tribune, January 31, 1981, 3.

Gwertzman, B. "Major Shift by Reagan." New York Times, May 10, 1982, 1, 13.

Habermas, J. Communication and the Evolution of Society. Boston: Beacon, 1979.

Halloran, R. "Pentagon Draws Up First Strategy for Fighting a Long Nuclear War." New York Times, May 30, 1982, 1,6.

Harvey, J.H. & Smith, W.P. Social Psychology: An Attributional Approach. St. Louis: C.V. Mosby, 1977.

Inglehart, R. The Silent Revolution. Princeton: Princeton University Press, 1977.

Inglehart, R. "Post-Materialism in an Environment of Insecurity." American Political Science Review, 1981, 75, 880-900.

Kahn, H. Thinking about the Unthinkable. London: Weidenfeld and Nicolson, 1962.

Kelman, H.C. "Violence without Moral Restraint: Reflections on the Dehumanization of Victims and Victimizers." Journal of Social Issues, 1973, 29, 25-61.

Kelman, H.C. & Cohen, S.P. "Reduction of International Conflict: An Interactional Approach." In W.G. Austin and Worchel (Eds.), The Social Psychology of Intergroup Relations. Monterey, California: Brooks/Cole, 1979.

Kissinger, H. "Continuity and Change in American Foreign Policy." Society, 1977, 15, 97-103.

Lane, R.E. "The Legitimacy Bias: Conservative Man in Market and State." In B. Denitsch (Ed.), Legitimation of Regimes. London: Sage, 1979.

Lazarus, R.S. The Riddle of Man. Englewood Cliffs: Prentice Hall, 1974.

Lewis, A. "Who Are The Realists?" New York Times, June 3, 1982, 29.

Lindskold, S. "Managing Conflict through Announced Conciliatory Initiatives Backed with Retaliatory Capability." In W.G. Austin and S. Worchel (Eds.), The Social Psychology of Intergroup Relations. Monterey, California: Brooks/Cole, 1979.

Medvedev, R. & Medvedev, Z. " A Nuclear Samizdat on America's Arms Race." The Nation, January 16, 1982, 234, 38-50.

Miller, J. "U.S. Is Cool to Declaration by Soviet on Use of A-Bomb." New York Times, June 16, 1982, 9.

Myrdal, A. The Game of Disarmament: How the United States and Russia Run the Arms Race. Nottingham: Spokesman, 1976.

Newhouse, J. "A Reporter at Large: Arms and Orthodoxy." New Yorker, June 7, 1982, 44-103.

Rokeach, R. The Nature of Human Values. New York: Free Press, 1973.

Sanford, N. & Comstock, C. Sanctions for Evil. San Francisco: Jossey-Bass, 1971.

Schell, J. The Fate of the Earth. New York: Knopf, 1982.

Smith, M.B. Social Psychology and Human Values. Chicago: Aldine, 1969.

Taubman, P. "U.S. Tries to Back Up Haig on Terrorism But Repeated Intellegence Studies Find No Direct Link to Soviet." International Herald Tribune, May 3, 1981, 1, 36.

United Nations Document A/34/540 and A/AC 206/14. United Nations, 1981.

Wiesner, J. "A Way to Halt the Arms Race." New York Times, June 13, 1982, 25.

Wilford, J.H. "U.S.-Soviet Space Cooperation Ends." New York Times, June 6, 1982, 11.

American Anti-Semitism Now: A political psychology perspective

Mervin B. Freedman

After World War II a remarkable thing happened. Anti-Semitism declined in the United States, declined to levels of tolerance, and even perhaps social benevolence, unique in Jewish history. The following essay propounds some explanation of this uncommon set of events.

The Historical Image of the Jew

Paul Johnson (1984) writes,"Anti-Semitism is one of the oldest and most persistent forms of human irrationality . . ." He goes on to provide some information about its origins in antiquity and its subsequent history.

> The first layer of anti-Semitism, itself a form of anti-Zionism, was laid down by Manetho, a priest from the intellectual community of Heliopolis in Ptolemaic Egypt, about 280 B.C.E. He presented the Jews as wanderers by nature, descendants of an outcast tribe of lepers, who had no natural land of their own. His theory underlay the response of Hellenistic intellectuals to the disquieting phenomenon of Judaism: they argued that the Jewish rejection of Greek syncretism and universalism was a form of misanthropy; the Jews were a dislocated people without true territorial title deeds, and their Diaspora was a conspiracy against humankind. This was the intellectual justification for the first systematic persecution of Jews by Antiochus Epiphanes in the 2nd century B.C.E. In Roman times a second layer of theory was added by both Greek and Latin writers: Lysimachus of Alexandria; Apion; Nero's tutor Chaeremon, who inspired the second great wave of persecutions; and by Horace, Martial, Tacitus, and Juvenal.
>
> A third layer was contributed by Christian writers, including some of the greatest doctors of the church, such as Gregory of Nyssa, John Chrysostom, Ambrose, Augustine, and Gregory the Great. Some Christians taught that the deicidal Jews were in both local and universal conspiracies with Satan, a no-

> tion later explored in innumerable plots and sub-plots by the investigators of the Inquisition. The writings of Luther added yet another layer of anti-Semitic theory which became the pattern for prejudice in Protestant Europe (p. 28).

Luther's attitude toward Jews was complex. In his younger days he wrote about them with a quality of benign consideration. "I would advise and beg everybody to deal kindly with the Jews and to instruct them in the Scripture; in such a case we would expect them to come over to us" Moellering, 1948: p. 921). When, however, Jews did not convert en masse to Christianity, they became blasphemers in his eyes, and in his later years he wrote: "The Jews are veritable liars and vampires . . . . A more bloodthirsty and vindictive race has never seen the light of day. . . . This race has been possessed by Lucifer and all his angels. . . . Cursed be the vile race of Jews and cursed be their iniquity. . . . It is our own fault that we have not annihilated them"(Moellering, 1948, p. 921).

When the intellectuals of the Enlightenment came to undermine Christianity in the eighteenth century, they produced the first secular layer of anti-Semitism. Diderot, and still more Voltaire, engaged in the most virulent attacks on Judaism, partly as an indirect but safer way of attacking the more dangerous target of Christianity. Describing the course of this movement, Johnson (1984) wrote,

> This meant that the intellectual foundations of the modern world were warped by anti-Semitism, for virtually all modern writers were influenced, directly or indirectly, by Voltaire. So at a time when the old Christian myth of the Jews in conspiracy with the Devil was losing its force, at least in Western and Central Europe, anti-Semitism acquired a non-religious dynamism. It was at this point that a connection between the Left and anti-Semitic theory was first established. The early French socialists linked the Jews to the new Industrial Revolution and the vast increase in world commerce which marked the beginning of the 19th century. In a book published in 1808, Francois Fourier identified commerce as "the source of all evil" and the Jews as "the incarnation of commerce." The same line was taken by Pierre Joseph Proudhon: In a world poisoned by greed and materialism, the Jews were "the source of evil," who had "rendered the bourgeoisie, high and low, similar to them all over Europe." "We should send this race back to Asia or exterminate it." Fourier's pupil, Alphonse Toussenel, worked out in detail the notion of a worldwide financial conspiracy against humanity, run by Jews. If one

> conflated these various conspiracy theories, the Jews were revealed as simultaneously in league with Freemasons, Protestants, and Jesuits. Satan might be dead but Rothschild had taken his place. Jewish intellectuals abandoning their Judaism were almost as prone to these fantasies as Christian intellectuals abandoning their Christianity. It was Heine who coined the characteristic epigram of the epoch: "Money is the God of our time and Rothschild is his prophet" (pp. 28-29).

The Historical Image of the Jew in America

In the 1850's Rabbi Isaac M. Wise stated that one reason for publishing his magazine, The Israelite, was to counteract the current stream of abusive Jewish stereotypes. "A rascally Jew," he explained, "figured in every cheap novel, every newspaper printed some stale jokes about Jews to fill up space, and every backwoodsman had a few such jokes on hand for use in public addresses; and all this called forth not one word of protest from any source" (Harap, 1974, p. 5).

Harap, in an extensive treatise concerned with the imagery held of Jews in England, and primarily the United States, noted characteristics he discerned as having been deeply ingrained in the nineteenth century: peddlers, old clothes dealers, pawnbrokers; the deicide people condemned to eternity; a people imbued with a preoccupation with money and an inhuman hatred of Christians; harbourers of vengefulness, an inherent trait since biblical times; possessors of repellent physical qualities, such as an extremely heavy beard, greasy hair and skin, humpback, and "Jewish eyes," the latter probably derived from the "evil eye" attributed to Jews during the Middle Ages; perpetual wanderers with supernatural and diabolic powers and extraordinary, perhaps sinister, intellect; revolutionaries;manipulators of political power through command of money.

By 1940 one could say that negative imagery of Jews had coalesced as follows: Jews were the deicide people. Aliens wherever they lived, they were offensive in manner and appearance, unpleasant, disturbing. They were seen as seclusive, clannish, subversive, foreign, dangerous, threatening, and corrupting, preoccupied with wealth and power, and driven to attain these goals at whatever cost. Although looked on as unmanly, Jewish men were nevertheless believed to be practiced in seducing Gentile women by means of deceit and trickery. For the most part, it was Jewish men who were the target of this assault. Jewish women fared better. Ambrose Bierce said: "I hate Hebrews, but I adore Shebrews" (Harap, 1974, p. 344). For men, dark-eyed Rebeccas have had an attraction that goes back at least as far as the Crusades.

By 1986, most of this troubling imagery has faded. Jews receive high marks for intellect, achievement, literary and artistic accomplishment. They are not perceived as physically offensive, unmanly, foreign, subsersive, or corrupting. A negative set of images centered on money, wealth, power, and influence still persists, however. An appreciable minority of Americans perceive Jews as preoccupied with money, stingy, clannish, and extremely wealthy. They tend to exaggerate the wealth and power of Jews; some professional people, for example, think that Jews are heavily represented on the boards of most of the major American banks. Even among those who are well-disposed toward Jews, there is a certain questioning of Jewish influence, wealth, and power. Is there some danger in the control attributed to Jews of financial resources and the communications and entertainment industries? Do Jews dictate governmental policy, particularly foreign policy? The influence of Jews as holders of wealth and arbiters of power seems to be the one domain that is still troublesome for many. Clearly, however, between 1940 and 1986 the image of Jews in the American mind has changed considerably, and "for the better."

Lessening of Anti-Semitism in the United States

To the liberal mind, the decade of the 1950's in the United States was a wasteland. Senator Joseph McCarthy stalked the land while President Eisenhower, an indolent and complacent war hero, did little to oppose him. Figures from the world of art, film, theater, and literature were pilloried, forced to recant their political beliefs and name former colleagues or suffer blacklisting or comparable ostracism or punishment. The intellectual establishment was dealt a severe blow with the conviction of Alger Hiss. The legal upholding of the civil rights of blacks translated, in practice, into little more than an end to blatant violations. A seemingly rigid ideologue, John Foster Dulles, was vicar of foreign policy, and the Korean war, particularly with the participation of the People's Republic of China, raised the spectre of nuclear war. Self-satisfaction, the grey flannel suit, two cars in every garage, four children in every household symbolized the era, although recently revisionist historians have begun to cast a somewhat different light upon those times (Ambrose, 1984).

It was during the years 1945 to 1960, however, during this period of apparent conformity, conservatism, and stagnation, that anti-Semitism began to decline significantly. Consider the changes that took place and have taken hold since then. Quotas governing admission of Jews to universities and professional schools now are rare. Jews are prominent in American political life. An index of massive social change in the world of politics and public opinion was the presidential nomination by the Republican Party of Barry Goldwater in 1964, an action that hardly would have been seriously contemplated even a decade earlier; for Goldwater, although raised Episcopalian, had had a Jewish father. While Goldwater's campaign was not politically memorable, it did produce some of the better jokes of recent political times. "Can a man who is half-Jewish be all bad?" and "I always knew that the first Jewish president of the United States would be an Episcopalian." To a considerable extent Jewish writers, filmmakers, and the like define American middle class sensibility. Unlike the film stars of former eras, entertainers and celebrities who cultivate a glamorous image do not find it necessary or expedient to change Jewish names or hide Jewish origins. In her history of Jews in America from 18881-1981, *On Equal Terms* (1982), Lucy Dawidowicz entitles one of her chapters, "The Golden Age in America, 1945-1967." Based on extensive analysis of data concerned with "beliefs, attitudes, and experiences of Jews and non-Jews," Martire and Clark say, "While there are many worrisome signs, there are also solid reasons to believe that anti-Semitism may be on the wane in the United States" (1982, p. 2).

One does not want to carry this vision that Jerusalem has indeed been built in the United States too far, of course. As I write these words, black-Jewish tensions are considerable. From time to time, one has cause to wonder whether anti-Semitism has been displaced from American Jews to Israelis. Here and there in the United States a posse comitatus, the Klan, or Nazis surface. On the fringes of far right political sentiment, "hate literature" is published and disseminated. Jews, whose antennae can detect disaster with the discrimination of a heat-seeking missile, are not likely to take these good times for granted. If history has a message for Jews, it may well be that this period of peace and tolerance is as brief as a bubble.

Nonetheless, in the history of Western civilization, such alteration in the lives and social circumstances of American Jews represents remarkable cultural, social, and personal change. Although Jewish organizations and Jewish leaders were not sanguine about the fate of Jews in the Western world or in the United States after World War II (the Nazi era and World War II having served, after all, to confirm what any perspicacious person could readily see, that Jewish survival was perhaps more perilous than ever), American anti-Semitism began to fade after World War II, unexpectedly and unselfconsciously. It is true that in the years following World War II, the founding of the State of Israel received considerable attention. But otherwise Jewish experience was not prominent in the public eye. Harper's Magazine, for example, an important middle-of-the-road or perhaps slightly left-of-center opinion, published not a single article concerned primarily with the circumstances of Jews, either in Europe or the United States, from the end of World War II until 1953. The Rosenberg treason trial of 1951 was alarming to Jews in that the activities of Julius and Ethel Rosenberg seemed to confirm to the public-at-large the validity of the imagery of Jews as dangerous radicals, agents of suversion, international conspirators. In fact, it is even likely that the harsh outsome of the trial, sentences of death for both defendants, owed much to the circumstance that the judge, being Jewish, was motivated to demonstrate the loyalty and patriotism of American Jews. Political or social movements that capitalize upon or border upon anti-intellectualism are likely to incorporate anti-Semitic elements. So it was that Jews were wary of Senator Joseph McCarthy (although his chief aides were Jewish), and of the House Un-American Activities Committee; but overt anti-Semitism did not emerge.

The Political Psychology of Anti-Semitism

This extraordinary set of events, the very significant decline of anti-Semitism in the United States, calls for more explication than it has received thus far. In recent years, the psychological sciences have devoted little attention to anti-Semitism as compared to several decades ago when, for example, the monumental psychological works, The Authoritarian Personality (Adorno and colleagues, 1950) and the Nature of Prejudice (Allport, 1954) were published. In their An Introduction to Social Psychology, Lindgren and Harvey (1981) paid no attention to anti-Semitism except somewhat peripherally in the context of a discussion of The Authoritative Personality (Adorno and colleagues, 1950). In The Social Animal (Aronson, 1980), black-white and male-female relations were given much more attention than Jewish issues. As compared to the period of 1940-1960, psychoanalysts of late have paid surprisingly little attention to anti-Semitism; few books and articles have emerged. An exception is The Israel Journal of Psychiatry and Related Sciences. It may be that black-white relations have taken precedence, exacting greater social urgency as they do. Nonetheless, even if anti-Semitism is not now a major social concern in the United States, it is surprising that psychoanalysts direct so little attention to anti-Semitism, considering the numbers of Jewish psychoanalysts and patients. Inadequacy of explanation may be a factor. Psychoanalytic interpretation circa the 1940's and 1950's, based essentially on psychoanalytic theory of the 1920's, is not adequate to the task of accounting for anti-Semitism in its many and varied manifestations, including its decline.

In recent years, attention to anti-Semitism has been the province primarily of historians, philosophers, theologians, social psychologists, and survey researchers. Particular attention has been paid to the Third Reich and to the Holocaust. Kren and Rappoport (1980) demonstrated the efficacy of integrating historical and psychological perspectives in explicating the staggering genocidal endeavors of Nazi Germany. Referring to their work, Kelman (1982) wrote, "The authors use psychohistorical analysis in a responsible and persuasive way. They employ different kinds of psychological interpretations--appropriately geared to the level of the phenomena--as the discussion moves from cultural dispositions to situational reactions and on to individual personality (and psychopathology)" (p. 86). It is in psychohistorical and political psychology literature, as opposed to psychoanalytical books and journals, that one is likely these days to encounter psychodynamic psycholgical attention to anti-Semitism. Rather striking on examination of the literature is the absence of empirically based studies of anti-Semitism, after the fashion of the authors of The Authoritarian Personality (Adorno and colleagues, 1950). They set out to utilize psychological, or more precisely psychodynamic perspectives, in explaining anti-Semitism and fascistic tendencies within the framework of academic psychology, with its concerns for empiricism, system, measurement. In the last two decades survey researchers have dominated empirical studies of anti-Semitism (Glock and Stark, 1966; Selznick and Steinberg, 1969, Quinley and Glock, 1979; Martire and Clark, 1982). Social psychologists with interests in attitudes and attitude change have been involved in empirical research and experiments concerned with prejudice, ethnocentrism, or intergroup relationships, but in recent years attitudes toward groups other than Jews have occupied their attention for the most part (Sears and McConahay, 1973; Pettigrew, 1980; Schönbach, 1981; Tajfel, 1982; McConahay, 1983).

To this endeavor of addressing the state of anti-Semitism in the United States after World War II, with special attention to the period of 1945 to 1960, I bring five years of empirical research consisting of interviews with officials of various Jewish agencies about their perceptions of the circumstances of Jews and their activities designed to improve the lot of Jews (including the nation state of Israel); interviews with various Jewish populations--for example, reactions of Holocaust survivors in Skokie, Illinois, to the threat of a Nazi march in 1977 and 1978 (Freedman, 1980); interviews with mothers who describe what they convey to their children about being Jewish; interviews with various non-Jewish populations, including members of explicitly anti-Semitic or quasi anti-Semitic organizations; administration of adjective check lists(La Forge and Suczek, 1955), sentence and phrase completion tests, projective tests (primarily variants of the Thematic Apperception Test) (Morgan and Murray, 1935), and a picture-frustration test (Brown, 1947) for purposes of assessing imagery of Jews and non-Jews. (By way of a caveat, I should say that these empirical studies have the limitation of being confined to California, and primarily to the San Francisco area.) In the course of this research, moreover, I have gained considerable insight into the perceptions and imagery of various ethnic groups--Hispanic, black, Asian, and white, in addition to Jews--that is, into both self-imagery and imagery of other groups.

My approach to these issues is that of political psychology (Knutson, 1973). I am concerned, that is, to integrate personality processes in the individual--including inferred intrapsychic processes--with situational or social processes, including macro-social processes, political, economic, and the like. Wheels within wheels, whorls within whorls, open-systems interacting with other open-systems (Campbell, 1958; Bertalanffy, 1967; Churchman, 1968; Gochman, 1968). Isaiah Berlin writes, "Everything is partly the fault of the individual character, partly the fault of circumstances, partly in the nature of life itself"(Brown, 1985, p. 34). Saul Bellow says of Israel, "But no one is at ease in Zion. . . . The world crisis is added to the crisis of the state, and both are added to the problems of domestic life" (1976, pp. 56-57). Self versus other, Jewish versus non-Jewish, inner versus outer, the individual versus the environment, personality versus social process, cognitive versus affective, history versus the present. Anti-Semitic attitudes and behaviors are overdetermined, if they are anything. Linear relationships, or cause and effect relationships, simply will not serve as sufficient explanation. Only the mind of God, however, can encompass all of the salient features of a system at any one time. Our concern, then, is to discern those elements of the system that have particular explanatory value for the issue or question at hand. At one time, we may look primarily to macro-political process for explanation, for example, mass ideology; at another time we may look primarily to inferred unconscious personality process in the individual, for example, projection and displacement. Churchman (1968) emphasized the importance to systems thinking of goals or objectives. Our goal is enhanced understanding of the phenomenon of anti-Semitism (including its decline), a degree or kind of understanding that may be functional in meliorating anti-Semitic thinking and behavior and comparable kinds of ethnocentric disposition.

The Role of the Victim

Customarily, thinking about ethnocentrism and prejudice focuses on the characteristics and behavior of the "victimizer." To do otherwise, to look to the objects of victimization for clues as to their contribution to unfortunate or vicious systems, touches on one of the cardinal sins in the eyes of liberals, "blaming the victim." In writings concerned with anti-Semitism, one frequently encounters such statements as, "Anti-Semitism is a Christian problem. It has nothing to do with Jews," or "Anti-Semitism is the most pernicious form of prejudice because of the invisibility of Jews." In recent years, however, various perspicacious observers of the nation state of Israel (Alter, 1973; Stein, 1984) have raised questions about how it may be that certain of the more unfortunate aspects of Israel's circumstances are in part a function of what could be termed a kind of historical repetition compulsion. Like individuals communities, aggregations of people on whatever basis--race, ethnic origin, religion, even nation states--may collude unconsciously to produce an outcome or fate they ostensibly are trying to escape or avoid. The history of a people, even when disastrous, may determine the future of that people; people can be mired in their history. The original impulse for Zionism came from the desire to escape the perils of the ghettos of Eastern Europe. Yet in a way the medieval ghetto has been recreated in Israel. There are the Jews surrounded by enemies; there is the prince, the protector, the United States. One does not want to carry such analogies too far, of course. The history and fate of Israel have been determined by a multitude of forces, a complex system to which the citizens of Israel are but one contributor. Yet one wonders. At some deep level of the mind or heart, do Israelis need enemies, persecutors, a sense of victimization? In a perverse way, are these circumstances necessary to the security or even the survival of many Israelis?

Hannah Arendt (1968) has passed on the information that in the fifteenth and sixteenth centuries European Jews began to perceive themselves as a race apart. How else to explain the mistreatment, frequently murderous, of Jews? So it was that in the nineteenth century, when various theories of racial differences made an appearance on the intellectual, social, and political scene, Jews showed a certain readiness to acquiesce, although not, of course, on the basis that they were an inferior or pariah race.

Prior to World War II, a host of pejorative images, as indicated earlier, were cast upon Jews by non-Jewish society. Inevitably, of course, people subjected to such negative attribution are likely, in time, to internalize or introject the stigma attached to them; they become a component of the self-image. Prior to World War II, it is difficult to think that many American Jews escaped absorbing some elements of such a congeries of qualities into the self. Jews were a different people, and even in their own eyes a flawed people, at least to some extent.

When one looks at the estate of American Jews in 1945 and later, the prospects for reversing their circumstances would seem to have been dim. Hitler was dead and the Third Reich in ruins; but even though Western Civilization has been preserved, the Jews had lost the war. Six million of them were dead and the whole world of Eastern European Jewry had been wiped out. Renascence via the birth of the nation state of Israel was dubious indeed. Britain actively restricted immigration into its mandate, Palestine, and support for the founding of Israel by the United States in the United Nations--a necessity--was at best uncertain. One would presume that the morale of American Jews in 1945 would be low, that their disposition to accept pre-World War II circumstances would be considerable. Things could be a lot worse, after all, as Nazi Germany had well demonstrated.

That is not how matters evolved, however. Toward the end of World War II Jews and Jewish agencies began to take active measures to combat discriminatory actions and conventions that had gone unopposed, or but little opposed, for decades--such as quotas limiting entrance of Jews into certain schools, agreements that Jews could not reside in certain areas, work in certain companies or occupations, or become members of certain social and business organizations.

Such formal legal militancy and obduracy flowed from a significant change in morale, spirit, confidence, and self-image of American Jews, the Jews in some countries of Western Europe, and perhaps among Jews in the British Palestinian Mandate, later Israel. The collective psyche of American Jews, their conscious state and the imagery, urges, and impulses bubbling up from the personal and historical unconscious in the period, following hard upon World War II, deserve much more research and systematic attention than they have been given. It may be that in a brief period of time Jews in America began to slough off the coils of millenia of Jewish history of persecution.

I first became aware of such a contingency when I carried out the research mentioned earlier on Skokie, Illinois, centered on the threat of a march by a group of self-styled Nazis from Chicago (Freedman, 1980). Among other activities, I interviewed a number of survivor families (of the Holocaust)--parents and adult children--who comprise a significant proportion of the Skokie population. My reading of the events that took place in Skokie as reported in magazines, newspapers, radio, and television did not prepare me for the reactions of the survivors. To my surprise, much as they detested Nazi uniforms and swastikas, they wanted the Nazi march to take place so that they might engage in a counter-demonstration. Consider the following remarks of survivors: "I wanted to be there standing up to the Nazis at City Hall when they marched." "I wanted to face them. I would be letting down my loved ones who died, if I didn't stand up and face them." A woman who lost her parents and sisters in Dachau said, "Violence does not frighten me. Years ago, in Europe, when Nazis marched, we were afraid. We hid in our houses. I am not afraid now, I want to face them. What can they do to me now? This time they won't put us in gas chambers." The director of the Warsaw Ghetto Uprising Coalition said, "We felt it would have been important that Jews and other anti-Nazis be there to confront Nazis with a counter-demonstration that they could see. It is important to show the Nazis that Jews can't be pushed to the side, hiding in cellars, allowing their leaders to pick which of them will stand up and which will cower in the high school stadium as they did when living under Hitler."

In 1980 I wrote,

> The Jews of Skokie, or the survivors among them, were certainly disposed to reinforce one another in active response to Nazi aggression. They seem even to exaggerate the passivity of European Jews during the Holocaust. The image of Jew as the helpless scapegoat for all seasons is being profoundly altered. My informant, keen observer of such matters over decades in Europe and in the United States, tells me that the old masochistic ghetto humor is dying out. Rarely do we hear: "To be a Jew is impossible;" or "To be a Jew it's better not to be born at all, but not one Jew in 10,000 has such luck." Perhaps before long we'll be hearing Jews in bars singing Jewish equivalents of, "It's the same old shillelagh my father brought from Ireland" (Freedman, 1980, p. 176).

The origins of such a profound change in self-conception and outlook are obscure. Jews, and particularly Jewish survivors of Hitler's Europe, have been sensitive indeed to charges that the Jews of Europe submitted supinely to their annihilation. As mentioned earlier, some Jews exaggerate the passivity of Hitler's victims. Others, by way of reaction against such aspersion, emphasize and perhaps exaggerate instances of resistance. It is true that the uprising in the Warsaw ghetto in 1943 was the first rebellion of consequence by subject peoples in the long night of the Nazi occupation of Europe. But although they knew they were doomed, the resistance fighters did not choose suicide, after the manner of the defenders of Masada as depicted by the Jewish general and later Roman historian, Josephus--the subject of much Israeli mythologizing. Undoubtedly the repulsion by the Israelis of the invading Arab armies in 1948 contributed to a sense of control and mastery among Jews. Jews as such had not borne arms since the destruction of the Temple, although some Jewish communities were permitted arms during medieval times, and a Jewish brigade served in the British army in World War II. The sense of Jews as brave, heroic, and above all victorious warriors probably reached its zenith with Israel's stunning and crushing victory in the 1967 war.

A significant aspect of the victimization of Jews was the widespread conception of the men as feminized. Jewish men were regarded as weak and impotent, students and intellectuals, in contrast to the virile Nordic, Aryan, or non-Jewish male, and inevitably, of course, these negative attributes were internalized to some extent. So it was that in earlier years of this century American Jews depended heavily upon Jewish athletes to counter such unmasculine imagery. Israeli military success, however, has probably almost eliminated such stigma. Recently a columnist for the San Francisco Chronicle (Carrol, 1982) interviewed a local dairy farmer, a representative of the old virtues--attachment to family, place, and tradition, respect for hard work--a disapprover of much of what he saw about him. And what did he admire?--Ronald Reagan, George Blanda (a former professional football player), and the Israeli army. My empirical researches--the sentence completion tests and adjective check lists, for example--revealed little disposition to attribute to Jewish males negative physical characteristics such as weakness, impotence, or "feminine" qualities. And, of course, comparable self-attribution on the part of Jews has diminished. Some critics of Israeli military actions, Jews included, may argue, in fact, that a reaction formation has set in, that Israel too readily displays the power of the gun of which Jews have so often been the victim.

At the Passover Seder, the ritual of the Jew as victim is reenacted as if it happened yesterday. One may say that injustice and victimization--particularly the experiences of the Holocaust--live on in the timeless unconscious of many Jews. With the threat of the appearance of swastikas in Skokie in 1977, for the survivors it was no longer 1977; it was 1944. History has kept alive in the Jewish psyche the sense of threat and menace that has been the lot of Jews for millenia. "History is a butcher block," said Hegel. And yet, perhaps American Jews have now broken with history. It may be that the personality of American Jews now constitutes part of a different historical system.

In the decades of the 1970's and 1980's, the Holocaust has been the subject of considerable attention in the United States, as, for example, on television. Jewish interest in this public observance of the Holocaust suggests a certain ability to master the trauma, akin to the phenomenon that occurs in psychoanalysis, when repressed memories become conscious or new relationships among memories or events are fashioned in accord with increments of insight. The American Jews' ego mastery and coping processes are evidently now such that they can begin to affix a level gaze upon an event that defies explication and explanation. They can now outstare the emptiness so to speak. One may ask in this connection whether this phenomenon of public "disclosure" concerning the Holocaust has removed the sense of stigma that inevitably, albeit unconsciously, attaches to being a victim. A few years ago, I wrote,

> A victim to some degree cannot escape, at some level of self perception, the conviction that one deserves one's unfortunate fate. Overt, public victimization enhances the sense of stigmatization stored in the privacy of the unconscious. Such a prominent public phenomenon, however, as the showing on television of a film on the Holocaust tends to open doors into this concealed or private nurturing of a personal sense of damage. Jews do not deserve this. Allied to the sense of victimization is the sense of contamination. Victims of trauma often feel this very keenly--cancer victims, for example. Flood victims often feel contaminated by dirty water. Public events, such as the Holocaust on television, can modulate the power of investment in such a sense of contamination (Freedman, 1980, pp. 176-177).

A disposition to contribute to the system of one's own victimization is based in part, although primarily unconsciously as a rule, on the consideration that guilt feelings in oppressors may give victims some power over them. Within some limits this is probably true. At least as far back as Tacitus, however, we have been reminded that it is the disposition of wrongdoers to hate the people they have wronged. This is a consideration of moment when public attention is focused on the history of anti-Semitic evil, and particularly on the Holocaust. To some extent, such attention arouses a degree of collective guilt among non-Jews that probably has some prophylactic value; beyond some point, however, guilt may well be replaced by resentment and anger.

The imagery of Jews held by the general populace exaggerates the power and wealth of American Jews, thereby generating a considerable body of envy. Do resentment, fear, envy of Jewish wealth and power contribute to anti-Semitic impulses? Should American Jews play down their realistically favorable status? Some Jews and friends of Jews would have it so. Hannah Arendt (1968) pointed out, however, that historically Jews have been most vulnerable not when they were powerful but when their power was declining. A while back I was reminded of her observations when I talked with a prominent official of an American Jewish agency about a ceremony that had been sponsored by the Polish government to commemorate the fortieth anniversary of the Warsaw Ghetto uprising. He remarked that this support, given by a governemnt with powerful anti-Semitic proclivities, was in considerable part based on an assumption (and a hope) that American Jewish bankers would influence Western creditor countries to be lenient about the repayment of Polish debts.

History is, after all, a vision of the past that we find useful in making sense of the present. In one sense, Jewish history is an unending series of fines, levies, massacres, social ostracism, ghettos, the Holocaust. Yet the remarkable energy of Jews, the facility with which they have managed to take advantage of favorable social circumstances, suggests that buried in Jewish history is another story. I say "buried" in the sense that a cast of misfortune and tragedy has obscured an obverse side of Jewish existence in the history of Western civilization. According to Riesenberg (1979),

> It is easy to understand why this particular view of an unabating Jewish misery persists through the ages. There has been extensive and dramatic persecution of the Jews throughout history, and anti-Semitism is one of the oldest identifiable social attitudes or prejudices in the western tradition. Moreover, in the last century, in the more or less immediate experience of all who write about Jewish subjects, first the Czarist and then the massive Nazi assault on the Jews have quite understandably colored views of earlier relations between Jews and other peoples. Indeed, a variety of negative experiences over the long-run development of Jewish consciousness has played an important role in stimulating Jews to an awareness of their identity and in creating an almost instinctive assumption that what has recently been horrible has always been that way. My belief is that these ideas have come to obscure contrary evidence about the quality of Jewish life. I will try to discard the black Hitlerian lenses and see the Jewish experience somewhat differently. My basic position is that the Jewish experience was not very different from that of other small peoples, and that, indeed, the Jews were remarkably and almost uniquely, successful in preserving their identity, adapting to a great variety of environments, and in attaining a high level of material, moral, and intellectual achievement (pp. 402-403).

The estate of Jews in America today is unique in history, and yet, assuredly, it rests upon some awareness of the kinds of experiences to which Riesenberg refers. How else to account for such circumstances as the considerable personal and social "successes" of the survivors living in Skokie, a single generation after the devastation of the Third Reich, or the extraordinary achievements of European Jews, after the gates of the ghettos were opened in the eighteenth and nineteenth centuries?

Social Change and Personal Change

To argue that the status of Jews in the United States is to some extent a function of the self-concept, the social outlook, and the behavior of Jews is, of course, to deny the validity of the view that prejudice is entirely a social phenomenon, an external imposition upon a minority population. That there is such a social phenomenon as oppression cannot be denied. But involved in prejudice much of the time is also a phenomenon equivalent to neurosis, a process by which individuals or groups contribute, often unconsciously, to outcomes they neither foresee nor are aware of desiring. Undoubtedly there are societies in which anti-Semitism is independent of the behavior of Jews--such as Russia and Eastern Europe today, perhaps--but I believe that the United States clearly offers to Jews the prospect--not always realized, of course--of a society in which they can prosper; and in recent decades most Jews have taken advantage of this beneficent environment.

Although I am deeply committed to a psychoanalytic vision of human nature and social existence, a vision that emphasizes pessimism, irony, complexity, tragedy, I am nonetheless convinced that inherent in American culture are deep and powerful impulses of tolerance and generosity. These proclivities have contributed to substantial changes in Jewish life in the United States. What processes or mechanisms bring such changes about? How do personality processes in individuals interact with cultural forces or influences so as to produce consequential social change?

Intrinsic to The Authoritarian Personality (Adorno and colleagues, 1950) is the sense, after the fashion of pre-World War II psychoanalysis, of the fixity or perdurability of the adult personality. To a very considerable degree, the personality is fully formed by about age sixteen, when the vicissitudes and vagaries of puberty have diminished. People who develop "normally," that is, with relative freedom from unconscious conflict and fixation, are capable of developing to higher levels of functioning. On the other hand, individuals (authoritarian personalities, for example) whose inner world is peopled by troubling ghosts of the past, which cannot readily be exorcised, are not likely to change short of extensive and systematic intervention into the personality, something on the order of psychoanalysis. In line with such thinking, the expectation would be that authoritarian dispositions in a culture or society are intimately bound to authoritarian characteristics in individuals. And the further expectation would be that since changes in such individuals are produced only with considerable difficulty, then authoritarian tendencies in culture and society can be reduced only with comparable difficulty.

It happens, however, that personal change and social change do not operate in this parallel fashion. Very slight changes in individuals, large numbers of individuals, to be sure, can result in massive social change. Undoubtedly, such a process accounts in considerable measure for the significant decline in anti-Semitism in recent decades. A good example of this process is the changes that took place between 1928 and 1936 in the United States. In 1928 Herbert Hoover was in the White House, and social conservatism was the keynote--laissez faire economics, caution in social intervention. Under Franklin Roosevelt, first elected to the Presidency in 1932, programs of social and economic intervention and experimentation were instituted that radically altered American society.In 1936, when Roosevelt carried all but two states, Maine and Vermont, his smashing electoral victory hardly signified that the great majority of Americans had radically transformed their social and economic outlook between 1928 and 1936. Rather, there had been small shifts in the beliefs and attitudes of millions of citizens. The person who in 1928 would have considered a program of social security an instrument of the devil and the equivalent of communizing American society was still opposed in 1936, but his opposition was less fervent, and less firmly linked to attitudes about the overall social and economic climate.

American Ideology

When we look at the systems in the environment, society, and culture in which attitudes, opinions, values, and behavior of American non-Jews toward Jews are embedded, it is useful to start with the system of American ideology. To be an American is to receive a measure of the ideology of the Bill of Rights and the Constitution as one's inheritance, in one's bones, so to speak, regardless of the other influences--regional, ethnic, racial, or religious--that may impinge. Consider the comments of Alexis de Tocqueville about a reading of the Declaration of Independence in a Methodist Church in Albany, New York, in 1831, as part of the civic celebration of the Fourth of July. "This was not, I assure you, a theatrical performance. There was not in the reading of these promises of independence so well kept, in this return of an entire people toward the memory of its birth, in this union of the present generation to that which is no longer, sharing for the moment all its generous passions, there was in all that something deeply felt and truly great" (Reeves, 1982, p. 43).

Voices are frequently raised to remind us that the authors of the Bill of Rights and the Constitution were patricians, many of whom owned slaves, and that various historical American injustices, among them the treatment of blacks and Indians, for example, amply demonstrate that ideal and reality have by no means fully meshed. Yet, the power of the American Revolution and its accompanying ideology cannot be discounted. Often the title of Robert Middlekauff's highly praised account of the American Revolution, The Glorious Cause (1982), is taken to be ironical. This was not, however, the author's intent. He envisioned the American Revolution as an epochal event in human consciousness and social experience: "The title that I have given this book may be misunderstood in this day--when all is suspect--as irony. I do not intend that it should be. The Americans, the 'commom people,' as well as soldiers and great leaders, who made the Revolution against Britain believed that their cause was glorious. And so do I" (p. vii).

By way of concern with anti-Semitism, it is relevant to note that American Jews were accorded full rights of citizenship from the inception of the Republic. This was not the situation in Britain until well into the nineteenth century; and while citizenship rights came to French Jews in the course of the vagaries of the French Revolution, they came with a caveat. Jews were clearly admonished to be French first, and Jews secondarily. The prerogative of the nation state of France clearly transcended any collective Jewish concerns.

In Germany, the concept of universal human rights never fully took hold, at least prior to the establishment of the Federal Republic of Germany after World War II. This principle was operative in theory but not in practice in the Weimar Republic, a consideration of importance when one contemplates the Holocaust. By contrast, at levels of ideology and governmental procedure, American Jews clearly were made to feel welcome on American soil, as witness the touching letter sent to General Washington by the congregation of America's second synagogue in Newport, Rhode Island, on the occasion of his inauguration as President. It included the following statement: "Deprived as we have hitherto been of the invaluable rights of free citizens, we now (with a deep sense of gratitude to the Almighty Disposer of all events) behold a government . . . which to bigotry gives no sanction, to persecution no assistance--but generously affording to all liberty of conscience, and immunities of citizenship--

deeming every one, of whatever nation, tongue, or language equal parts of the great governmental machine" (Harap, 1974, p. 3). In a letter to the Jewish congregations of Philadelphia, New York, Charleston, and Richmond, Washington wrote, ". . . the liberal sentiment towards each other which marks every political and religious denomination of men in this country stands unrivalled in the history of nations" (1974, p. 20). John Adams, Thomas Jefferson, and James Madison strongly affirmed these liberal sentiments. In this connection it is important to appreciate the significance of the search for religious freedom in America's early origins. Various Puritan divines likened the experiences of their sects to those of the Israelites of *The Old Testament*. They were Hebrew scholars; Hebrew was, in fact, required of students at universities such as Harvard and Yale, on into the nineteenth century. The Puritans held Jews in high regard, and when they made efforts to convert them to Christianity, it was only to lead them to a higher phase of religious development, not a matter of coercion.

"All men are created equal." As compared to Europe, status and hierarchy are not such prominent features of American life, and lessened anti-Semitism is a consequence. In a short story, Isak Dinesen (1981) asked why it was that as late as the middle of the nineteenth century, in an age of superb craftsmen, the upper classes of Scandinavia lived such uncomfortable lives--in cold and drafty rooms with uncomfortable furniture. The answer, she concluded, was that they were simply conforming to the expectation of how people of their social station should live. Gregor von Rezzori, in *Memoirs of an Anti-Semite* (1981), described the anti-Semitism endemic to the aristocracy of the pre-World War I Austro-Hungarian empire. By virtue of one's social status one looked down upon "Jew-boys." This disposition came with one's mother's milk. No amount of experience, education, or sophistication could eradicate it.

Consideration of the power of ideology in America to foster tolerance or mute anti-Semitism, particularly in the decade or two after World War II, certainly calls for attention to the ethos of the United States during that war. It was in some ways a recapitulation of the American Revolution--a time and a nation informed by historical resonances of the brotherhood of man, death to the tyrant, the salvation of the oppressed and the persecuted. And this time, unlike some other American military adventures, the United States had got it right. The fate of democracy and Western Civilization versus despotism and barbarism was truly at stake. In a study of alumnae of a women's college over various graduation classes from 1904 to 1956, which I (Freedman, 1967a) carried out in the late 1950's, the results were that the alumnae of the classes of 1940 to 1943 were the lowest of all groups on the California E (Ethnocentrism) and F (Authoritarianism) Scales (Adorno, and colleagues, 1950). Even by the late 1950's, the influence of the passionate reaffirmation of the United States to democratic ideals generated by the war had not diminished. The scores on the E and F scales of the alumnae of the classes of 1940 to 1943 were lower than those of the alumnae of the class of 1956 (tested two years after graduation), but not significantly so. Nevertheless, this generally liberal position of the alumnae of the early 1940's with respect to social and political issues was not accompanied by anything approaching economic liberalism or radicalism; a full ninety-two percent of the group, for example, rejected the statement, "It is up to the government to make sure that everyone has a secure job and a good standard of living." Comparably, although young people of today tend to be liberal in racial, ethnic, and religious issues, they supported Ronald Reagan in the election of 1984.

A substantial body of thought has it that economic inequality is at the heart of ethnocentrism. Addressing the issue of how to lessen American anti-Semitism, Cary McWilliams (1949) wrote, ". . . what the task involves is the creation of a society in which production is organized on some basis other than individual self-aggrandizement. . . . Freedom from fear is the best way to cure group prejudice. This means freedom from the fear of war, from the fear of economic insecurity, from the fear of personal unworthiness . . ." (pp. 224-225). Yet anti-Semitism began to decline in the 1950's, a decade not notable for radical social change, nor has it increased during the tenure of President Ronald Reagan.

The Significance of a Difference

The American ethos has supported tolerance and accommodation, although only marginally in some respects, in that Americans by-and-large are expected to become Americans. The melting pot design sets certain limits on differences. Improvement in Jewish social circumstance owes much to the Jewish facility to fit in, to become productive citizens, primarily middle and upper-middle class, like non-Jews of comparable status. Unlike the fervently visible ethnic character that flourished, for example, on the lower East Side of Manhattan at the turn of the century, today Jews are indistinguishable in appearance from non-Jews. Exceptions, like the Hasidic Jewish communities in Brooklyn, New York, and Los Angeles, for example, are few. In this connection we must take note of the ubiquitousness of circumcision among young American males of all faiths as compared with former eras. Freud wrote: ". . . among the customs through which the Jews marked off their aloof position, that of circumcision made a disagreeable, uncanny impression on others. The explanation probably is that it reminds them of the dreaded castration idea and of things in their primeval past which they would fain forget" (1939, p. 144).

Any perceptual difference is, in a sense, an invitation to discrimination. In this respect, Jews, by virtue of being Caucausian, are spared a considerable degree of instant perception of difference. Unlike the Jewish populations of many European countries, where until well into this century they constituted a singular "different people," in the United States Jews have not been the only conspicuous minority. In most of Europe in medieval and earlier times, however, Jews were indeed the only "different" ones. Because travel was rare for most Europeans, their experience with any other race or religion was limited to the Jews. And they, confined to ghettos, were effectively prevented from casual social interaction with Christian society. Jews were likely to dress differently, often required to do so by order of local authority. Jews spoke another language, followed many different customs. Small wonder, then, that they were objects of curiosity, often morbid, and projection, often virulent. By contrast, from early on the United States has had an even more distinct minority--the blacks. In the nineteenth century, the poet, James Russell Lowell, observed that the lot of Jews in the United States would be easier than their life in Europe by virtue of the presence of blacks. In Europe, Jews served to satisfy the need of the greater society to establish superiority, "this peculiar craving of the supreme Caucasian nature," to use Lowell's phrase (Harap, 1974, p. 96). In the United States blacks have better served this purpose. Some social critics have asserted that the decline in American anti-Semitism after World War II is to some degree a function of a diversion of hostile attention away from Jews to blacks, as blacks became more "visible" by way of the civil rights movements and political and social prominence.

As a most significant contributor to prejudice, the simple fact of perceptual differences has received insufficient attention. The great historian of the Jews, Salo Baron (1964), was called upon to testify at the trial of Adolf Eichmann in Jerusalem. When asked why anti-Semitism was so persistent a phenomenon, he replied, ". . . dislike of the unlike. People dislike people who are not quite like they are" (Berger, 1985, p. 18). Studies of development in infancy and childhood indicate that perception of difference occurs early and often engenders fear (Brooks and Lewis, 1967; Bower, 1977; Brooks, 1981). From an ethological and evolutionary perspective, such disposition to respond negatively to difference probably has survival value for the human species; thus are potential enemies identified. Various anthropologists account for the incest taboo primarily on the basis that it promotes marriage among differing, sometimes potentially hostile peoples, thereby promoting peace or coexistence, and countering suspicion of strangers. Self-definition is not only a matter of determination of what one is; it is also a matter of determination of what one is not. National, ethnic, racial, or religious self-consciousness is of necessity exclusionary. There must be aliens--or in some cases, enemies--to be excluded (Armstrong, 1982). So by virtue of minimizing maifestations of differences or exclusivity, Jews have assimilated into middle-class American life. The journalist, Richard Reeves, has reported an interview with a Jewish professor and editor. Professor: "The Federalist Papers are the most morally impressive documents in the history of the world. The United States offered Jews the greatest space we ever had. But of course we had to pay a price." Reeves: "What was the price?" Professor: "We had to be like everybody else." (1982, p. 282)

Education, Information, and Anti-Semitism

To emphasize the role of awareness of differences in cognitive development in childhood and infancy and in the process of arriving at self-definition is also to maintain that a disposition to ethnocentrism, intolerance, and prejudice is an inevitable human quality. It is, in some respects, like original sin. Anti-Semitism cannot therefore be laid solely at the door of a flawed society, and social, political, and economic reform cannot of themselves eliminate it, although social conditions can exacerbate or moderate prejudicial tendencies, just as increases in cognitive complexity can counter them.

Studies indicate that about one-third of Americans harbor significant negative opinion about Jews (Martire and Clark, 1982). These "anti-Semites" tend to be in their fifties and beyond, older than the general population. Although any explanation for the decline in anti-Semitic outlook in younger age-groups would clearly be complex, undoubtedly the higher educational levels of the younger population is a central factor. More accepting attitudes toward Jews tend to be associated with higher income and education, and a decline in ethnocentrism and authoritarianism has been found to be among the important outcomes of college education. Higher education, therefore, can be seen to have exerted a profound influence on American life and society, notably since the Depression years and especially since World War II, a period during which college attendance increased dramatically. Research has clearly shown that students have emerged from commencement exercises with a greater commitment to the liberal view than they had as freshmen, that is, with a greater appreciation of the complexity of people and social events, more openness to new experience and flexibility in thinking, greater forbearance in judgment of people, and the like. These changes are large in some students, small in others. But few go through college these days without acquiring at least a tinge of liberalization. And the social consequences of such changes are enormous (Sanford, 1962; Webster and colleagues, 1962; Freedman, 1967b; Axelrod and colleagues, 1969; Feldman and Newcomb, 1969).

Research by Plant (1965) indicated that a decline in ethnocentrism and authoritarianism during the college years is not entirely a function of stage of life or maturation. The college experience plays a key role. Other investigations (Freedman, 1962, 1967a,b; Feldman and Newcomb, 1969) have revealed that these changes in attitude and opinion that develop during the college years have considerable perdurability; they are likely to persist over a lifetime. Individuals of elite persuasion may scoff at American standards of higher education, but mass higher education unquestionably has contributed significantly to such progress as the United States has made in the area of civil rights and social tolerance.

Comparably, in the domain of religion and theology, lessened anti-Semitism is related to increases in the amount and complexity of information provided to the public-at-large. I refer, in particular, to the decline in the imagery of Jews as killers of Christ. In the United States in the nineteenth century, and on up to World War II, the aura of deicide surrounded the Jew. As Mark Twain (1985, originally published 1899) pointed out, it was fostered in most of the Sunday schools in the land. Since World War II, however, Christian churches have tended to dwell more on Christ's Jewish origins and to explain the circumstances of the Crucifixion in ways that do not reflect primary guilt onto Jews. The devastating image of Judas Iscariot as a deicide figure, which has been attached to Jews for millenia, has thereby been much diminished.

Beginning in 1933, when Hitler took power, the constant barrage of slander directed at Jews in German film, radio, newspapers, and the like contributed to and facilitated their slaughter. Today, the propagation of negative imagery of Jews is a prominent feature of Russian public life. The nature and degree of publicly disseminated information are intimately connected to the extent to which inhumane, even murderous actions are visited upon various peoples. At some level of awareness most citizens of the Third Reich, although not privy to the details, knew that terrible things were happening to Jews. Newspapers and radio were silent on the subject, however, and the worst atrocities were carried out in restricted areas. This lack of public attention enabled the civilian German population to preserve its guilty secrets in isolation, or in small pockets of shared guilt. To some degree, even active perpetrators of atrocities could escape guilt feelings thereby. It happens, when public attention is focused upon grossly inhumane behavior in a reasonably civilized society, that feelings of shame are elicited, as witness the effect of various scenes on television and reports in newspapers during the Civil Rights Movement in the 1960's. A free press and free communications can significantly induce shame on a mass scale and contribute to humane public behavior. (In the case of individual development, guilt reaction may represent a higher stage, but it often can be quietly sequestered without influencing public behavior, whereas shame can more effectively control uncivilized dispositions among large groups of people.)

Anti-Semitism and Political and Economic Alignments

Prior to 1945, the Jew as radical, subversive of the established order, was a common American image. Stereotypes are likely to have a kernel of truth, and indeed, Jewish commitment to liberal and radical causes was conspicuous. In the past decade or so, however, Jews have tended to vote their class interests to greater extent, giving Presidents Nixon and Reagan a larger proportion of their votes than they had given any Republican candidate since 1933, when Democrat Franklin Roosevelt began his tenure in office. (This proclivity was apparently reversed in the election of 1984.) The onetime attraction to the Soviet Union, based on the belief that it was a beacon of hope for liberals and radicals, has by now plummeted to just about zero. The clear knowledge of Russia's internal anti-Semitism and hostility to Israel has indisputably turned most Jews against Russia and communism, and a substantial body of Jewish intellectual and political conservatism has been generated in recent years. In the ways in which macro-social processes influence personal imagery, it is much easier now to envision the Jew as protector of and contributor to rather than underminer of American welfare, hearth, and home. Such an assumption presumes that enmity to Jews in the United States is primarily the province of right-wing sympathizers. Unlike Europe, the United States has no tradition of left-wing anti-Semitism, although in recent years, perhaps, certain black groups have been so disposed, and one is sometimes compelled to think very carefully, and at least twice, about certain left-wing criticisms of Israel.

Beginning with the victory of Israel in the 1967 war, European sentiment toward Israel, for complex reasons, has grown increasingly hostile. Israel is hardly beyond criticism, of course, but the extremely hostile fervor and irrationality of some of the condemnations of Israel suggest underlying motivational forces at work that are seriously occluding political judgment. In the plethora of criticism directed at Israel it is not hard to detect a degree of displaced anti-Semitism--that is, anti-Semitism displaced from Jews to Israelis. Some elements of the European far right can, of course, excoriate Israelis, as they may European Jews, simply for being Jews. People who inhabit other political positions that do not tolerate anti-Semitism so readily have more difficulty expressing hostility to Jews. Israelis, however, by virtue of what is opprobrious behavior in the eyes of many Europeans, offer a fair target. They are seen as militant bullies and oppressors, and given the hostility to the United States endemic to many Europeans, it is a simple matter to label Israel as America's puppet, America's agent in imposing its imperialist designs on the world. Such positions are readily taken by the European left, for example, in France and Germany, where left-wing anti-Semitism has a long history. As mentioned earlier, Voltaire, a prince of the Enlightment, was hostile to Jews, as were many of the foremost French writers and social critics of the nineteenth century. The "sins" of Israelis, moreover, help to alleviate the residue of guilt left in the wake of the Holocaust in Europe. If the Israeli Jews of today are so bad, perhaps European Jews were equally reprehensible and therefore deserved their fate. In inchoate but significant ways condemning Israel seems to ease some guilt and grant some serenity to many Europeans, compensation for the troubled sleep brought on by the ghastly fate of Jews in World War II.

In recent decades in the United States the shifts in attitude toward Israel among various groups have been remarkable. People who admire power and toughness and advocate hostility to Russia, usually found on the political right, who in the past were likely to be equivocal at best in support of Jews, are now supporters of Israel. Out of eschatological concerns various fundamentalist Christian sects now promote Israeli causes. In the past such congregations, of relatively lesser education and sophistication, were likely to harbor considerable negative imagery of Jews. As Fischel (1982) has pointed out, their enthusiasm for Israel does not mean that negative stereotyping of Jews has completely ended, but for the most part they are favorably disposed. Given the inevitable tendency to transpose Israeli and Jew, Israel has great significance for the imagery of all Jews, and a favorable attitude toward Israel is likely to be reflected in the attitude toward American Jews, and vice versa.

The new phenomenon that has emerged in the United States in the last decade is left-wing condemnation of Israel. This represents a response to actions of Israel to some degree, but also, and perhaps more centrally, it is related to the negative imagery of the United States--regarded as the world's bete noire, a reactionary bully responsible for most of the misfortunes, sins, and injustices to be found on this planet, with Israel its ally. Given the fluidity of Jewish versus Israeli identity, this phenomenon bears watching.

Stages of Development and Anti-Semitism

Although personal development over the life cycle has received much attention from psychologists, sociologists, and psychiatrists in recent years, the vicissitudes of ethnocentrism over time have been given little attention. The conception of stages of development after the fashion of Erikson (1963), Loevinger and Wessler (1970), Kohlberg (1971), Piaget (1932, 1972), and Gilligan (1982) obviously has implications for ethnocentric attitude and behavior. Loevinger and Wessler posited six stages of ego development based on data derived from a sentence completion test: (1) the presocial and symbiotic, (2) the impulsive, (3) the conforming, (4) the conscientious, (5) the autonomous, (6) the integrated. Stages one and two are associated with ethnocentrism, as is stage three in certain social circumstances. People whose level of ego development has attained stage four or higher are likely to be of a moderate or low ethnocentric disposition. For Loevinger and Wessler then, authoritarianism and the accompanying ethnocentrism are characteristics of all individuals during early stages of development. Some develop beyond these early stages; others are mired in early developmental stages and are thereby prone to ethnocentrism.

As Erikson (1968) and Greenberger (1984) have reminded us, adolescence is often a time of confusion as to self-identity. Fierce loyalties to the groups that seem to foster certitude of identification and fierce antagonisms to the groups that seem to threaten it are likely to be hallmarks of adolescence. Not long ago a high school student of recent Asian immigrant origin was murdered by a fellow student, a Caucasian, in a university town in California. Contributing considerably to the assailant's hostility was not so much the victim's race but rather that he had made no attempt "to fit in." The victim and a small group of recent Asian immigrants were said to keep to themselves and were noticeably different. Since most Jewish youth are indistinguishable from their peers, they are less likely to be subjected to such primitive in-group versus out-group distinctions. It happens, however, that most of the vandalism of recognizable Jewish properties--synagogues and graveyards, for example--is carried out by persons under the age of 21. The youth in this age group are also responsible for a major share of American crime in general, of course.

Many of the numerous studies concerned with anti-Semitism published in the decade after World War II viewed it from a psychoanalytic perspective (Loeblowitz-Lennard, 1947; Kurth, 1947; Zilboorg, 1947; Ackerman and Jahoda, 1948; Loewenstein, 1951; Bird, 1955; Simmel, 1946). Among psychologists, the authoritarian personality dominated theoretical attention to anti-Semitism from a psychodynamic perspective. Essentially the concept of the authoritarian personality addressed personality structure and processes in accord with the dominant psychoanalytic themes of the 1940's--the interplay among the systems of ego, superego, and id, and the vicissitudes of the mechanisms of defense as they mediate among these systems (Freud, A. 1946). The Oedipal themes of rivalry, power, and desire predominate, with contributions from the anal stage of development as well. The prototypic authoritarian personality resembles Fromm's (1941) sado-masochistic character--submission to an authority figure perceived as all-powerful, repression of the hostility engendered by such submission, displacement of aggression to an aggregate of people who are "deserving" of such hostility. Projection of undesirable qualities onto the despised or hated out-group justifies sadism and obviates guilt. For Hitler, Jews were "the bacillus in the blood of mankind;" simple self-preservation, therefore, demanded their extermination. Typical of traditional Freudian psychoanalysis, the prototypic authoritarian personality is a male. Among women, authoritarianism derives primarily from conventionality--the need to idealize parents, the disposition to repress hostile tendencies so as to maintain a proper "lady-like" persona. Mitscherlich-Nielsen (1983) has written one of the rare articles to address anti-Semitism among women.

By the 1980's the authoritarian personality is rarely adduced to account for racist tendencies. Among psychologists, racism or ethnocentrism has become much more the province of the social or cognitive psychologist than that of the depth psychologist. Consider _Sanctions for Evil_ (Sanford and Comstock, 1971), in which the authors addressed the issue of sanctioned mass cruelty. To some extent the massacre at My Lai in Vietnam was the catalyst for the book. What social and psychological processes underlie or contribute to such uncivilized behavior? It is interesting to observe that in _Sanctions for Evil_ psychoanalytic explanations are given modest attention, only a score or so years after publication of _The Authoritarian Personality_. In the United States and perhaps in the Western world generally, authoritarian personalities en masse seem to be considerably less in evidence than in earlier decades of this century. The phenomenon resembles the changes in clinical symptomatology that have occurred over the course of the twentieth century. Whereas, for example, in World War I conversion hysterias were common in the British army, they were but little in evidence in World War II, replaced apparently by physiological sequelae of prolonged stress, such as gastric ulcer. In the United States today eating disorders are much more common than they were several decades ago.

Because the authoritarian personality is less likely to be adduced these days than it was several decades ago in addressing personality contributions to anti-Semitism, does this mean that the basic concepts on which the construct, the authoritarian personality, is based--that authoritarian and ethnocentric behavior has roots deeply based in the personality--are now invalid, and perhaps were erroneous even in 1950? Hardly. Evidence that a body of theory has come to have diminished usefulness in different social circumstances does not mean that it did not serve to elucidate in the past, nor that it cannot continue to illuminate in various context in the present and future. Does one explain Hitler and Goebbels, for example, primarily on the basis of social influence, without attention to forces in the personality? To the last, in Hitler's bunker in Berlin in 1945, both men were faithful to their commitment to racial purity and the necessity for countering the worlwide Jewish conspiracy. Or how do we account for so-called revisionist historians today, some of them of considerable intellectual and professional stature, albeit not in the field of history, who assert that the Holocaust never occurred, that a phenomenon--like typhus epidemics--killed off several hundred-thousand Jews. One of these "historians," a professor at a university of some prominence, informed me that Jews were, "like a disease. Wherever they went, they infected people." Almost daily, in 1985, newspapers reported another arrest of members of a violent anti-Semitic and anti-black loose confederation of groups, which go by various names--The Order, The White American Bastion, Brüder Schweigen, Aryan Nations. Although little personal history of these individuals has been made public, they seem to resemble various of Hitler's bullyboys in the early days of the SS and SA--Ernst Röhm, for example.

Addressing the issues of social processes versus personality processes in explicating authoritarianism and anti-Semitism, Sanford (1973) said,

> It follows that differences in F scale scores from one culture or subculture to another do not by any means contradict or downgrade the role of personality in authoritarianiam. Selznick amd Steinberg, however, would leave personality out altogether, relying simply on the learning of cultural norms

> or elements as an explanation for authoritarianism. No doubt such learning, or nonlearning, influences F scale scores and may even be largely responsible for high scores in the "surface resentment" type of "authoritarianism" and the "rigid" type of low authoritarianism. But any alternative theory of authoritarianism must explain the major finding of the original study--the patterning of the component dispositions. Why should anti-Semitism be associated with anxiety about sex, with self-glorification, with submissiveness toward authority? To say that this is "in the culture" or is due to a general lack of enlightenment (as Selznick and Steinberg do) is not an explanation. Why should the dispositions go together in a culture? I would argue as we did in _The Authoritarian Personality_, that they go together because they constitute a dynamic system, in an individual or in a social group. In any culture the common emotional impulses of individuals are shaped through shared experience in the social group, and ways of controlling these impulses are developed in the individual and in the group, thus forming and favoring cultural values. In any culture some individuals accept prevailing values and social codes without necessarily needing them for defensive purposes, but such individuals most quickly adopt the cultural elements they do need for such purposes; and any individual may develop methods for coping with the problems of life in the same way they were originally developed in his culture. Culture and personality continuously interact, in mutually supporting ways (p. 160).
>
> . . . Thus today, although I find little in the facts or theories of _The Authoritarian Personality_ that seems fundamentally wrong, I have no difficulty in urging that we now stress the _interaction_ of personality and culture, of psychodynamic and cognitive processes (p. 161).

It does seem that cultural and social conditions in the United States have so changed as to reduce the likelihood of producing authoritarian personalities, and to reduce their influence when they do appear on the social scene. The fearsome father who dominated the household in the nineteenth century is now just as likely to be something more on the order of a more competent and knowledgeable older brother. The world of politics and finance is less likely now than earlier in this century to tolerate--or even foster--curmudgeons on the order of Henry Ford, who financed the publication of _The Protocols of the Elders of Zion_ and promulgated their distribution in the 1920's (Sykes, 1967). The closely-knit, patriarchical family of Freud's day that produced people who knew who they were or were supposed to be, but had trouble fitting in, has been replaced to a considerable degree by family circumstances that produce people who do not know very well who they are (Erikson, 1963). The latter syndrome can predispose to ethcocentrism also, of course, but probably patterns of ethnocentrism that differ somewhat from those exposited in The Authoritarian Personality.

Object Relations Theory and Anti-Semitism

If we look to psychoanalysis from an historical perspective, we may observe that somewhere in the second generation of the movement, in the 1920's and 1930's, primarily in the United Kingdom, attention began to shift from the Oedipal and anal stages of development, expressed in drives accentuating desire, power, and competition, to earlier periods of development, expressed in drives accentuating need, attachment, and separation (Little, 1984). The emphasis shifted as well from Freud's focus on the father to the relationship with the mother. Object relations theory offers much by way of explication of ethnocentrism, but in this connection it has received little attention from most psychologists and others in the psychological sciences. The index of the Handbook of Polical Psychology (Knutson, 1973) contains no references to Melanie Klein (1975), the doyenne of the object relations movement, nor to any other prominent figures of like persuasion, for example, Fairbairn (1954), Winnicott (1958), or Bion (1970). In the past several years, however, some historians, psychologists, psychiatrists, and persons in related professions have begun to focus attention on anti-Semitism and ethnocentrism generally from an object relations perspective. As Clegg (1981) put it,

> Klein put forward the idea that early in life, each of us experiences a phase, which remains partially with us all of our life, in which thinking is dominated by the conviction that external persecutors are threatening death at every turn. This infantile "paranoid phase" of development in the first months of life is characterized by confusion of self and other to the point that affects originating in the baby are felt to come from outside; a sense of life-threatening vulnerability, dependence and weakness; a corresponding but opposite sense of enormous power, omnipotence and ideas of reference; the simplification of situations into "good" or "bad," life supporting

or life threatening respectively, so called object splitting (p. 11).

Object relations theory contributes to understanding why xenophobia or ethnocentric disposition is a universal human characteristic. It helps to explain the phenomenon of fear of strangers in infancy as discerned by developmental psychologists. By virtue of very early childhood experiences, a powerful need to identify and define enemies is common to all human beings (Klein, 1946). This need is activated not so much on the basis of competition and struggle to achieve power as on the basis of the need for security, a predictable and safe environment. Volkan (1979) has described how such primitive splitting evolves into "sociocultural behavior patterns" in the case of Greek and Turkish enmity on the island of Cyprus. For Greeks, Turks and their world are "all bad," and Greeks and their world are "all good." Turks perceive Cyprus, Greece, and Turkey in comparably opposite ways. Such primitive splitting underlies the images of "the rascally Jew" and "the idealized Aryan," Shylock versus Siegfried. Given sufficient stress, regression to the paranoid state of infancy with its concomitant splitting is a common phenomenon. The degree to which the United States has provided biological, psychological, social, and economic security and orderliness has served to reduce ethcocentric, or at least anti-Semitic bias.

Bion (1970) delineated patterns of behavior of individuals in groups in response to anxiety--which can readily be translated into useful ways of looking at ethnocentrism. Without entering into the ramifications of such considerations in depth, we note, when we entertain some of Bion's ideas, that phenomena centering on involvement with siblings are brought center stage, and yet sibling rivalry tends to be neglected in consideration of ethnocentrism in favor of imagery focused on aggression toward and destruction of authority, primarily father, figures. The Jewish patriarch is, of course, an archetypal father figure, and in the Nazi era rabbis and comparable men often were prime targets of humiliation and torture by sadists among their captors and guards. In the United States, however, prejudice directed toward Jews emanates frequently out of imagery of Jews as unwanted siblings or more successful siblings, thereby arousing envy. Some of my ongoing research suggests that among American blacks who harbor negative sentiments toward Jews, particularly more socially successful and better educated blacks, imagery centered on sibling rivalry is at the heart of their hostility.

Bion's work serves to emphasize the complexity of ethcocentrism, or the variegated imagery that underlies it. In research undertaken to compare the imagery among white people of various black figures I found that Dr. Martin Luther King, Jr., is envisioned as almost a maternal figure, thereby one that aroused hope or promise of meeting needs for security and attachment. On the other hand, Jesse Jackson, with a younger and more masculine image, is often envisioned as a rival or competitor, something on the order of an unwanted sibling (Bird, 1955), thereby engendering hostility.

Psychoanalytic Theory and Anti-Semitism

In _Totem and Taboo_ (1950, originally published 1912) and in _Group Psychology and the Analysis of the Ego_ (1959, originally published 1922) Freud focused on the killing of the primal father by the sons. This act of patricide, the argument goes, contributes to the formation of cohesive groups and to the reduction of aggression within the group, thereby advancing civilization. In _Civilization and Its Discontents_ (1946, originally published 1930) Freud again addressed this theme, but in a somewhat different way--"narcissism in respect of minor differences." Enmity between groups is sometimes "a convenient and relatively harmless form of satisfaction for aggressive tendencies, through which cohesion among members of a group is made easier" (p. 133). As Bird (1955, p. 493) commented, ". . . intergroup rivalry, according to Freud, thus acts in the service of the growth of civilization and culture."

Proponents of the liberal tradition in the United States deplore any sign of intolerance in groups. Yet American racial, ethnic, and religious diversity, and the tensions that accompany it, are in many ways responsible for such stability as the United States has achieved in its history. The very disparateness of the population is a barrier to the kind of unification necessary to produce radical social change (a French or Russian revolution, for example). The "siblings" of such a society will not put aside their rivalries to a degree necessary to overthrow constituted authority, an intransigence which must be considered in a positive light if one values continuity and is dubious about abrupt or radical social action. In the United States, as compared with Europe, the existence of a multiplicity of potential victims and victimizers reduces the likelihood that any one particular group will be the sole or primary target of discrimination.

Freud's words about narcissism are more important in other ways, however. They bring us to the third chronological phase of psychoanalysis--self-identity (Erikson, 1963; Mahler, 1975; Kohut, 1977; Lichtenstein, 1977)--and its implications for ethnocentrism and anti-Semitism. It is likely that self-identity is the crucial issue of modern times--

how to enhance a sense of self while retaining functional involvement with society. Kohut has propounded that the child needs a center in itself, a sense of being a singular or emergent agency from the beginning. This sense of self is not entirely reducible to the resolution of the self-other confusion of object relations theory nor to the residues of Oedipal desires and competition expounded by traditional psychoanalysis.

Since self-identity is in many ways a matter of defining what one is not, self-definition for American Jews was easier when prejudice was rife and assimilation much more difficult. So it is that perhaps one now encounters among Jews less concern with anti-Semitism as such and more concern with the personal and social definitions of a Jew, with the evolution of ritual and religious communities appropriate to the current state of Jews, with "Jewish identity." Assuming that current assimilative tendencies are not reversed, can American Jews still maintain their religious identity? Or in a Tolstoyan sense, are the forces of history on the side of ever-increasing mergence--personal, social, religious?

In this essay I have assumed, as one of my tasks, the restoration of depth psychological perspectives to a consideration of anti-Semitism because aside from whatever else it may be, psychoanalysis is imbued with the power of irony, the recognition of unanticipated consequences of actions and events, however benevolent and well-intentioned. So it is that as life in the United States becomes easier for Jews and their collective self-confidence increases, a certain sense of angst is aroused: What is a Jew? Can a special sense of Jewishness be preserved? And added to these uncertainties there are, of course, the vagaries of the nation state of Israel, the fate of which is tied so intimately to the state of American Jews.

The history of the Jews cautions against complacency and emphasizes wariness. Berger writes of Salo Baron's ". . . caution in assessing the propects for Jewry, despite its relative security today. He (Baron) recalled that in Spain in the 13th century Jews were diplomats and government leaders. Yet by 1391 they were experiencing pogroms and by 1492 they were expelled. They thrived in England in the 11th century; yet by 1290 they too were expelled. 'We can't be too sure that things will last,' he said" (1985, p. 18). Ignoring or minimizing anti-Semitism has its perils. But overemphasizing it in the cultural and political climate of the United States can be both troublesome and self-defeating.

REFERENCES

Ackerman, N. & Jahode, M. "The Dynamic Basis of Anti-Semitic Attitudes." Psychoanalytic Quarterly, 1948, 17, 240-260.

Adorno, T., Frenkel-Brunswik, E., Levinson, D., & Sanford, R.N. The Authoritarian Personality. New York: Harper, 1950.

Allport, G. The Nature of Prejudice. Cambridge, Massachusetts: Addison-Wesley, 1954.

Alter, R. "The Masada Complex." Commentary, 1973, 56, 19-24.

Ambrose, J.E. Eisenhower. New York: Simon and Schuster, 1984.

Arendt, H. Antisemitism. New York: Harcourt Brace Jovanovich, 1968.

Armstrong, J. Nations before Nationalism. Chapel Hill, North Carolina: University of North Carolina Press, 1982.

Aronson, E. The Social Animal. San Francisco: Freeman, 1980.

Axelrod, J., Freedman, M., Katz, J., Hatch, W., & Sanford, N. Search for Relevance. San Francisco: Jossey-Bass, 1969.

Baron, S. A Social and Religious History of the Jews. New York: Columbia University Press, 1964.

Bellow, S. To Jerusalem and Back. New York: Viking, 1976.

Berger, J. "Salo Baron--Another Workday." The New York Times, February 27, 18.

Bertalanffy, L. von. Robots, Men and Minds. New York: Braziller, 1967.

Bion, W. Experiences in Groups. New York: Basic Books, 1970.

Bird, B. "A Consideration of the Etiology of Prejudice." Paper presented to the American Psychoanalytic Association, New York, 1955.

Bower, T. The Perceptual World of the Child. Cambridge, Massachusetts: Harvard University Press, 1977.

Brooks, J. The Process of Parenting. Palo Alto: Mayfield, 1981.

Brooks, L. & Lewis, M. "Infants' Responses to Strangers: Midget, Adult, and Child." Child Development, 1976, 47, 323-332.

Brown, C. "Jangling Man." The New Republic, 1985, 192, 33-35.

Brown, J. "A Modification of the Rosenzweig Picture-Frustration Test to Study Hostile Interracial Attitudes." Journal of Psychology, 1947, 24, 247-272.

Campbell, D. "Common Fate, Similarity, and Other Indices of the Status of Aggregates of Persons as Social Entities." Behavioral Science, 1958, 3, 14-25.

Carroll, J. "A Dairyman." San Francisco Chronicle, August 31, 1982, 12, 15.

Churchman, C.W. The Systems Approach. New York: Dell, 1968.

Clegg, H. "A Synopsis of Kleinian Theory." Paper presented to the American Psychological Association, Los Angeles, 1981.

Dawidowicz, L. On Equal Terms. New York: Holt, Rinehart and Winston, 1982.

Dinesen, I. "Miss Sejlstrup's Question."Scandinavian Review, 1981, 69, 23-38.

Erikson, E. Childhood and Society. New York: Norton, 1963.

Erikson, E. Identity: Youth and Crisis. New York: Norton, 1968.

Fairbairn, W. An Object Relations Theory of Personality. New York: Basic Books, 1954.

Feldman, K. & Newcomb, T. The Impact of College on Students. San Francisco: Jossey-Bass, 1969.

Fischel, J. "The Fundamentalist Perception of Jews." Midstream, 1982, 28, 30-31.

Freedman, M. "Studies of College Alumni." In N. Sanford (Ed.), The American College. New York: Wiley, 1962.

Freedman, M. "Changes in Six Decades of Some Attitides and Values Held by Educated Women." In M. Jahoda and W. Warren (Eds.), Modern Psychology. London: Penguin, 1967a.

Freedman, M. The College Experience. San Francisco: Jossey-Bass, 1967b.

Freedman, M. "Psychological Destructiveness through Political Process." Political Psychology, 1980, 2, 168-180.

Freud, A. The Ego and the Mechanisms of Defense. New York: International Universities Press, 1946.

Freud, S. Moses and Monotheism. New York: Knopf, 1939.

Freud, S. Totem and Taboo. New York: Norton, 1950. (Originally published 1912.)

Freud, S. Group Psychology and the Analysis of the Ego. New York: Norton, 1959. (Originally published 1922.)

Freud, S. Civilization and Its Discontents. London: Hogarth, 1946. (Originally published 1930.)

Fromm, E. Escape from Freedom. New York: Holt, 1941.

Gilligan, C. In a Different Voice. Cambridge, Massachusetts: Harvard University Press, 1982.

Glock, C. & Stark, R. Christian Beliefs and Anti-Semitism. New York: Harper and Row, 1966.

Gochman, D. "Psychological Systems." In D. Sills (Ed.), International Encyclopedia of the Social Sciences. Vol. 15. New York: Macmillan, 1968.

Greenberger, E. "Defining Psychosocial Maturity in Adolescence." In P. Karoly and J. Steffen (Eds.), Adolescent Behavior Disorders. Lexington, Massachusetts: Heath, 1984.

Harap, L. The Image of the Jew in American Literature. The Jewish Publication Society of America, Philadelphia, 1974.

Johnson, P."Marxism vs. the Jews." Commentary, 1984, 77, 28-34.

Kelman, H. "Genocide as Social Policy." Contemporary Psychology, 1982, 27, 85-86.

Klein, M. "Notes on Some Schizoid Mechanisms." International Journal of Psychoanalysis, 1946, 27, 99-110.

Klein, M. Love, Guilt and Reparation and Other Works, 1921-1945. London: Hogarth, 1975.

Knutson, J. (Ed.). Handbook of Political Psychology. San Francisco: Jossey-Bass, 1973.

Kohlberg, L. Stages in the Development of Moral Thought and Action. New York: Holt, 1971.

Kohut, H. The Restoration of the Self. New York: International Universities Press, 1977.

Kren, G. & Rappoport, L. The Holocaust and the Crisis of Human Behavior. New York: Holmes and Meier, 1980.

Kurth, G. "The Jew and Adolf Hitler." Psychoanalytic Quarterly, 1947, 16, 11-32.

La Forge, R. & Suczek, R. "The Interpersonal Dimension of Personality III: An Interpersonal Check List." Journal of Personality, 1955, 24, 94-112.

Lichtenstein, H. The Dilemma of Identity. New York: Jason Aronson, 1977.

Lindgren, H. & Harvey, J. An Introduction to Social Psychology. St. Louis: Mosby, 1981.

Little, G. "Ambivalence, Dilemma, and Paradox." Political Psychology, 1984, 5, 553-571.

Loeblowitz-Lennard, H. "The Jew as a Symbol." Psychoanalytic Quarterly, 1947, 16, 33-38.

Loevinger, J. & Wessler, R. Measuring Ego Development. San Francisco: Jossey-Bass, 1970.

Loewenstein, R. Christians and Jews: A Psychoanalytic Study. New York: International Universities Press, 1951.

Martire, G. & Clark, R. Anti-Semitism in the United States. New York: Praeger, 1982.

McConahay, J. "Modern Racism and Modern Discrimination." Personality and Social Psychology Bulletin, 1983, 9, 551-558.

McWilliams, C. A Mask for Privilege. Boston: Little, Brown, 1949.

Middlekauff, R. The Glorious Cause: The American Revolution 1763-1789. New York: Oxford University Press, 1982.

Mitscherlich-Nielsen, M. "Antisemitismus." Psyche, 1983, 27, 41-54.

Moellering, P. "Luther's Attitude Toward the Jews." Concordia Theological Monthly, 1948, 19, 921-934.

Morgan, C. & Murray, H. "A Method for Investigating Fantasies. " Archives of Neurology and Psychiatry, 1935, 34, 289-306.

Pettigrew, T. (Ed.). The Sociology of Race Relations: Reflection and Reform. New York: Free Press, 1980.

Piaget, J. The Moral Judgment of the Child. New York: Harcourt Brace Jovanovich, 1932.

Piaget, J. "Intellectual Evolution from Adolescence to Adulthood." Human Development, 1972, 15, 1-12.

Plant, W. "Longitudinal Changes in Intolerance and Authoritarianism for Subjects Differing in Amount of College Education over Four Years." Genetic Psychology Monographs, 1976, 72, 247-287.

Quinley, H. & Glock, C. Anti-Semitism in America. New York: Harper and Row, 1979.

Reeves, R. American Journey. New York: Simon and Schuster, 1982.

Rezzori, G. von. Memoirs of an Anti-Semite. New York: Viking, 1981.

Riesenberg, P. "Jews in the Structure of Western Institutions."Judaism, 1979, 28, 402-415.

Sanford, N. (Ed.). The American College. New York: Wiley, 1962.

Sanford, N. "Authoritarian Personality in Contemporary Perspective." In J. Knutson (Ed.), Handbook of Political Psychology. San Francisco: Jossey-Bass, 1973.

Sanford, N. & Comstock, C. (Eds.). Sanctions for Evil. San Francisco: Jossey-Bass, 1971.

Schönbach, P. Education and Intergroup Attitudes. New York: Academic, 1981.

Sears, D. & McConahay, J. The Politics of Violence: The New Urban Blacks and the Watts Riot. Boston: Houghton Mifflin, 1973.

Selznick, G. & Steinberg, S. The Tenacity of Prejudice. New York: Harper and Row, 1969.

Simmel, E. (Ed.). Anti-Semitism: A Social Disease. New York: International Universities Press, 1946.

Stein, H. "The Holocaust, the Uncanny and the Jewish Sense of History." Political Psychology, 1984, 5, 5-35.

Sykes, C. "The Protocols of the Elders of Zion." History Today, 1967, 17, 81-88.

Tajfel, J. (Ed.). Social Identity and Intergroup Relations. Cambridge: Cambridge University Press, 1982.

Twain, M. Concerning the Jews. Philadelphia: Running Press, 1985. (Originally published 1899.)

Volkan, V. Cyprus-War and Adaptation. Charlottesville: University Press of Virginia, 1979.

Webster, H., Freedman, M., & Heist, P. "Personality Changes in College Students." In N. Sanford (Ed.), The American College. New York: Wiley, 1962.

Winnicot, D. Collected Papers. London: Tavistock, 1958.

Zilboorg, G."Psychopathology of Social Prejudice."Psychoanalytic Quarterly, 1927, 16, 303-324.

Changed Sexual Behavior and New Definitions of Gender Roles on the College Campus

Joseph Katz

Prefatory Note

The exploration of the impulse life has always been close to the center of Nevitt Sanford's work. Authoritarianism is impulse gone haywire, with the superego assuming the force of unconscious impulse, brutal and punishing. When Nevitt turned from authoritarianism to studies of the development of college students, his eye was again very much on the vicissitudes of impulse, from impulse-riddenness to free and creative expression. The Impulse Expression scale that he, Mervin Freedman, and Harold Webster developed at Vassar is one result of his abiding interest; the scale has proved itself extremely useful both in tracing the development of individual students and in assessing the differential impact of institutions. Nevitt has been fond of saying that higher education has relied too much on the superego and too little on the id. Enlisting the emotions and the imagination can be as freeing for the advanced scholar as for the entering freshman.

The impulse life of the student has often been disregarded in studies of higher education, and it was a sign of the times that even _The American College_, fashioned under Nevitt's direction during the 1950's, had little explicit discussion of students' sexual lives and the role of sex in their development. After Nevitt went to Stanford he and Mervin Freedman, in the early 1960's, were the instigators and leaders of discussions among students exploring the role of sex in their lives and the implications of sex for a redefinition of male-female relationships. These discussions as well as a series of seminars that Nevitt and his wife gave in the Santa Cruz mountains in the mid-1960's were one stimulus for the development of co-residential housing which was pioneered at Stanford in 1966.

At the same time this author, with the collaboration of Nevitt Sanford, Mervin Freedman, and others, was engaged in a longitudinal study of college students at Berkeley and Stanford. The study included very explicit and detailed attention to the sexual development of college students. These data, collected in 1963-64, still showed a traditional picture in regard to the definition of gender roles and the permissibility of premarital sex. The advent of co-residential housing heralded a new definition of gender roles as well as changed sexual behavior. Hence after 1969 this author engaged in a series of studies to trace the evolution of the new roles and the changed sexual behavior. By about 1975 the responses of students began to show a certain repetitiveness and by 1977 a plateau seemed to have been reached. Collection of the data, on which this chapter is based, terminated in 1978. At the present time there are again indications of changes in attitudes. Physical sexual behavior may not be greatly different now from what it was in 1978. But perceptions of gender roles may not have the freshness, elan, hopefulness, and idealism that characterized them in the first half of the 1970's. Relations between the sexes seem to have become more stabilized along more conventional lines, but no less groping and troublesome. This calls for fresh study to which this author plans to turn.

This chapter presents the exploration of one of the themes central to Nevitt's thought. Its discussion here is only one small facet of the many-sided stimulation I have received over many years from his intellectual and personal companionship.

From Custodianship to Laissez-Faire

Several times in this century it has been announced that a sexual revolution was taking place, and this was said particularly in regard to college youth. But until the 1960's, studies of student behavior consistently showed relatively low rates of intimate sexual activity on the part of female students and when compared with today, on the part of male students. Moreover, most college students did not approve of premarital intercourse, particularly for females. Things began to change in the first years of the 1960's. Students were demanding more liberal visitation rights allowing men and women students to see each other in their dormitory rooms. But even in the middle of the decade Rimmer's book The Harrad Experiment (1966), which described male and female students freely living together, seemed futuristic and unreal. Things began to change dramatically only with the advent of co-residential housing which began at Stanford in 1966.

College administrators offered much resistance to students demands for liberalizing the rules about visitation, or hours at which students, particularly women students, had to check in at their dormitories at night, or supervision of students once inside the residential walls. The implicit expectation was that if rules were liberalized students would engage in sexual activities and these were considered bad, immoral, or interfering with the normal development of the students. A vast supervisory apparatus was employed to ensure that students did stay chaste: housemothers, residential staff, white-clad women, dubbed "white angels" by the students, sitting watchfully at desks in the dorm lobbies. Students "caught" in sexual behavior were punished, often severely. Expulsion was not uncommon--the degree of discretion varied with the college.

Besides external supervision, there was also the internal control of the mores--among them the "date." The date was a rather ritualized affair: A well-dressed male calling upon a well-dressed and perfumed female and going to some fairly stereotypical event, a movie, a restaurant, a dance; there was a prescribed return hour by the time of the dormitory's closing. In many ways the ritualized date took the place of a chaperone of old; it allowed superficial acquaintance, but made deeper knowledge of each other difficult and prevented for a while more intimate sexual contact. Some sororities would enshrine dating behavior in very specific rules. For instance, they prescribed that only on the third date was it even permissible to kiss the boy.

Things changed at the end of the 1960's when many campuses followed Stanford's example and allowed co-residential living. At the same time, and to some extent independent of the move toward joint residences, there was a great increase in the rate of sexual activity among college students, and a particularly strong increase among women. Why was there such a rapid change just at that time? The answer points to a varied set of factors. The 1960's had been years of intense activism among students who felt that they should have a greater share in the running of their society and their colleges. The rationale and conduct of the Vietnam war, of racial discrimination at home, curricular contents and styles of teaching and learning became topics of student thinking and action. Students felt an increasing sense of not wanting to be treated like dependent children and wanted to be more like participating adults; the call for "participatory democracy" emanated from a student manifesto early in the decade. Students who had worked for voter registration in some embattled states, at times at the peril of their lives, did not easily take to continued custodial treatment, including imposed rules about sexual behavior. An eventual reflection of this new independence was the lowering of the voting age to 18.

College women, in particular, were developing a much stronger sense of autonomy. In the earlier days of the student movement they had found themselves once more relegated to the auxiliary tasks. They did the clerical, housekeeping, and menial tasks while the men made the speeches. But eventually they rebelled against this traditional division (Keniston, 1968, pp. 160-161). They insisted, for instance, that typing was not their natural domain and asked that all tasks be shared by men and women alike. As a consequence one saw the emergence of very young women as effective political leaders chairing mass meetings of hundreds if not thousands of students. This new sense of their role made women question the imposition of a double standard, of special sexual supervision addressed to their gender alone.

Two factors contributed powerfully to the emergence of new norms for women's sexual attitudes and behavior. The birth control pill came into prominence in the 1960's and allowed for a control of conception felt to be more apt than preceding ones. The pill dispensed with apparatus to be put in operation at the moment of passion and, at a time when older attitudes still persisted, allowed the woman (and her partner) to feel that intercourse had been spontaneous, not due to premeditation. In the late 1960's there was much agitation about whether pills and other birth control devices should be dispensed by student health services. Many physicians and other college authorities were reluctant to do so but eventually student pressure won out. With enhanced control over pregnancy and the consequent avoidance of the psychological and social consequences illegitimate pregnancy had once entailed, women's sexuality was freed considerably. One of the dramatic outcomes has been that college women in the 1970's engaged in intercourse more frequently than men, a dramatic reversal of the situation that had obtained before.

A second factor furthered the liberalization of sexual behavior. The 1960's were marked not only by student interest in political and social action but also by many attempts at a more sustained exploration of feelings. Encounter groups of various sorts were rampant on college campuses and, sometimes with the help of drugs, students were seeking to enlarge their consciousness of themselves and of other people and to be freer in the expression of their feelings. Even in the midst of some sit-ins and the height of political excitement, students on some campuses would temporarily divide into small "affinity groups" designed to explore their feelings and motivations for participating in the action. Occasionally this showed a rare willingness to submit the motives for political engagement to the psychological test. We know that the encounter groups raised expectations of psychological magic with consequent disappointments; but their lasting contribution was some opening up of the affective and affectionate side of students, and they led to a freer expression of sensuality and sexuality.

The Emergence of New Sexual Attitudes and Behavior

The 1970's have seen the consolidation and expansion of what was begun at Stanford and elsewhere; so that by now co-residential living is the rule rather than the exception. The changed living arrangements are themselves more effect than cause of new sexual attitudes and behaviors. The author and his associates have undertaken seven surveys between 1970 and 1977, collecting data from 6,098 male and female students at 13 colleges and universities differing in size, location, and academic status. These data furnish much of the base of what is said in the pages of this chapter. The results of our study are congruous with those of other investigators (Hopkins, 1977; Jessor and Jessor, 1975; Robinson, King, and Balswick, 1972).

The surveys taken by us in the 1970's register enormous changes. In 1970 only about half of the college students believed that "Full sexual relations are permissible before marriage." By 1975, 90% thought premarital intercourse permissible for <u>both</u> genders. Student behavior is in line with their attitudes. In 1970 about half of the men and women students reported having had sexual intercourse, but in 1977, 78% of the men and 72% of the women reported having had sexual intercourse. The incidence of intercourse is lower for freshman, but we have found no great differences between sophomores and seniors. The figures for college students are in line with those for the population at large. In 1978 in the United States 8 in 10 men and 7 in 10 women had had sexual intercourse by age 18 (Alan Guttmacher Institute, 1981). These changes are even more remarkable when compared with what surveys reported a few decades earlier. Before 1950 surveys report the incidence of sexual intercourse for college women in a range between 13% and 33% and for college men, between 52% and 58% (Bromley and Britten, 1938; Ehrmann, 1959; Freedman, 1965; Kinsey and colleagues, 1948, 1953). With the rates for men and women nowadays being nearly the same, the double standard seems to have considerably reduced. In some respects, the differences between the genders have been reversed. In our 1977 survey, 52% of the women students and only 40% of the men students reported having intercourse five times a month or more often. The difference is not only quantitative. Women also describe themselves as enjoying their sexual experiences more often than the men. In 1977, 66% of the women, as against 50% of the men described their current sexual relationships as very satisfying emotionally.

One of the consequences of the changed sexual behavior seems to be the near-vanishing of sex with prostitutes. The Sarrels (1979, p. 99) estimate that in the mid-1950's, in the Northeast, close to 50% of college men had sex with prostitutes by the time they graduated. In surveys they conducted between 1970-74 they found less than 5% of randomly selected men to have had such experience (p. 100).

The increase in sexual activity has not led to the orgies and promiscuities that some administrators and other adults had feared. There is constancy in the sense that sex involves relatively few partners. In the author's surveys, half of the sexually active people reported no more than two or three partners over the entire course of their sexual history; an additional 30% reported up to 10 partners. In the most recent survey, three-fourths of the women and a slightly smaller proportion of the men reported only one sexual partner for the preceding year; most of the rest reported two relationships.

While there is constancy in sexual relationships there is also a more relaxed attitude to "casual" sex. As one of our interviewees put it: "I do not idealize sex to the extent that it is purely an expression of love. It can be an expression of friendship." Casual sex can be a relatively unencumbered seeking of pleasure--which may have further utility in contributing to a feeling of sensuality. The Sarrels (1979, pp. 104-105) on the basis of their extensive experience with college students describe it well: "Positive 'recreational' experiences (casual sex) are particularly valuable in increasing the capacity for playful nonguilty erotic pleasure, but they can influence other aspects of sexual unfolding as well. When a person approaches another, even when the stated aim is 'just for sex,' there can be pleasant surprises. Besides being a shared moment of erotic pleasure, the experience can turn out to be one of special meaning: closeness, empathy, a mutual influence. The personality may be subtly or profoundly affected. Something the other does may change one's perceptions of oneself or one's feelings about sex. The 'after' feeling can be a glow, a sense of having learned something, an expanded awareness and an eager anticipation of more." Another sign of the heightened acceptance of erotic pleasure is the increase in masturbation. The Sarrels (p. 109) report an increase in masturbation among college women from one-third in 1970 to approximately three-fourths in 1976-77.

It is of particular importance to point out that the opportunities for freer access of men and women to each other have led not only to increased sexual activity, but also to increased non-sexual contacts between men and women, to more acquaintance, talk, friendship, sharing of work. In the author's 1977 survey only negligible percentages of men and women said they had no close male and female friends--friends being defined as people with whom one feels comfortable to talk about intimate things. But women still tend to have more female than male friends and the reverse is true for men; further, women spend more time with female friends and men more time with male friends (The Brown Project, 1980, p. 98). In the past we did not realize clearly enough that the rules and customs separating women and men from each other sexually also separated them from each other in other areas of life. Greater sexual freedom has led to a de-emphasis of sex, while the suppression of sexual activity in the past led to a psychological overvaluation of sex in which both genders tended to regard each other more as sex objects than as people with many other diverse interests.

The greater ease of access of the genders to each other has at times brought a flourishing of activities not previously possible. The experience at Stanford beginning in the late 1960's is exemplary. The establishment of co-residential living units was immediately accompanied by a differentiation of living units according to "themes." Some houses oriented themselves toward themes of social inquiry, including the rendering of social service. Others focused on artistic endeavors, others on teaching, others on a variety of studies from mysticism to revolutions, still others on dietary practices (Stanford, 1974). Residences developed a character of their own and involved a large part of their people in the relevant activities. Having observed the evolution of the Stanford residences from close by, I came to the conclusion that the removal of restrictions and the freeing of energies due to the non-ritualized and unencumbered relationships between men and women students led, with relevant help from adults, to an astounding flourishing of student self-education. Other institutions have not been quite so fortunate. Co-residential living or freer sexual expression do not by themselves yield an enlarged cultural life. There is behavior that might be described as mindless sex.

Still, the abolition of the old custodial rules has brought great changes in the relations of men and women students to each other. It has allowed more satisfying relationships in work and play with both men and women, less stereotyped conceptions of masculinity and femininity, even higher self-esteem (Katz, 1974; Reid, 1974). It has considerably diminished the old "rating" game in which male and female relationships were means for gaining status, and sex was used as an instrument for the man's attempt at a sense of self-worth, power, or domination and for the women's sense of desirability and catching a male. The opportunities for non-sexual acquaintance and friendship have enabled young people to learn more about the other gender. They have opened up the possibility in the students' later lives for more unencumbered relationships at work and at play. One need only to consider that even today a certain suspiciousness still attaches to informal contacts between men and women colleagues in and around their workplaces to realize how much male-female relationships have been viewed under the aspect of genital sex, of seduction, and illegitimacy. Moreover, the current situation makes possible the selection of future mates on the basis of a deeper knowledge, a considerable improvement when compared with the superficial relationships provided by the "date" and the choices made under the pressure of sexual frustration and desire.

Because men and women have been able to meet more freely they have been able to learn more from each other. Traditionally, women have linked sex and affection more fully with each other than men have--a trend that as the author's data show is continuing but diminishing. (In 1977, 67% of the sexually active women and 42% of the men described their current relationship as one of great mutual affection.) Women in our society have been more aware and expressive of their feelings, more in touch with their inner life, less given to a more abstract and stereotypical view of relations. Elizabeth Douvan (1981, p. 203) has vividly described the traditional difference between male and female sex talk. "Young woman learn about sex--and the nature of their own sexual responses--in their intimate friendships with other women. This is the stuff of college women's late night talk sessions: How did he act, what did you do, how did it feel, how did you handle it, and so on. The inexperienced learn from their more sophisticated sisters. But such talk involves a great deal of self-disclosure and expression of vulnerability. While young women share their sexual knowledge and experience, young men compete with theirs. Sex is a topic for asserting one's prowess, for boasting, not for candidly exploring feelings and experiences.

It is part of the new situation that college women have turned into teachers of the men. They ask their men whether their physical desires are at the service of some machismo and they try to awaken dormant capacities for affection and caring. As one woman student expressed it: "I have had an enjoyable sex life. Part of it is luck and part of it is taking a close look at your partners. It takes courage when you are sitting in a dark room and someone makes aggressive moves to say: 'Wait a minute, let us talk about it and find out if we both feel the same way about the situation.' It takes a lot of courage to say, if our attitudes differ, that we should not go out any more. You have to be honest with people even if it involves a tense confrontation, but it pays off."

It is not only in regard to sex that women have encouraged men to become more aware and to free their emotions. In other areas as well--in choice of career, lifestyle, political and social arrangements--men are moving toward a more feeling approach. In recent work with the "Masculinity-Femininity" scale of the Omnibus Personality Inventory (OPI), which measures such dimensions as openness to feelings in literature and forms in art, sensitivity, emotionality, my associates and I have found that college men are moving in the direction of "femininity." At the same time there is a trend on the part of the women to move in the direction of "masculinity." Many studies of gender differences in the past have shown men to be stronger in assertiveness, sometimes called aggressiveness. In this regard women are going in the opposite direction. This has also brought about, as the author's surveys show, that women frequently take the initiative in sexual relationships as well. Some people speak of a movement toward androgyny. I think that we are indeed moving away from stereotypical definitions of the genders. But a movement toward unisex seems to me unlikely. New differences and a new differentiation between the genders seem to be in the making, but the difference no longer based upon invidious definitions and no longer ruled by the domination-submission principle.

There are other important aspects of the redefinition of gender roles. Large percentages of college men support women's desire for seeking an important fulfillment through having a career. Most college men in the author's surveys favor equal job opportunities even if it should mean fewer jobs for men. Both genders show little diminution of the desire for marriage and children, but fewer children are desired than 20 or 25 years ago and the age of having one's first child is later. Somewhat more women (87%) than men (82%) say that having a career is important to them and a considerable proportion of women, as of men, put career above marriage and children. This seems a reflection of many women's sense that validation does not come through marriage alone.

The men expect to take on the responsibilities that go with their new attitudes. Sixty-nine percent of the men expect to spend as much time as their spouses in bringing up their children, and a devoted 6% expect to spend more time. They also favor the sharing of other domestic tasks. Some gender differences still exist. There is a greater tendency for men to expect to do the more mechanical tasks around the house. They also expect more often than the women to be the primary breadwinners while large numbers of women, consistent with their new self-conception, expect to be equal contributors financially. But this gap has been narrowed during the 1970's. In 1977, 53% of the men said they thought it likely that they and their spouse would share equally in providing the family income and 67% said they would ideally like to do so. (The corresponding figures for the women are 68% and 80%.)

There is some difference between men and women in regard to what each gender thinks is the appropriate time when a mother can return to either part-time or full-time work. Women tend to set this date earlier (The Brown Report, 1980, p. 102). This is probably an expression of women's greater readiness to draw out consistently the consequences of their striving for equality. It must be borne in mind that current arrangements in the workplace make it often very difficult for women to combine the task of child rearing and work. It is of interest, therefore, that there are indications of some movement in the direction of greater paternal participation in the nurturing of children. The three-fourths of college men who expect to spend as much time as their wives in bringing up their children may be idealistic but they testify to a changing view of paternity.

One might wonder whether the college men express attitudes that they will deny in the realities of married life. But a recent survey (Benton and Bowles, 1980) of younger (under 35) and older (over 35) husbands shows important differences. Younger men take on a wider variety of household tasks, such as cooking, vacuuming, food shopping. Younger men (61%) are much more likely than older men (37%) to think that it is a good thing that women are working. This constitutes some evidence that college attitudes in regard to marriage carry over into later life. Still a word of caution is necessary: While many males wish to support female occupational aspirations, others do not. In a recent survey of six Northeastern colleges many more females prefer to have a full-time career 10-15 years hence than there are males who have that preference for their future partners (The Brown Project, 1980, p. 102). This discrepancy indicates the potential for conflict.

To briefly sum up this entire section, the developments since the 1960's have not only brought an increase in physical sex but also have led to profound redefinitions of gender roles, have deepened acquaintance of men and women with each other, and have considerably enlarged the range of activities that men and women engage in with each other. Something like a progressive evolution of the relations of the sexes is taking place.

Homosexuality

Thus far I have talked only about changes in heterosexual relations. But there have been profound changes in the status of homosexuals as well. The 1970's witnessed the public coming out of gay groups on campus, contrasting with the prior furtiveness of such relationships and the often severe consequences to people discovered in homosexual acts. One result has been that even more than in regard to heterosexual relationships, the non-physical aspects of homosexual sex are given a chance of greater development. Because it is possible to avow openly one's sexual orientation, people can cultivate aspects other than the physical ones in their relationships with each other.

It is true that homosexuality has not found as ready an acceptance among college students as premarital heterosexual activities or as other aspects of sexuality, such as abortion. Many students are still ill-at-ease with homosexuality and more frequently express disapproval than they do of other sexual behavior. In a recent survey at Stony Brook (Leslie, 1978), 47% of the students disapproved of open homosexuality. By contrast only 7% of the students disapproved of sexual activity by unmarried college students, and 22% of abortion. Observations show that when college students become acquainted, through literature or other exposure, with homosexual ways of thinking and feeling, their own understanding even of heterosexuality becomes deepened. The removal of prejudices and fears about this form of sexual orientation can lead to a lessening of one's own restrictive attitude to heterosexuality.

There are no very definitive figures about the extent of homosexuality on college campuses. In the author's most recent survey 8% of the female and 9% of the male respondents described their preference in sexual partners as being exclusively for members of their own sex; 4% of both genders described their preference as bisexual. On the basis of a re-analysis of Kinsey data, Gagnon (1977, p. 254) estimates that 9% of college men had homosexual experience between puberty and age sixteen and/or between ages sixteen and eighteen. This figure for college women is about 10%. Gagnon estimates that about 3-4% of adult males have an exclusively homosexual orientation and about 2-3% of adult females, with an additional 2-3% of adult females having a mixed experience.

One thing that is clear is that the liberalized attitudes toward homosexuality and the courage of homosexuals themselves to openly avow their orientation have diminished much suffering brought by the old situation of clandestineness and even semi-criminality. Homosexuals now have a better chance to develop their other human capacities more freely. The case of a student who was the subject in a research study directed by the author provides a poignant illustration. I quote from a written communication to his interviewer.

> My first homosexual contact was at the age of twelve and from that first encounter throughout high school there were repeated encounters. In spite of that, I refused to consider myself homosexual. I knew I had litte desire for women and as my peers each found their own heterosexuality I became aware of a widening gulf between them and me. My reading told me that homosexual desires, and even manifestations, were not uncommon in puberty--I seized on that and convinced myself that I was simply a little late in making the transition. I went off to college fully expecting, like Saul on the road to Damascus, to be struck

down by heterosexuality. It did not happen my freshman year. During my senior year I had my first, last, and only intimate heterosexual encounter. The only way I could consummate the affair was to fantasize about a man while "doing it" with a woman. That left me really mixed up as I felt I had just negated my identity. This was followed the next summer by an incredible affair with a fellow student who was not homosexual before or after the summer we spent together.

I came away from that summer having experienced my first real love affair with anybody--one that was reciprocated in every respect. I remember the joy and serenity it gave me. But in all of this, neither my friend nor I talked about being "homosexual," not identifying ourselves or each other as being that. The termination of the affair was one of labelling and stereotyping ourselves, not each other. We both decided that being homosexual would be incompatible with our other goals. For me that became the operative policy--plus more celibacy. I again refused to consider myself homosexual, now because I didn't practice. That lasted through graduate school and on through my career until finally I couldn't hold the tiger in chains any longer and I began a process of self-analysis and self-acceptance which culminated in my "coming out" three years ago. In spite of the "victories" of that summer, I do not consider myself to have "integrated" my personality and achieved a workable level of self-esteem and self-confidence until the coming out.

I want to emphasize the overwhelming importance that the issue of self-acceptance played in my college years. It was <u>the</u> problem which preoccupied me. School work was an escape from that problem. Until the resolution of the self-confidence business, studies were an escape from that too. Things might be easier now for a person in my predicament. There is more acceptance by others, more understanding.

The eventual unencumbered avowal of this young man's sexual orientation not only made possible his greater flourishing as a person and brought about much enlarged self-esteem and peace of mind but also had beneficial consequences for the people that he works with. (This shows the societal benefits of enlarged "tolerance.") During his undergraduate days he was described by a staff member in his college residence as a troublemaker and as not getting along well with his fellow students. He now is a man who is a warm and concerned boss and appreciated by his fellow executives for the brightness and practicality of his ideas. While he still yearns, like many heterosexuals, for a many-sided relationship with another man, he does not openly indicate his homosexuality to his colleagues at work and to their wives socially. This capacity for discretion and recognition of other people's feelings, even if they are prejudicial, is another mark of his maturity. But the need for discretion is also a sign of continuing restrictive attitudes to homosexuality. Still, in the past our young man probably would have experienced his homosexuality more fearfully or might have expressed it more povocatively.

The New Sexuality and its Problems

The picture drawn thus far has left out some of the problematic aspects of the changed situation. Some of the problems are due to the newness of the situation itself; others have always existed but their frequency has increased because of the high incidence of sexual activity. Foremost among the problems are unwanted pregnancies. In the author's 1977 survey 15% of the female college students who had ever been sexually active reported themselves as having been pregnant and 12% reported having had an abortion. In surveys of metropolitan-area women aged 15-19 Zelnik and Kantner (1980) found an increase in premarital pregnancies from 9% in 1971 to 16% in 1979. It has been estimated (Alan Guttmacher Institute, 1981, p. 16) that "if there is no change in our current rates, four out of 10 girls who are now 14 will get pregnant in their teens."

Our data also indicate that sizable percentages of students either do not use contraceptives at all or do so irregularly. In the author's 1977 survey 21% of the sexually active females said they never use contraceptives; 50% say they always use them and the rest fall in between. (In Zelnik and Kanter's 1979 survey 27% said they never used contraceptives; 34% said they always do.) The chief reasons students give are that contraceptives interfere with sexual activity and that they have possible medical side effects; a much smaller percentage (15% of the women) say they hesitate to consult a physician.

While much of the social stigma has been removed from unwanted pregnancies and while abortions have become legal, much psychological trauma can still be associated with an unwanted pregnancy and abortion. The issues here are complex. Information about contraception is easily available and not using this information is likely to be psychologically motivated because of inhibitions, confusion, or guilt connected with sex. Some students probably continue to hold older attitudes according to which sexual intercourse is permissible as an act of passion while premeditation and preparation make it less justifiable. On a deeper plane the non-use of contraceptives may well reflect half-conscious or unconscious wishes for a child or a defiance of presumed or actual parental wishes and prohibitions. A consciously unwanted pregnancy may reflect hidden wishes and anxieties. As the Sarrels (1979) have suggested the desire to impregnate and be impregnated may stem from anxiety about femininity or masculinity, striving for adulthood and independence, conflicts between career and private life. They think that in some cases an unwanted pregnancy may even be an indirect cry for help. All these factors point to a need for increasing student awareness--a matter to which we will return.

Another problem--and this one is directly due to the abolition of custodial rules--is violation of the feelings and privacy of others. Various surveys, including the author's own, indicate that something like 20% of college seniors of both genders have not yet experienced sex to the point of intercourse. (This is a group incidentally that deserves a special study.) It is a significant proportion of college students. One may surmise that for a portion of these people the timetable of sexual development is prolonged. Not all parts of a person develop simultaneously. Some developmental tasks, including sexual development, may be postponed. Reassurance and counseling would help these people to be comfortable with their own pace and not to be scarred by invidious comparisons. There are other students whose inactivity betokens more severe inhibitions of their sexuality and their personality in general. This group of students requires more sustained help for the sake of their maturing as people.

Observers still report traditional pressures exerted by males upon females derogating the woman's femininity if she is not willing to give in to the sexual demands of the man--a pressure that is probably enhanced by the greater openness and greater frequency of sexual activity of these young women. The narrow quarters of the dormitory and the absence of custodial rules make it common enough to have a roommate present while a couple does have sexual intercourse. In my 1977 survey 11% of the women and 14% of the men said that other people were present often or sometimes when they were having intercourse. David Riesman, in a letter to the author, describes an instance: "An entering women student moved in her boyfriend on arrival, and her roommate, strictly raised in the old-fashioned way, moved to sleep on the couch. It took six months before this young woman was brave enough to talk to anyone about her situation. She came to see me, and I encouraged her to seek a change of room, which she finally felt able to do--previously, she had felt this would seem too square."

At times informal accommodations are made by which a roommate will switch rooms at certain times or even more permanently. But when this is not the case, given the tenseness that sex can arouse and the fact that sexual development is intimately tied to other aspects of emotional and intellectual development, such intrusion is not only an unjustified violation of one's private sphere, but may have some injurious consequences for the growth of the person's sense of identity at his or her own rate. At the present time neither custodial rules nor attempts at enforcement coming from the outside may have much effectiveness. Clearly the best way would be self-regulation by students based upon increased awareness of the consequences of their acts for others. Such increase in self-awareness, supported and perhaps stimulated by student affairs professionals, is one of the new and challenging tasks set by the present situation.

A tiny percentage of undergraduates in the traditional age range of 17-22 are married. Much larger proportions of graduate students are. They have not been much studied. However, one recent study (Hartshorn, 1978) shows that a majority of couples report graduate school to have had a negative influence on their marriages. This is less true when both partners are graduate students (see also McKeon and Piercy, 1980); however, in that situation, problems concerning childcare become more often a source of conflict. Graduate students who have been married longer report more harmony and satisfaction. One may assume that this is due to their greater maturity and the fact that their marriages have stood the test of a longer time.

The perceived negative impact of graduate school highlights once more the particular exigencies of the graduate student role, the hard apprenticeship, the work demands, the relationships with professors who are authoritarian, the professional and occuaptional insecurity (Katz and Hartnett, 1976). The problems of married graduate students antedate the changes in sexual mores and gender relationships. But as there seem to be more graduate student marriages now where both partners are students, the lessened conflict engendered by school and the heightened conflict engendered by children is of interest.

Faculty-Student Sexual Relationships

We turn now to the vexed question of faculty-student sexual relationships. Such relationships occasionally reach public attention and also the courts. In the author's 1977 survey students were asked what their experiences had been. Three percent of the male and 5% of the female students, who are sexually active, reported having sexual relations with a faculty member, and 5% and 6% of male and female students respectively reported such activity with teaching or research assistants. More work would need to be done to be sure that these percentages are representative. In a 1978 nationwide survey of members of a division of the American Psychological Association (Pope, Levenson, and Schover, 1979) 17% of the women reported having had sexual contact, such as genital stimulation or intercourse, while they were graduate students, with at least one of their teachers or supervisors. When the investigators compared recent graduates with those who graduated seven or more years ago, they found a dramatic increase in faculty-student relationships. (It must be borne in mind that the students surveyed were much older than traditional undergraduates. On the average the women began their graduate training at age 27.) Some of the rationale of the respondents is noteworthy. While only 2% affirmed the statement, "I believe that sexual relationships between students and their psychology teachers, administrators, or clinical supervisors can be beneficial to both parties," 21% circled "perhaps" (and 77% said "no"). In another inquiry (Pope and colleagues, 1979, p. 687) directed to the faculty of a Western state university (response rate 25%) the following results were obtained: About one-half of the respondents claimed they would never have an affair with a student; one-fourth reported that they had had relations with students; and the remaining one-fourth indicated that although they had not yet been sexually involved with their students, they would not turn down the right opportunity. By comparison the percentages of students who reported sexual relations with faculty in this author's survey may seem small. But it must be realized that the possibilities of intercourse with a faculty member are rather limited by the small faculty to student ratios.

The problem is not only vexed but also complex. In evaluating any particular situation one must take into account the age of the faculty member--some teachers are rather close in age to that of the student. A very important factor is the degree of psychological or other coercion that may have been exerted by the faculty member. At other times it is the case that the student is more of the seducer than the faculty member, particularly if one takes into account that faculty members may not be emotionally at the same level of maturity as they are in the intellectual domain. Emotional and cognitive development may vary considerably. In many cases a good many unresolved psychological problems are brought to a student-faculty relationship. The most obvious one is the student's not having worked through his or her infantile sexual attachment to the parent of the opposite sex and so the attachment to the faculty member is one of infantile dependency. A quite different situation obtains when a student, who may even be somewhat seductive, actually looks to the faculty member for appreciation of her intellectual capacities--often the relationship is initiated around some academic task or conversation. When the faculty member moves toward sex the student may feel invalidated in her intellectual sense of self, feel herself stereotyped as being primarily desirable as a sex object. This may lead to a more or less conscious disappointment and devaluation of herself as an academic or intellectual person.

Faculty members, therefore, who engage in sex with their students, particularly if it leads to more prolonged relationships, may be asking for more trouble than they realize. The infantile dependency and inevitable rage when the student's longing does not get fulfilled may make them objects of some painful abuse. The relationship may give some pleasure to the faculty member, but he may gain it at the expense of not only diminishing the student's own sense of intellectual worth but also of demonstrating to her that even respected adults do not have sufficient ego strength and are liable to fall right in with the student's infantile pattern, including lack of capacity for passing up an easy gratification.

What is needed is more awareness by faculty members of the ramifications of sex with students. At the present time much talk is of the cocktail party variety and faculty have been overheard referring to sex with students as a fringe benefit. The awareness of consequences to themselves and to their students and appealing to their sense of responsibility may go some way toward mitigating the situation. It would be nice if one could design clear-cut administrative rules. But like the custodial rules of old for students they would be too gross and could not do justice to the individuality of the situation. If on the other hand administrators were to deal with the situation in a more individual fashion, it would require rather complex psychological expertise of those who render the judgement. Hence faculty awareness and self-regulation seem preferable. But faculty will need expert help to articulate the problem and move toward self-regulation. More extreme cases of sexual coercion can, of course, more easily be dealt with; gross abuse of power and of authority can be more readily defined and the proper consequences attached. Finally, having focused on the pathology and abuse, we must also remember that the possibilities of relationships between people are quite varied. There are occasional situations where a relationship between a faculty member and the student is largely free of the neuroticisms that have been suggested here.

The Role of Administrators and Faculty

What is the rule of administrators and faculty vis a vis students' sexual lives? The waning of parietal rules has obviated the need for large armies of custodial officials watching over the more or less presumed chastity of their students. While college personnel staff and student residential assistants (RA's) have continued to live in dormitories, much of the supervisory function of erstwhile housemothers, "white angels," and others is gone. While administrators initially put up some resistance to giving up their role of being in loco parentis, after a while institutions felt relieved that they no longer needed to fill this role. This was facilitated by the harder budgetary conditions of the 1970's when being able to cut down on staff was almost always relished. The new situation also relieved colleges of responsibilities to parents that occasionally had been troublesome.

The question is whether we have given up too much. It is true that students want to be more autonomous, and to some extent are, and it is certainly true that they have been regulating their own sexual lives. But this does not mean that they are not in need of new and different kinds of support. They may not need the old style prohibitions but they need the counsel of those adults who have some maturity. Generational segregation is a particularly strong, if not insidious, aspect of American life. In recent years this segregation has assumed even sharper proportions when in so important a sphere of life as sexuality students are largely bereft of adult counsel and adult example. Part of the difficulty is that many adults are not particularly good examples and guides, and adult sexuality itself has been going through changes, experimentation, and self-searching: But the ineligibility of some adults to serve as models is no excuse for an educational institution not to provide other adults who are capable of giving guidance.

What form should the guidance take? It obviously cannot be, in form and content, something like the old chastity rules. Whatever one may think of current student sexual behavior, it is clear that students have determined to have control of their sexuality. In most institutions control by external authority would be doomed to failure, if not ridicule. One also needs to consider that the student culture has moved into what appears to be beneficial directions, that is, deeper understanding of the genders of each other, the freeing of imagination from a frustrated preoccupation with sex, the deepening of feeling and intimacy in the relationships of men and women. These changes were made by the students' own initiative, against the initial opposition of adult administrators. Through its adolescents society has an opportunity to renew itself, and often college students discover, in response to changed societal and historical circumstances, the possibilities for psychological advance and for new forms of living.

This provides a first clue for administrators. Before rushing in with rules and advice, it is eminently desirable to find out first what new thinking, what new attitudes, what tastes, desires, styles characterize the present generation. This is not as easy as it may sound because often there is no ready-made articulation by the students themselves; adult inquirers must often develop such articulation if they are to understand what is going on. As everybody who has watched students from close by knows, there can be rapid changes, even on a year-by-year basis, of students' styles of interactions with each other, their expectations of the classroom and their teachers, their leisure time activities. Knowledge of students does not stay fresh for very long.

The enhanced sexual freedom, the possibilities of students getting to know each other more intimately have also brought about fresh problems and fresh pains. In the past the harder problems of living together were faced in the years after college when students got married, and the difficulties and pains of making marriages work are sufficiently known. Challenge to one's capacity for caring and for empathy with and understanding of others, inevitable disappointments and breakups when people do not measure up to each other's expectations and their more mature or more infantile needs--all these can now be part of the college student's experience. Decisions for the future can now not as easily be made by oneself alone, but often involve another person and bring up all the possible conflicts of which partner will get preference in regard to where to settle, what graduate schools to go to, and many others. Parents need to be taken into consideration or confronted earlier in regard to the choice of partner and the implied future life style. Moreover in close relationships capacities for hurting others--even sadism, and other forms of aggression--can be mobilized leaving deep scars in both parties. Difficulties in relating to others may find expression in various forms of sexual dysfunction. Sexual self-doubt may follow. There is the increased risk of venereal disease. All in all, we confront a panoply of problems that seem too big to put upon the frail identities of college students alone.

Colleges have not done enough to respond to these problems, with the exception of some ample psychological and health services (Arnstein, 1973) or some well-designed courses on human sexuality. The Yale Sex Counseling Service has demonstrated the capacity of a program to render the effective help to students with a great variety of sexual and relationship problems. Among other things the service has been able to help students reduce unwanted pregnancies to a minimum (Sarrel and Sarrel, 1979). Essentially the Yale service manifests the university's giving priority to the task of employing competent professionals for the purposes of sexual instruction.

The need is to enlarge information and awareness of students. There are many different ways:

(1) Periodic discussions, competently led at the appropriate times in the students' lives, could lead to enhanced awareness, particularly if students are encouraged to speak up about their experiences and submit them to clarifying comments by their peers and by more mature adults.

(2) More academic faculty could be enlisted. The human sexuality courses have already shown the way. But other courses in departments ranging from biology to philosophy could, if appropriately taught, help students sort out some of the complex issues of sexuality.

(3) Selection of staff for the residents, including RA's, could be guided by the principle of picking at least some people of special maturity in the area of human sexuality so that they can use the informal opportunities of the dormitory to converse with individual students about particularly salient individual problems and anxieties, at the very moment when these come into focus.

(4) Students may be trained as peer counselors. Surveys show both that students go predominantly to peers for help with their emotional problems and that they find many of their peers insufficiently competent. Some academic course might be devised to train students better for the tasks they already perform, including a sense of the limits of their capacities and when it is desirable to refer a student to professionals. Such a course would wed theory and practice for which there usually are limited opportunities in the college curriculum.

(5) For students with more severe sexual and relationship problems referral to competent counselors and psychotherapists should be available. Specialized sex counseling services, staffed by people from within or outside the institution, could be established. A cadre of able people could probably be found in or near most institutions if the will to find them is there.

(6) The activities here suggested would best be based upon constantly updated knowledge of student life to help determine the appropriate contents and timing of discussions and other interventions. One needs to look for the conditions, motivations, interests, and attitudes, from which the behaviors stem. The results of inquiries into student attitudes and behavior should be made the continuing subject matter of an ongoing seminar of staff concerned with the care of students. It is crucial to

avoid both the appearance and the reality of "snooping." It is equally crucial not to violate the growing autonomy of students and their increasing capacity for making their own discoveries and decisions.

(7) I have thus far suggested "talking" interventions, whether discussions or therapy. But, on the basis of inquiry, it is possible to set up structures that facilitate or discourage certain behaviors. To give two examples: Offering a choice of housing--single-sex and coeducational residences--allows students, particularly freshmen, an option consistent with their developmental timetable and other preferences. Providing opportunities for men and women to work together on common tasks, as in Stanford's "theme" houses, can circumvent the establishment of psychologically more regressive relations between the genders. Ultimately the best arrangements are those that are characterized by student self-regulation and a mature peer group consensus. Adults can help the young in this task if they find the appropriate middle ground between laissez faire and attempted coercion.

(8) When they are reasonably sure of their psychological and sociological grounds and also know what is enforceable, administrators can define the limits the institution wants to set for student behavior.

These suggestions may imply an enlargement of the activities of student affairs professionals. At the present time the resources of student affairs offices are being reduced in many cases. These offices are thus more than ever taken up with their day-by-day tasks that may leave little time and psychological energy for exploration of the more fundamental patterns and changes in the student culture. There need to be both external incentive for and internal self-scrutiny by student affairs professionals to free time for these tasks. Too often in the attempt at remediation of casualties opportunities are lost for prevention and for furthering the growth of the students.

The Future

Leonard Glass (1980), a psychiatrist and 1964 graduate of an Ivy League college--for men only in his days--recently reflected on his student days and the attitudes engendered when women peers are not part of the everyday lives of college men. He reports a feverish and brutal sense of masculinity, a rejection of thoughts, feelings, or actions arising from the "feminine" aspect of the male self. The insufficiently integrated male ego was mirrored in the Madonna/whore split: "There are two kinds of women: one virtuous, the other sexual. The Madonnas are maternal, idealized, and sexually unexciting. The whores are held in contempt; they are good for sexual conquest and as audiences for exhibitionist display but unthinkable as mothers, sisters, or daughters. . . . For men who view women through the Madonna/whore split, emotional closeness is as impossible with any women as it is for such men to come to know the feminine aspects of themselves" (p. 35). In reading this disquisition on the "hypermasculine myth" one realizes that we have traveled some distance in a relatively short time. But where are we going?

Predictions about the future are always hazardous. It seems that the new sexual attitudes, the greater liberalism and freedom of expression, are firmly anchored in the personality and attitudes of large numbers of today's college students and hence perhaps irreversible. Yet history shows great fluctuations over time in sexual attitudes from periods of relative openness, even lustiness, to Victorian-type repression and prudery. Still there is a possible firm base for making predictions and that is _the new self-concept of women_. It is difficult to see how women, once having discovered that they can have equal chances for personal and professional assertion, would want to go back or accept being pushed back. Surveys have found that even quite traditional college women are at least firm about having a career. The fact of being able to be self-supporting and of having a position in life economically and in status quite like that of their husband necessarily affects relationships, the sexual one included.

The prospects for the future seem to be in the direction of more egalitarian and harmonious relations between men and women. A wiser choice of marital partners based upon longer and more intimate exploration of compatibility is possible now. Men and women are moving toward developing capacities that once were considered more exclusively masculine or feminine, such as assertiveness, empathy, awareness and expression of emotions. Both genders share more of the same kinds of activities in the home, at work, in politics, and elsewhere. Men and women talk more, share more feelings and experiences with each other, while it is not so long ago that the notion of the "battle of the sexes" was almost taken as axiomatic. Greater cooperation of the genders also holds out the possibility of freeing men from too strong a concentration on the world of work, often to the detriment of their capacities as intellectual, aesthetic, and emotional beings. For both genders there has been considerable movement toward the notion that sex is pleasant, not dirty.

REFERENCES

Arnstein, R. "Psychiatric Services on Campus." In J. Katz (Ed.), Services for Students. San Francisco: Jossey-Bass, 1973.

Benton and Bowles, Inc. Research Services. Men's Changing Role in the Family of the 80's. New York, 1980.

Bromley, D.D. & Britten, F.H. Youth and Sex: A Study of 1300 College Students. New York: Harper, 1938.

The Brown Project. Men and Women Learning Together: A Study of College Students in the Late 70's. Providence: Brown University, 1980.

Douvan, E. "Capacity for Intimacy." In A. Chickering (Ed.), The Modern American College. San Francisco:Jossey-Bass, 1981.

Ehrmann, W.W. Premarital Dating Behavior. New York: Holt, 1959.

Freedman, M.B. "The Sexual Behavior of American College Women." The Merril-Palmer Quarterly, 1965, 11, 33-48.

Gagnon, J.H. Human Sexualities. Glenview: Illinois: Scott, J.F. Foresman and Company, 1977.

Glass, L.L. "The Dartmouth Animal and the Hypermasculine Myth." Dartmouth Alumni Magazine, 1980, 73 (1), 34-36, 45-46.

Alan Guttmacher Institute. Teenage Pregnancy: The Problem That Hasn't Gone Away. New York: Alan Guttmacher Institute, 1981.

Hartshorn, K. "Perceived Effects of Graduate School on Couples' Relationships." Unpublished doctoral dissertation, University of California at Berkeley, 1978.

Hopkins, J.R. "Sexual Behavior in Adolescence." Journal of Social Issues, 1977, 33 (2), 67-85.

Jessor, S.L. & Jessor, R. "Transition from Virginity to Non-virginity Among Youth: A Social-Psychological Study Over Time." Developmental Psychology, 1975, 11, 473-484.

Katz, J. "Coeducational Living: Effects Upon Male-Female Relationships." In D.A. DeCoster and P. Mable (Eds.), Student Development and Education in College Residence Halls. Washington, D.C.: American College Personnel Association, 1974.

Katz, J. & Hartnett, R.T. Scholars in the Making. The Development of Graduate and Professional Students. Cambridge, Massachusetts: Ballinger Publishing Company, 1976.

Keniston, K. Young Radicals. New York: Harcourt, Brace and World, 1968.

Kinsey, A.C., Pomeroy, W.B., & Martin, C.E. Sexual Behavior in the Human Male. Philadelphia: W.B. Saunders, 1948.

Kinsey, A.C., Pomeroy, W.B., Martin, C.E., & Gebhard, P.H. Sexual Behav-in the Human Female. Philadelphia: W.B. Saunders, 1953.

Leslie, R. "The Stony Brook Experience: A Survey of 1142 Undergraduate Students." Working Paper No. 10. Research Group for Human Development and Educational Policy, State University of New York at Stony Brook, 1978.

McKeon, D.M. & Piercy, F.P. "Factors in Marital Adjustment of Graduate Students." Journal of the National Association for Women Deans, Administrators and Counselors, 1980, 43 (3), 40-43.

Pope, K.S., Levenson, H., & Schover, L.R. "Sexual Intimacy in Psychology Training--Results and Implications of a National Survey." American Psychologist, 1979, 34 (8), 682-689.

Reid, R.H. "Effects of Coresidential Living on the Attitudes, Self-Image, and Role Expectations of College Women." American Journal of Psychiatry, 1974, 131 (5), 551-554.

Rimmer, R.H. The Harrad Experiment. Los Angeles: The Sherbourne Press, 1966.

Robinson, I.E., King, K., & Balswick, J.O. "The Premarital Sexual Revolution Among College Females." Family Coordinator, 1972, 21, 189-195.

Sarrel, L.J. & Sarrel, P.M. Sexual Unfolding. Boston: Little, Brown and Company, 1979.

Stanford University. Stanford Residences 1974-75, A Descriptive Guide to the 1974 Undergraduate Spring Housing Draw. Stanford, California: Stanford University, 1974.

Zelnik, M. & Kantner, J.F. "Sexual Activity, Contraceptive Use and Pregnancy Among Metropolitan-Area Teenagers: 1971-1979." Family Planning Perspectives, 1980, 12 (5), 230-231, 233-237.

The Lonely Presidency

David Riesman

There may be a few hardy presidents left, of the style of former President Herman B. Wells of Indiana University, for whom the personal side of the presidency is peripheral. They accept his mandate that the president should "always be available," and "always attend as many informal social gatherings as possible," and yet be capable of carrying extraordinary workloads so that they can be available; they also possess the quality Wells thought indispensable: namely, to have the stomach of a goat! That expression should be metaphorical also; they must stomach a great deal of abuse and respond with contagious good humor and wit. In an earlier day, as in the corporate world also, presidents were often ambitious, immersed in their work and in improving themselves. What has changed in our day is the more than incremental increase of pressures on the president, which are apt to absorb virtually all of his or her time and energy, so that the personal side of the presidency has become a side issue. I have known a number of celibate presidents from Catholic religious orders who can throw themselves into the work of the presidency and as well into many extramural civic and educational efforts wholeheartedly, while maintaining their lives in their religious communities and their private devotions as Christians. I should add that the religious communities are not invariably supportive; one of the members may be one's religious superior and academic subordinate, which can be awkward. But in the best cases, the vocation as priest or sister--generally as a member of a religious order rather than drawn from a diocese--helps sustain the president in the private troubles some of us can shrug off but few of us can escape.

The Interplay Between Personal Life and Institutional Life

But for virtually all the presidents I have known in recent years, the quality and duration of their presidencies depend in high degree on a

----

I am indebted for support for my research on college and university presidents to the Carnegie Foundation for the Advancement of Teaching, the Mellon Foundation, and the Exxon Education Foundation.

stressful interplay between their personal lives, including the lives of family members, and their institutional lives. To be sure, this is true in some measure of all of us who lead busy and active lives. It is true for those who chair boards of trustees, and must at times face extra burdens and pressures in that capacity simultaneously with pressures in their regular occupational roles and in their personal lives. A trustee who merely reads the agenda for board meetings or minutes of such meetings might assume that what goes on in a college or a university is reasonably predictable, that emergencies arise only at stated intervals and that, with careful management and planning, there are few surprises. In fact, presidents are often reluctant to confide in members of the board, even in the person chairing the board, that they have been surprised by some development, or that a situation has arisen either in their professional or their personal lives that they are having difficulty managing. After all, the president has been chosen because he or she is supposed to be able to cope. It takes that development of trust between those who chair boards and those who are presidents for the latter to be able to admit periods of professional or personal stress. A president wants to maintain an image of strength such as that projected during the search process, and this cannot lead to much ease in honest exchange. It may be that women presidents both in women's colleges and in coeducational institutions find greater difficulty than men do in admitting any conflicts. Perhaps the most difficult career for the woman who wants, as the phrase goes, to "have it all"--that is, husband, family, and a full professional career--is that of being a college president. And of course women college presidents, no matter what their ideology, have difficulty in admitting to anything that might be seen as signs of femininity and frailty. (I recall as an apparent exception the shrewd and agreeable Sister-President of a small Catholic women's college who exploited her apparent lack of budgetary and financial acumen to elicit strong countervailing support from a group of influential businessmen. But this was uncharacteristic then and more so now of the remaining Sister-Presidents.)

Relationships with the Board of Trustees

Members of boards of trustees understandably see themselves as making a sacrifice at least in some measure, whatever benefits they may derive from their contacts with the college. Most trustees are busy men and women in professional or corporate life, victims of the maxim that if one wants to get something done, go to the busiest person. With the growth of litigation and generally of federal and state intervention, the honor and colleagueship of being a trustee (perhaps particularly at one's alma mater) may be outweighed for some by the fear of legal liability and the personal and political pressures resulting not only from extramural forces but from diminished academic hierarchies and greater democratization of governance. Nevertheless, I would be inclined to presume that most trustees in their professional lives take fewer anxieties home from the office with them and carry lighter briefcases than presidents do, who commonly, like a few big city mayors and high civil servants, get "home" ever later and less often.

Of course there are exceptions. I know of one board chairman of a liberal arts college who is a surgeon at a major university-related medical school and whose hours are longer, pressure as intense, and decisions even more delicate than that of most presidents. But a surgeon can deal with things as well as with people, and while the president, of course, must master a great deal of paper work, most of those materials ultimately concern people, just as most of his or her life involves interactions with people.

Trustees, of course, come from institutions so diverse that many of my generalizations will necessarily apply only in limited degree to any one in particular. What trustees and faculty members should realize about presidents is that even modestly capable presidents are something of a non-renewable resource. They need to be preserved. Instead they are often eroded by mistrust in which many faculty see the president, if he or she comes out of academic life, as a failed academic rather than a superior one with understanding and concern for the institution. Faculty greatly overestimate the power of the president; students do so as well. The egalitarian, anti-elite, and non-hierarchical style of contemporary America influences many to see the president as a symbol of formal structure--conceivably decent personally, but inevitably compromised by the title and role.

It can be particularly difficult for the president and his or her spouse to seek to maintain close friendships with faculty members whether one is promoted at one's own campus or has known these faculty members in other contexts. The charge of favoritism is bound to arise. Perhaps the most obvious thing to say about the personal side of the presidency is that, while it is a professionally crowded, it is personally a lonely position.

Loneliness, of course, varies with the setting. The president is not likely to be isolated, nor is the presidential family, in a small church-related college, where the faculty are generally more loyal to the institution than to their disciplines and even to their departments.

But in such settings, it sometimes happens that collegiality is purchased at the price of claustrophobia. Furthermore, some of the community colleges are able to recruit faculty members oriented to the college and the community they serve as well as to their academic or technical specialty. In addition, community college presidents, often united in a district as in parts of California, in St. Louis, or in Cuyahoga County, Cleveland, often have closer ties with each other and also with school superintendents, corporate officials, union leaders, and others in their localities than is typical for the president, to give a contrary example, of a selective liberal arts college located in a small community from which it draws virtually no students. Correspondingly, the community college presidential spouse is in a different situation in metropolitan Los Angeles than in, for example, rural Maryland.

I have had students at the Harvard Graduate School of Education seeking a doctorate in education with the aim of becoming a community college president, moving up through positions in institutional research, student services, or other "middle management" positions. But in most instances men and women on assuming their first presidencies discover that they have joined a new league. However, this league varies a great deal, for there is no such thing as a "presidential profession." In other words, there is no regular career line. In the new milieu of the presidency, it takes time to discover colleagues among other presidents and among their trustees, and there are some meetings which presidents and their spouses attend just to find and maintain such company.

Presidents who come from corporate life are accustomed to making friends in the corporate, financial, and journalistic worlds, and have an easier time if they are in metropolitan locations. It is the majority of presidents who come out of academia with little experience beyond that who find themselves suddenly without peers.

It takes a while for a president and his or her spouse to cultivate friendships among the trustees and their spouses, and in any case meetings with trustees are generally infrequent--hence the relation with the person chairing the board can become all-important, as someone with whom one can try out ideas and be less guarded than with one's inherited and as yet unfamiliar administrative team, as well as with faculty and staff.

The search process itself may set the initial tone for the relation between the president and the person chairing the board of trustees. I have found it fruitful to interview both successful and unsuccessful candidates about their experiences of the search process, and the candidate's spouses as well; and it is rare in these settings of mutual and wary courtship that either the board or the presidential partners find out what would be helpful to know about each other, or to establish a relationship on which to build further trust and mutuality.

The President's Spouse

I am suggesting that presidents are likely to be more vulnerable than big-city mayors, or cabinet officers, or even Foreign Service officials in hardships posts. Politicians can be friendly with each other (and often with lobbyists) across ideological and partisan lines, while presidents may wish for but cannot achieve camaraderie with members of the professoriate out of which most of them have come. A good president is a person of sensitivity and feeling who must often make tough decisions. He is not accustomed, and his family is certainly not accustomed, to a life of little privacy and almost no free time. In this situation, the role of the spouse as a supportive, sympathetic, and understanding person is all-important for both male and female presidents. In a memorandum written to the search committee chosen to find a successor to her husband, Theodore Friend, President of Swarthmore College, Elizabeth Friend wrote, ". . . one of the most important things I do (is) make myself available to talk with Dorie (Friend) whenever he needs a consultant. He may want me to edit a speech he is about to give; he may have a sensitive letter which requires typing; and he certainly needs a great deal of uninterrupted, empathic listening. After eight years of practice, I feel that my value as a consultant is a crucial and probably irreplaceable part of my job and of this particular presidency." (1983, p. 29) It is understandable that the role of the male spouse of a woman college president is not symmetrical. Virtually all male spouses have their own careers, in some cases at a distance. Most offer emotional support and try to help with children. But unlike a female spouse, they cannot serve as visible lubricators of social events, nor readily substitute for their wives at campus and community events.

The role of the volunteer tends to be deprecated by the women's movements today. Thus it all right for a professional person to serve on a board of trustees, but not allright to involve herself in invisible and unpaid institutional service for her husband. To create an environment in which the spouse-volunteer can be helpful to the president and to the institution, extending the network of influence and connection, maintaining friendships outside of the institution, pinch-hitting and supporting on the road--all the myriad ways described in recent books and articles by former presidents' wives--these comprise the most significant personal side of the presidency. But it is hard for the spouse to ignore the women's movements. Ever so many presidents' wives in the more liberal academic institutions have reported to me their dismay about the antagonism they receive from prefessional women on the faculty or the staff. (For fuller duscussion, see Riesman, 1984). The development office and the public relations people may attack her for other reasons; they may see the spouse as an inscrutable if not interfering factor in their own professional linkage to the president, and these discomforts are maximized for female staff.

The Search Process

I have already indicated my view that concern for the personal side of the presidency must begin with the search process itself. As the search narrows down, and finalists are brought to campus, the question arises as to how to handle the spouse, and I shall treat here that majority of cases where the spouse is a woman. In the minority of cases the spouse is not brought to campus at all. In a few cases, this non-benign neglect may reflect fear on the part of the search committee that it will be seen as extravagant in a time of retrenchment. More often today, Affirmative Action officers and representatives of women's organizations insist that candidates be considered as individuals and judged on their merits as such, without reference to whether they are married or not, or whether they have a spouse prepared to help in institutional development and in humanizing the office of the president. This insistence that couples be treated as if they were two isolated atoms reflects ideology rather than reality, and search committees undoubtedly inquire about the existence and qualities of a spouse, whether brought to campus or not. When as in most cases couples are brought to campus, members of the search committee and of the board of trustees should already be alert to the different kinds of agenda that will concern different kinds of spouses. Some wives may appreciate the separate tour often provided to give them a sense of potential schooling for their children or even being taken to see the art museum or other local attractions. But other wives, though they may be concerned as mothers of school-aged children, would prefer to be involved in the substantive issues of the university--in part to help their husbands decide on whether the position will be agreeable for them as partners. A wife may want to meet some of the same important figures with whom her husband will be dealing to be able to add her judgment to his concerning the hazards and opportunities of a new position about which enough is never known on either side of the negotiations. And some wives may also be concerned about future possibilities of part-time or full-time employment when the children have reached an appropriate age. They may also be interested in the opportunities the new location offers for friendships with people of similar interests outside the university, whether chamber music groups, local poetry workshops, tennis and swimming facilities--in fact the whole cultural ambience of the community, including what the college or university itself provides.

Nadine Skotheim, the wife of the President of Whitman College, reports the story of a new presidential wife who asked several trustees what was expected of her in the new position and was told that she could do whatever she liked. She took this remark to mean that it did not matter at all what she did, as if taking for granted that there were no contribution she could make as a wife. It seems likely that the trustees who responded in this way were alert to the possibility that the woman might have in mind a full-time career, but in the context it was an insensitive response, depriving the wife of recognition of the contribution that wives can and do make, not only to maintaining their husbands' sanity in myriad ways, certainly including meetings with alumni and alumnae and with potential donors.

The president's wife often is a conveyor of messages. Seen as a less formidable or threatening person, she will hear some important, if not always pleasant, things about her husband--as indeed, in a crueler way, will the president's children in school, from insensitive teachers as well as from peers. But she will also hear kindly and generous things, not said to the president out of fear of seeming to curry favor, or out of diffidence. She will have different connections from those of the president, perhaps a network of women faculty and of faculty spouses some of whom are on the college payroll. She extends the president's antennae and to some degree his influence. She will be sought after for community activities to which her presence lends legitimacy, many of them activities in which she has previously been concerned, but in a less salient way. In some cases she can help the president's image that is inevitably more aloof than students and faculty would like; for example, students are apt to expect the president to come at a moment's notice to have lunch or come to a particular game or artistic production just that day or tomorrow, while the calendar is booked up for weeks and months in advance. In such a situation the wife may make herself available as his representative.

To return to the search process, the basic practical questions are seldom touched on in the final interview with the candidate. Though often suggested, it seems impractical to expect such matters as retirement pay, or ownership of a house, to be easily settled at the time of final choice. Moreover, if one has been away from one's academic field for a long time, and has not become eminent enough or the timing is not right to head a consortium, or a foundation, or a federal or state education agency, there may be no easy post-presidential passage when the time comes for resignation or retirement.

Donald Mundinger, in "What a Presidential Candidate Needs to Know" (1982), gives a list of tough questions about housing, degree of trustee financial support, and other protections, which it seems to me are far too probing and awkward for a candidate to raise as the time of final choice approaches.

Perhaps what we need is someone like a Japanese go-between to try to deal with such issues, if not at the point of actual recruitment, then perhaps shortly thereafter. But some things can be accomplished in the last stages of recruitment. One illustration is a recent search for the first woman president of a college previously headed by men, in this case a single woman. The male chairman of the board brought with him to the final negotiation a woman trustee who could talk in fact like a go-between to the new incumbent about particular anxieties she had concerning the dual role she would face, having to be both the president and the president's spouse. What arrangements might be made for a hostess for entertaining? Were there questions which the candidate had which were more easily expressed to a sympathetic woman than to an impressive and somewhat imperious board chairman? An issue that arose was the new incumbent's desire to keep for a time her summer place in New England, though the campus is in the South. One search committee member had suggested, in fact, that the candidate might want to find a retreat or getaway cottage nearer to the institution but still in pleasant country. But the woman trustee recognized the need of someone moving to a new location and a new part of the country to hang on for a time to sources of emotional support and friends from her previous position, until well enough established so that, as she said, the time might well come when she would believe she had enough support and friendships to move her retreat to a more accessible spot.

I believe that there are many advantages to employing professional search consultants who are more likely to help the search committee maintain confidentiality, and whose courtship of candidates may have more credibility than someone from the institution itself. Moreover, such consultants may help faculty members and trustees to make a more realistic evaluation of their institution, realizing, for example, that to become their president is not something that every capable dean and academic vice president would jump at. Moreover, a professional search consultant can continue, after the completion of a search, to act as a tactful negotiator between the successful candidate and the board of trustees. To be sure, most search committees and consultants believe their job complete when they have found an appropriate candidate. But the Presidential Search Consultation Service, sponsored and partly subsidized by the Association of Governing Boards and the Association of American Colleges, recently changed its designation to Presidential Search and Assessment Service, in part to reflect recognition of the ability to continue assistance to an institution after the completion of the search, whether in negotiations with the new incumbents or in their evaluation.

The President in the Office

As I have already indicated, I fully appreciate that to some members of boards of trustees, such considerations may seem relatively minor in comparison with the business of the presidency which, in these days, so often is business, or rather, as I would prefer to put it, entrepreneurship. (But we must appreciate that it is entrepreneurship without a recognized career ladder.) Indeed, concern with the personal side of the presidency may seem trivial because of the general focus of professional people on work. But a president's personal life is not entirely separate from work.

Corporate executives are probably somewhat more protected from the endless telephone calls, early and late, from cranks and cranky parents, or alumni, or faculty, or students than are college and university presidents who are believed endlessly accessible and who want indeed not to appear inaccessible. Even today, moreover, there are threatening letters and calls and, on some campuses, demonstration which can be terrifying for the presidential family, especially for small children.

Trustees may not appreicate that an inside candidate, seemingly fully at home, is in a new situation vis-a-vis faculty friends, or may come from a part of the university, for example, the law school, which has quite a different style from the faculty of arts and sciences, both in its social and intellectual life. I still have to meet a president, including those who were inside candidates, who has not encountered some shocks and surprises.

Though surprises are the stuff of the presidency, perhaps after ten years some presidents begin to experience redundancy. Each generation of students has both new and old issues to raise, whether South African investments, or women's studies, or gay rights, or complaints about tuition, dormitory assignments, library hours--and so on. With retrenchment, faculty members' anxieties lead them to become more rather than less obdurate, even in some of the more prestigious institutions. Where applicant pools are shrinking and where there is not a substantial endowment, presidents find it difficult to strengthen the already strong departments while allowing weaker ones to decline further through attrition. In such a task, presidents more often find hazards than renewals and opportunities. But a resilient president can enjoy surprise where it is not overwhelming; it helps make the job interesting. But I cannot imagine a president who enjoys the surprise of discovering at a selective liberal arts college that students who had completed all arrangements to register, including an agreed-upon financial aid package, had suddenly decided in August that the financial picture was too hazardous, and signed up instead at a nearby public institution, creating a sudden deficit of tuition and room rentals too late in the season to repair. The admissions office had predicted some shrinkage, and taken the risk of overbooking the airplane, but had not allowed sufficiently for the no-shows.

A surprise of this latter magnitude may throw into disarray the plans of the president for faculty pay raises, sabbaticals, and other long-planned improvements. But when a president reaches the more typical state of finding few surprises, perhaps the very best ones are those who, in a sense, create their own surprises by recognizing changes that have occurred since their incumbency began, and setting out to confront trustees, faculty members, state coordinating councils, and other outside authorities with plans to reshape the institution, in the process renewing the presidency itself.

One surprise I have just recently heard about is the practice of creating a sabbatical leave for the president as a means of renewal. This was the idea of the trustees of a small college where appreciation of the president was high. He had been there ten years and they felt it was a way of preventing burn-out as well as a way of expressing their concern and appreciation. All too often institutions wear out their presidents and then either dismiss them or hope they will depart "voluntarily." In my judgment, the average terms of presidential service today are much too short. Presidents sometimes barely have time to learn their way around when they find they are out. But it is understandable that board chairmen and board members rarely think that the presidents, and their spouses as well, need sabbaticals. Trustees also face stress, and sabbaticals are very rare in corporate and professional life. But they have for many years been a regular feature for faculty of the better academic institutions, along with an extended summer vacation, whereas presidents and other administrators typically work an eleven-month year. If one agrees with my judgment that the average terms of presidential service today are too short, then a sabbatical, perhaps for a half year, is a way of prolonging the useful incumbency of a capable president. I disagree with Frederic Ness (1981) of the Presidential Search and Assessment Service who said a year or so ago that he thought three or four years was about the right length of service for a president (see also Riesman and McLaughlin, 1984). When I challenged this, he was willing to grant that what is now the average length of service, seven years, might be about right. I still disagree.

For a good president that is too short. Perhaps at that point it would be time for a sabbatical as a mode of renewal for a further term of service.

Another word about the length of terms needs to be said. Here there can be no fixed rule. I have seen ever so many instances where a board of trustees has waited much too long, and should have realized almost immediately that its search committee had made a mistake, which it had confirmed. To buy out the president's contract would be a wise course. It is seldom taken--all sorts of expedients are tried instead. It is hoped that people will improve. This does happen and facilitators can sometimes make it happen. But once trustees have concluded that the president is inadequate, the chances for redemption are slim, and the sooner the action is taken to find a new person the better. Often, a new search starts out with little sensitive understanding of what went wrong with respect to the previous candidate, or there is an overreaction toward the incumbent in a search for someone very different, without analysis of all the complex reasons for failure.

With longer terms, whatever the lack of community in the cmapus as a whole, not to speak of the surrounding communities, the successful president can develop some sense of trust and camaraderie with members of the board of trustees, and these members can in turn provide contacts outside the institution for the president and his or her spouse. This may sound trivial, but it is not. This personal relationship and concern--like the giving of a sabbatical leave--affects the quality of life for both the president and the trustees. The president will have the opportunity to meet nonacademics, especially if he or she has lived entirely within the unevenly permeable academic enclaves, just as for many trustees the opportunity in their role as trustees to meet people who are different from themselves is one of the satisfactions to compensate for the obligations, the redundancy of some trustee meetings, the wear and tear of attending them.

Of necessity, I have overgeneralized. The relation between the president and the board chairman differs in degree, often very large degree, between the independent sector, where the board is self-perpetuating, where a president who stays for any length of time can help influence the composition of the board, and that of the public sector, where the board may be elected or appointed by the governor and may in the majority of cases be a system-wide board rather than an institutional board, in either case only marginally if at all influenced in its selection by the incumbent president. An analysis by Robert Berdahl and Samuel K. Gove (1982) indicates that only about thirty percent of senior public institutions are still governed by individual boards, while only the three states of Vermont, Delaware, and Wyoming have no state-wide coordinating or governing board. In system states, the campus heads of a public institution may or may not have their local board of trustees. Hence, not all presidents are in the position of establishing a close relation to someone chairing their board of trustees--in the best cases, an essential personal and professional tie.

In this as in other contexts, it is obvious that the size and location of the institution make a vast difference. Presidential families can be more anonymous in a metropolis, even on a residential campus, and find it easier to make and keep friends who are not involved with the institution and with whom therefore it is possible to be at ease and not too guarded--and where the other people are also not guarded, because they are dealing with the person who may be their nominal superior. In general, though there are many exceptions, the personal side of the presidency exhibits, in the midst of claimants and constituencies, the loneliness due to a degree of isolation from academically engaged and intellectual peers.

REFERENCES

Berdahl, R. & Gove, S.K. "Governing Higher Education: Faculty Roles on State Boards." _Academe_, 1982, _68_, 21-24.

Friend, E. "The President's Spouse." _Change_, 1983, _15_, 24-33.

Mundinger, D. "What a Presidential Candidate Needs to Know." _AGB Reports_, March-April 1982, 41-45.

Ness, F. "The Search for a College President." _AAHE Bulletin_, 1981, _34_, 1-16.

Riesman, D. "Epilogue." In D.M. Magrath and J. Clodius (Eds.), _The President's Spouse_. Washington: National Association of State Universities and Land-Grant Colleges, 1984.

Riesman, D. & McLaughlin, J.B. "A Primer on the Use of Consultants in Presidential Recruitment." _Change_, 1984, _16_, 12-23.

Wood, M. _Trusteeship in the Private College_. Baltimore: Johns Hopkins University Press, 1985.

Personality Development in Highly Educated Women in the Years Eighteen to Forty-five

Emily J. Serkin

This study addressed personality development in the early adult years of women, specifically the development of women oriented to some degree to a career. Based on five open-ended interviews with each of twelve women Ph.D.'s, the study took an in-depth approach to the understanding of their life experience.

The impetus for this research was a longstanding interest in the problems of women who are relatively conventional in their orientation toward family life but who have creative talents and intellectual interests that involve them in the world outside the home. The change in the roles of women--and, of course, of men as well--in recent years has already been well documented. The participation of women in the labor force generally and particularly in the professions increasingly compares to that of men (van Dusen and Sheldon, 1976; Press 1978), and career-minded women of today are not likely as they were in the past to expect to remain single. This emerging pattern makes it relevant, therefore, to investigate a phenomenon frequently found in women with careers--an apparent discrepancy between their intellectual competence and their sense of personal self-worth. Consequently the study focuses on the relationship between personal and professional identity, and how they are harmonized.

To understand how the personal and professional aspects of life are integrated, and to arrive at some systematic insights into the adult lives of intellectually oriented women, I adopted, as a coherent and comprehensive framework, a systems-based and object relations-oriented perspective.

In modern psychology, Jung's article (1971, originally published 1933) was the first attempt to chart the terrain of personality development in adulthood. Other attempts followed--most notably those of Bühler (1935), Erikson (1963), and Jaques (1965)--but only in recent years has adult development become a significant concern in the discipline of psychology.

Contemporary research in adult development, like most research in personality, has largely concerned itself with discrete aspects of personality. Examples of some of the more prominent approaches in such research include Loevinger's (1966) studies of ego development, Kohlberg's (1973) studies of the development of moral reasoning, Vaillant's (1977) study of mechanisms of defense, and the research of Lowenthal, Thurnher, and Chiriboga (1975) on stress. In addition, a large proportion of the psychological literature on adulthood deals with changes in the quality of life, such as Gould (1972), and change and stability in personality traits (Schaie and Parham, cited in Helson and Mitchell, 1978).

A relatively "holistic" or psychodynamically-oriented or systems-based approach is not commonly taken in research on adult development. Levinson (1978) and, to a degree, Vaillant (1977) took such an approach in major studies of the adult development of men, as did Stewart (1977) and Henning and Jardim (1977) in their more limited studies of the adult development of women. However, none of these four studies reflect either a systematic, comprehensive conception of personality, or of personality development in adulthood.

To simplify the analysis of the data, I limited the twelve interviews to women with Ph.D.'s in the social sciences or humanities who were between the ages of 30 and 45. Choice of age range and discipline was dictated by the goal of studying the integration of personal and professional identity of women in relatively "feminine" fields of study who were affected by recent social change in their roles as women. I interviewed each woman five times, for an average of eight-and-half hours each.

The interviews were open-ended, and subjects were invited to speak freely about their lives. I anticipated that personality development in adulthood would unfold in an ordered sequence of some kind and that I would be able to discern at least something of this process.

To analyze the data, I developed both a typology and a model of personality development in adulthood. The following typology emerged from the study of the twelve women in the sample. The lives of two of the women were oriented in large measure toward achievement in their profession, while encompassing marriage and motherhood as well--"achievement-oriented integrators." Three of the women were married, had children, and were predominantly oriented toward family relationships, although they also had careers--"family-oriented integrators." Two of the women were neither family- nor career-oriented. They were single, and their life orientation was toward independence, with a measure of both personal and professional satisfaction--"independence-oriented non-integrators."

The achievement-oriented integrators had conventional academic careers. Three other women had similar careers; but they were single or married without children. (These three women constitute a subtype of the achievement-oriented integrators.)

The family-oriented integrators had unconventional careers by customary academic standards; they worked as researchers in part-time or non-tenure positions, and were not on a conventional route to academic advancement.

The independence-oriented non-integrators were not committed to a career. One other woman was similarly uncommitted; she was married, however, unlike those of the main type, and she constitutes the subtype of this group.

From the interviews and data, it seems evident that there are distinct stages in adult life, and that these are bounded by "turning points" --periods of marked dysphoria of about a year's duration. The stages alternate between relative stability and relative fluidity and expansiveness in images of self and other. The malaise of the turning points suggests a kind of mourning for the earlier self-other images which are being discarded, and the stress of the reengagement with nascent images.

The conceptions of Erikson (1963) and Jaques (1965) lend themselves readily to an amplification of the nature of these stages. Erikson wrote of a sequence of three major crises in adult life. In the present study, the first two of these stages, as well as the adolescent stage, were divided into distinct and alternating periods of "crisis" and "consolidation." The turning points for the women studied fell approximately at the ages of 18, 23, 28, 33, and 38, and were assigned the stages adapted from Erikson as follows: crisis of identity--age 13 to 18; consolidation of identity--age 18 to 23; crisis of intimacy--age 23 to 28; consolidation of intimacy--age 28 to 33; crisis of generativity--age 33 to 38; consolidation of generativity--from 38 on. The "crisis of generativity" referred to here is commonly referred to as the "mid-life crisis." Jaques described a major reorientation, at mid-life, as a function of a new awareness of human mortality and of the limitations of oneself and one's achievement. Jaques' interpretation of the mid-life crisis is used here as the basis for a systematic conception of stages based on self-other images. After Jaques, idealized self-other images were attributed to the stage of consolidation of identity, partially idealized self-other images to the stage of consolidation of intimacy, and non-idealized self-other images to the stage of consolidation of generativity.

It was possible to synthesize the data of this study with reference to a developmental sequence of self-other images for each of the three main types of women in the sample.

For the achievement-oriented integrators, the predominant self-other images in the stages of consolidation of identity, consolidation of intimacy, and consolidation of generativity, in sequence, were: teacher-student, mentor-apprentice scholar, autonomous professional-autonomous professional.

For the family-oriented integrators, they were: exclusive mates, mates inclusive of children, autonomous mate-autonomous mate.

For the independence-oriented non-integrators they were: teacher-student with secondary peer images or exclusive mates with a sexual taboo, teacher-student and exclusive mates with a marriage taboo, mentor-apprentice scholar, if teacher-student in consolidation of identity, or exclusive mates with no marriage taboo, if exclusive mates in consolidation of identity.

Predominant self-other images of the subtype were split or undifferentiated relative to those of the main types. For example, the mentor of one of the women in the subtype with conventional career, at the start of the consolidation of intimacy, was also a lover. The woman in the subtype without commitment to career described her relationship with a mate in the stage of consolidation of identity as one comparable to a psychotherapeutic relationship.

Distinguishing between stages of crisis and consolidation, and delineating sequences of primary self-other images in the stages of consolidation, have lent an intrapsychic dimension and a more differentiated structural framework to Erikson's theory.

Characteristics of the Sample

A striking feature of the backgrounds of most of the women in the sample was the immigrant status of their parents, grandparents, or both. Of the two women for whom this was not so, the mother of one moved, at marriage, into a subculture markedly different from the one in which she was raised. The other described her father as a man who had not had a change in views since the Depression and who increasingly lost interest in the world as time seemed to pass him by. All the women, then, were heir to the experience of the outsider, which could be presumed to be a factor in their electing to function in academia, an arena in which they could use the tools of their discipline to reflect systematically on the experience of others.

Another important feature of the sample as a whole is that the women by-and-large established themselves professionally (in the late 1960's) at a time of expansion in higher education and concern for fair representation of women in fellowship awards and in hiring. As one women said, "I've been right on the crest of something." The historical specificity of the experience of the women in this sample compares to that of the women business executives studied by Hennig and Jardim (1977), who had been promoted to middle-management positions during the Second World War, when manpower was in relatively short supply.

Seven of the women were Jewish, five Catholic, Protestant, or mixed

Catholic and Protestant. They grew up for the most part in middle-class homes. Half of the parents were college-educated; five of the fathers had some postgraduate training, two of these having earned professional degrees. None of these five fathers had had careers in the field in which they did postgraduate work, and their unfulfilled ambitions sometimes figured in the ambitions of the women. The mean age of the women, at the time of the first interview, was 36. Two of them were only children, five first-born, two second and last-born, and three middle children. One was foreign-born.

All the women with unconventional careers--that is, family-oriented integrators and subtype--were Jewish. The achievement-oriented integrators and the independence-oriented non-integrators were Catholic, Protestant, or mixed. The women in the subtype with a conventional career and the subtype without commitment to a career were either Jewish or Christian.

Since some of the women in the sample were as young as thirty, it is possible that a woman studied as one type would move into another type some years hence--that one of the unmarried women, for example, in the subtype with a conventional career, would marry and have children.

The following presentation discusses each type, then the subtype, in four aspects of their lives: career, men and marriage, children, and personal and professional identity. Each aspect is linked to the stages of adult development--crisis and consolidation of identity, intimacy, and generativity, in sequence. The midpoints of the stages are often referred to as bellwethers of the new experimentation with roles in stages of crisis, and of the new consolidation of images of self and other in the stages of consolidation.

A caveat is in order with regard to these concerns. The twofold purpose--to describe various types of highly educated women and to illustrate the process of personality development in adulthood--was handicapped by the small numbers of women in each type, and by the fact that the description of the types and stages of development rested largely on a recounting of the life experience of individuals. While these were drawbacks that tend to obscure the overall conceptualization of the study, they seem unavoidable. The delineation of the process of development is also obscured by the presentation of data by type and by aspect of life. The stages and the turning points emerge in sharp relief only with reference to the overall life experience of all the women in the sample. This problem also seems unavoidable in a typological study.

Finally, the presentation that follows refers primarily to actual relationships and life experiences, rather than to images of self and other. It requires a leap of the imagination to bridge these two levels of discourse, and the material does not always lend itself to such speculation. It may help to think of a dialectic in the differentiation and integration of aspects of personality. A "masculine" or "agenic"[1] or "active" aspect of personality seems always to be differentiated in tandem with a "feminine" or "communal" or "passive" one--a process probably reflected most clearly in the development of the woman in the subtype with an unconventional career.

In sum, there seems to be an internal process of personality development at the heart of the life experience of adults. This process can be understood with reference to images of self and other, which become progressively less idealized in the stages of adult life. Images of self and other evolve through alternating stages of emergence and consolidation--represented in life experience by alternating stages of experimentation with, and consolidation of, new roles. The stages are articulated by turning points that seem to represent periods of mourning for the images of self and other of the previous stage.

One-third of the highly educated women in this study were primarily oriented toward professional achievement, and achievement for them was associated with an identification with their father. Another third was primarily oriented toward personal relationships, and for them, professional achievement was associated with an identification with their mother. The remaining third was oriented neither to career nor to family, but rather to the establishment of an independent life, with a measure of both personal and professional satisfactions. The sequential stages of the consolidation of identity, intimacy, and generativity were more fully delineated earlier.

The applicability of this typology to professional women other than Ph.D.'s in the social sciences or humanities and to non-professional women requires further research. But while the typology of this study merits further attention, the schema of adult development that also evolved from this research is potentially of greater significance, because it proposes an age-linked sequence of stages of personality development in adulthood.

Crisis and Consolidation of Identity

In considering the period of the crisis of identity, the data of this study refer significantly only to the latter part--assumed to begin at age 13, with puberty, and to end with the turning point at age 18. Never-

----

[1] The terms "agency" and "communion" are used by Bakan (1966) to describe a fundamental polarity in human experience.

theless, it is of some interest that two of the women in the sample described a marked change in their father's behavior toward them, beginning at puberty; a doting father became remote, and a benevolent one became excessively critical. A third woman also reported that her father became considerably more critical during her adolescence.

As one would expect, most of the women in this study first became interested in boys during the crisis of identity. In addition, or instead, some became interested in what they viewed as a "masculine" field of study. The turning point at age 18 was most commonly a period of disillusion with a field of study or with relations with boys, "And so I had an image of myself as being science-oriented. And so I started college in chemistry. And then after a year of those smelly labs I decided I didn't want chemistry. Then I didn't know what I did want to do." And, "I had a lot of problems with men that I dated . . . What happened was that they would be intimidated by me, and I'd get very irritated. It was just very bad."

In the consolidation of identity, age 18 to 23, relationships reflected an idealized image of self and other; truth could be found in the relationship with a teacher and happiness in the relationship with a mate. With regard to a teacher:

> He had a particular technique--just the way he presented information, the way he asked questions. Although he was extremely dogmatic. I mean, there was no possibility of holding an opinion other than his, although at that stage of the game I was an undergraduate who really didn't have enough knowledge of the subject matter to want to hold an opinion other than his. So I just sort of accepted what he said. He would present seven different opinions on a particular issue, and then proceed to demolish six of them and show you why the one that he espoused was unquestionably superior to anything else. But, I mean, he had a magnetism and a dynamism . . . And I often thought, boy, I'd really like to be able to do that.

And with reference to a mate:

> I married a man whose work I felt was so superior to anything I was capable of that in a sense it was the reason for the marriage. That it was like I don't have to do it now. He was everything I could possibly dream of being myself, and more. And therefore I could kind of ride along on his wake.

Borrowing from Erikson, I suggest that this stage is one of resolution of the polarity of identity versus role diffusion. The achievement-oriented integrators established a sense of identity in the commitment to a field of study. The earlier diffusion of identity, their interest in a "masculine" field, was eventually ameliorated by commitment to a field they felt was more genuinely their own. The family-oriented integrators established a sense of identity in the commitment to a mate. Their earlier diffusion of identity, often a result of a relationship with a man who did not appreciate them intellectually, was ameliorated by relationships with men of unusual intellectual abilities. The women's sense of having found themselves at this stage is reflected in the following: "I think the early orientation to very masculine subjects came more from that notion that I really didn't want to be like my mother and a certain amount of emulating my older cousin. But I think when I switched into (name of discipline) I really was doing something for myself." And,

> There was something very gentle about him--very, very sweet and very loving. And he was so bright and warm. And the combination of these characteristics--a man and being bright, and yet very kind of family-oriented, was just very appealing to me. And I remember after that evening saying to my mother, "That's it. He's the one I really want to marry."

While all the women studied seemed to have largely resolved the issue of identity versus role diffusion, at this stage some apparently experienced a greater degree of diffusion than others. Compare the above quotations to the following. With reference to a mate:

> It was like a therapeutic relationship . . . He was the only person that I let in to see all my different worlds, all my different segmented parts of myself. And so he became a unifying symbol for myself in some ways . . . And I always felt that I could get along in every one of those worlds. But no one knew me. No one knew who I was in all that. And so I think that that was a key point to my relationship.

And with reference to the decision to go to graduate school: "I had glommed on to him, and he had definitely not glommed on to me. And he being really kindly and actually having some reasonableness could see, which I didn't want to admit, that it was very reasonable for me to go off to graduate school. So he said, 'Go off to graduate school.' So I did."

The commitments of the achievement-oriented integrators and the family-oriented integrators in the consolidation of identity evolved into commitments to more fully adult roles in the consolidation of intimacy. The achievement-oriented integrators went on to have careers in their chosen field, and two of the three family-oriented integrators raised a family with their chosen mate. The relative retardation, so to speak, of the independence-oriented non-integrators was reflected in a greater commitment to peer relationships than to relationships with authority or romantic figures in the stage of consolidation of identity. Relationships with peers were as important a source of education as those with teachers, or a mate was viewed as a friend with whom a sexual relationship was taboo.

Age 23 was another period of disillusion, when the women reported they deeply felt the loss of the idealized images of self and other. For example, one of the women invested a kind of absolute authority in her mate, during the consolidation of identity, "I just let him run the show." She felt disillusioned with this relationship at the turning point at age 23. "We had very little in common. We couldn't sit in the apartment and talk to each other for two hours." Another of the women similarly became disillusioned with the conventional hallmarks of achievement, "I had all the training, but I wasn't equipped really to do what I wanted to do . . . I had those degrees. I had all the grades. It was all on paper. But it wasn't in my head. It was where somebody said I should be but not where I really believed I was."

According to Erikson (1976), the issues of one stage are more or less fully resolved only when those of the next stage begin to assume importance in life. Thus, the stage of crisis of intimacy, age 23 to 28, can be viewed as one of relatively final resolution of the issue of identity versus role diffusion and the beginning of the next stage--the contention of intimacy versus isolation.

Crisis and Consolidation of Intimacy

The achievement of a relatively firm sense of identity, independent of specific relationships, is reflected in the descriptions of several of the women of their experience during the crisis of intimacy. One woman described an experience at this stage as providing a sense of herself as an adult, independent of national, religious, or family identifications, "That was also a very big important growing up period for me. It was my first time away from home. The first time where I was alone in terms of my country, alone in terms of my religious upbringing, away from my family--I mean (away from) all those reference points." Another achieved a sense of herself as an adult, independent of professional identifications, "It was an integrity confrontation for me. That I had to use myself as a reference and not count on my professional group as one to tell me what was right and what was wrong and what was sound and what was not. So it was a real growing up experience for me, personally and professionally both. No question about it." A third evolved a sense of herself as an attractive woman, independent of an identification with conventional roles of wife and mother. With reference to the turning point at age 23 she says:

> I really was a different person in terms of thinking of myself as a career person, thinking of my personal needs. To a certain extent I saw myself as a traditional woman generally did, as having my primary function as being somebody's wife. And it was about time to get on with this business. And after he and I split up I became more conscious of the importance of my career. And my self-image really changed quite a bit.

Specifically, with reference to the change in self-image:

> It was (the transition) from the old me to the new me . . . I lost quite a bit of weight. I became more physically active and more healthy. And just had never thought of myself as a particularly attractive person. And all of a sudden here were all these men paying attention to me . . . And I'm not sure how much of that to ascribe to the ambiance, to where I was in my career, to dumping (name of boyfriend). I don't know. It just seemed to happen.

In sum, the internalization of identity became significantly enhanced during the crisis of intimacy. For the independence-oriented non-integrators, the evolution of an internalized sense of identity during the crisis of intimacy was reflected in a first love affair or in a first significant relationship with a teacher.

For the women who married during the stage of consolidation of identity, an aspect of the idealization of self and other was a sense of themselves and their mate as a unit sufficient unto itself. At age 23, however, they experienced a period of deep-felt sorrow at the loss of the self-sufficiency of their marriage. One says, "We were like leaves, blowing around in the wind . . . And being like leaves was getting to be a little disturbing."

Three of the four women who married during the consolidation of identity decided to have a first child during the crisis of intimacy. While this decision reflected, in part, a disillusion with the idyll, it also reflected a sufficient internalization of the identity of a mate to assume the identity of a parent. At this point, by having a child the women committed themselves to social and economic aspects of adult society that had impinged upon them only minimally during the consolidation of identity.

Age 28 was another period of particular distress for most of the women in this study. Jaquès (1965) describes the mid-life crisis as the loss of idealized images of oneself, and the data from this study confirm his view. However, the crisis of intimacy seems also to precipitate a partial loss of idealized self-other images, and what the women in this study related about their experience at age 28 reflect this loss. One of the independence-oriented non-integrators, who had been raised to expect fulfillment in life in a marriage and family, said that she sorrowed at the loss of this image:

> I felt more concerned about age when I was 27 and 28. I really did. Because at that time I really felt, I think, that I wanted to get married and have children, I think much more so than as I got older . . . And I'm not sure whether that wasn't at that time a desire for security and being taken care of . . . I had been disappointed with teaching, disappointed with a lot of things . . . (and) that's the way I was raised, (to expect) that I was going to be taken care of . . . And perhaps also the instinct for motherhood is stronger at that time. I don't know. But I felt much more concerned about getting older at that time than I ever did afterwards.

Another of the women described this period as the time when she first experienced a sense of menace in life, and a concomitant sense of her own vulnerability. She said, "That was a tough time, in a very brutal department, a very brutal city, that taught me fear for the first time in my life. It was the worst period of my life." Finally, one woman described her 27th birthday as representing a loss of a certain sense of magic in life:

> I actually felt the crisis happened when I turned 27. That was a difficult birthday . . . It was like wanting to make that birthday special, and nothing could make it special . . . It was like it couldn't live up to my image of what a birthday's supposed to be . . . It was like nothing could live up to my ideal of being extravagant.

Of the two stages of crises fully addressed in this study, the crisis of generativity generally involved greater turmoil, whereas of the three stages of consolidation, the consolidation of intimacy was likely to be the most stressful. In the consolidation of intimacy, age 28 to 33, the women were in some sense suspended between a sense of certainty in the goodness of life (an attribute of the consolidation of identity) and an acceptance and relative mastery of limitations in life (an attribute of the consolidation of generativity). In a manner of speaking, they no longer experienced a state of grace, but they had not yet crossed the path of the shadow of death. With reference to the period between the crisis of intimacy and the midpoint of the crisis of generativity, one of the women said, about the latter half of the crisis of generativity:

> There's years of pain and struggle in there, which in some ways are lost in this 'cause I can't re-create them as fervently now --which happens probably to be the best time in my life. The period of time up until I finished graduate school (during the crisis of intimacy) was golden, believe me. I had everything. The period of time since I've come to (name of university--where she accepted a position at the midpoint of the crisis of generativity) has been golden. Okay? You take between (age 26 and age 35), those years are hell. There are moments of beauty . . . moments of great productivity in there . . . But I cannot honestly remember a truly happy year.

In the consolidation of intimacy, the authority of teacher or husband was no longer absolute, and the felicity of a profession or a marriage no longer perfect. With respect to marriage and the stage of consolidation of identity, one of the women said of her husband, "He was bright, and he was affectionate, and he was loving, and all loving of me . . . Even now he says I'm the only woman he ever loved and the most wonderful woman he ever met in his life. And all that was very important to me." She continued to derive a sense of personal support from her marriage throughout the stage of consolidation of intimacy, "I could acknowledge with my husband my insecurities and my self doubts. And he was very comforting and very loving and very supportive in that way . . . It was always, 'Oh, you're such a good wife and such a good mother and all the other nice things that you do so well. How can you possibly feel inadequate about yourself as a person?'" However, her husband no longer seemed fully in control of his destiny, and her sense of security in her marriage was no longer absolute. About the start of the crisis of generativity she said:

> I had to go through that marriage in order to come to that way I'm feeling about myself now. And my sense of self-reliance. And I even needed to have a husband like that. Because he, in a sense, he forced me to be on my own. He was so demanding of

> me all along. If I were with someone very strong who'd been taking care of all my needs then I would never have--I needed to support him for a very, very long time. So now being by myself is a relief, more than a fear of being abandoned.

This same woman also described the drama of her marriage as having been compelling in the earlier stage of consolidation of identity, "My husband is a little bit crazy. He's a very complex person and very impulsive and really a little bit crazy. And I thought that at the time (of their marriage) to be very charming and very wonderful, because it made him so interesting . . . He was the most exciting man I met." In the stage of consolidation of intimacy, she still felt attracted to her husband's energy and creativity, but the attraction was no longer wholehearted, "He's a very dramatic character. And at the time I really enjoyed that part of him. Because so many of the other men I found very dull. Actually I should stop myself and say maybe even now if I were to split with my husband, I think I would also feel many men to be dull. But just living with that drama can be draining sometimes. And in that respect I'm thinking, just a little bit more stability would have been nice." By the start of the crisis of generativity, the drama of her marriage had lost its appeal, "People get involved in extramarital relationships and things because their relationships are boring. Mine, there was always too much drama. And I guess that there was some side of me that enjoyed that thing. The big thing for me was the realization that I can be by myself and love it."

Similarly, another of the women experienced her marriage as "the perfect love" during the stage of consolidation of identity. She felt secure in her future as the wife of a man with talents as great as those of her husband, "He was everything I could possibly dream of being myself, and more. And therefore I could kind of ride along on his wake." And in the stage of consolidation of intimacy, she continued to feel secure in the marriage. With regard to her own creative achievements, "He was doing it, or we were doing it together." However, she, too, no longer felt that her husband was in control of his destiny or that she was still as fully identified with his destiny. "As I felt my husband was not taking charge of his life--it was just happening to him--I had to take control . . . He was no longer the great (name of profession), so I could no longer be the great (name of profession)'s wife."

With regard to career, one of the women discovered a field of study in the stage of consolidation of identity that "dealt with all the things I just found fascinating." In the period of consolidation of intimacy, her commitment to the intellectual life had lacked this wholehearted sense of conviction. About her mentor, she said:

> (Name of mentor) feels being a high school teacher may be sometimes more important than a university professor, because of the impact you have on people, the way you mobilize attitudes and change lives . . . He doesn't say publish more books, or give you a socially-defined notion of success. He's someone who allows you license to explore fulfillment within a very individualistic framework and who will comprehend it.

Another woman felt secure during the consolidation of identity, in her membership in the "little private club" of her discipline, although later, during the consolidation of intimacy, she doubted her admission into the discipline. Near the end of the crisis of generativity, she said with reference to the years of the consolidation of intimacy, "I'm not so nagged with, 'Do I know what I'm doing? Can I do this?' Which I felt quite a bit . . . obviously not enough that it kept me from doing it, but I had to fight with that somewhat."

As another example of the partially idealized nature of images of self and other in the consolidation of intimacy, one of the women described this stage as the first time she experienced writing blocks. Another described visits home during the consolidation of identity as follows: "I was always arriving with the latest kind of (academic) triumph . . . and I would say, 'I'm never going to marry.'" In the consolidation of intimacy, she doubted the rectitude of the conduct of her profession and personal life both. Speaking from the first half of the crisis of generativity, she said:

> I don't feel that I need to run around to parties and go out with anybody who's around that I think's interesting, in some kind of vague search for a mate. Nor do I think that I feel the most important thing is finishing the next paper or I won't get tenure. And although those weren't constant pressures, they were there. And those added responses like I don't ever get enough work done; I'm not serious enough about my personal life. I don't build serious, enduring relationships with people. They were all those kind of self-criticisms that in some way kind of undermined one's sense of certainty or confidence that you knew what you were doing and that you were proceeding in a fairly well-ordered fashion toward certain goals.

At the age of about 33, the women were likely both to accept a relative professional success--that is, a modified version of earlier idealized images of success--and to regret the loss of the idealized images of self and other that they still valued. With regard to the acceptance of relative success, as a teacher, one woman asserted, "In that year I began to think maybe this is going to be all right. Maybe there isn't an absolutely right way of doing it. And I guess I began to think I was being too hard on myself, just with some sort of ideal notion that I had to do it perfectly . . . I got a sense that sometimes it was good and sometimes it wasn't so good, but it all sort of evened out." And with regard to progress in graduate school, another concluded that, "I thought whatever I had to prove to myself I've proven. I've gotten this far." The sense of regret is reflected in the following:

> When the world started falling apart, and I started really looking for people to blame, then, of course, I said, yes, how terrible this was. Here I have all this, I forget even what I was calling it, this whatever from my mother, and not been given the proper tools because of my father. So here I am in desperate straits of not having the tools with which to accomplish the great things that I could have done. Because this (academic success) is not an accomplishment compared--here I am, a third of a century old, I would say, or I would now say, and done nothing concrete yet towards being immortal. I'm not accomplishing anything real, not yet written the greatest novel on earth. And I also hadn't--the other fantasy was marrying this super-person, the sort of Nobel Prize winner type, who would sort of accomplish it for me. And I could settle down and have lots of kids and a nice warm home and elegant dinners. But I hadn't managed to accomplish that because I don't have the proper characteristics for that either. I mean, didn't have the accomplishments and the good fortune for that, either. So either way.

And:

> That was my issue, my existential crisis. I was not making decisions for my own life. I did not even realize that I made me happy. I always felt a man would make me happy. You see, if only I not only had the profession I had, and that was very important, but if I had somebody who loved me and took care of me also, then I would be happy. If only my knight would come and take care of all the other things. It was a generalized running around looking for something to fill certain voids. In many ways first saying I'm basically alone is a step to taking more charge of your own life and setting different priorities. But I think you have to remove yourself from all the other

> things before you say I'm really alone. It means you have to give up all these other dependency relationships . . . I think the depression occurred before. Once I got into the period of deciding to give it up., that was fine . . . It's that period when you don't know what in the hell's wrong that's painful. I don't think the fact of giving up is so hard. I think it's knowing that's what you have to do is hard.

Finally:

> Somehow I just always felt that things would work out. I was very unplanned. And things always did work out in some way or another. But when I got to (site of field research for dissertation) and realized I wasn't getting this thing done that I was supposedly there for, and began to think about it all, this kind of made me stop and think, maybe the world isn't all your oyster, anyway.

Crisis and Consolidation of Generativity

The crisis of generativity, age 33 to 38, was the stage of most profound reorientation in the adult lives of the women in this study; only the turning point at age 28 approached it in significance. Nearly all the women in the sample described a confrontation of some kind with the prospect of death, in this stage, and nearly all described a major change in their sense of self and their significant relationships. Two of the women suggested that there was a consequent reorientation in their life and an intensified sense of their mortality. For example:

> At that time it brought very concretely that nothing was forever . . . The cancer bout made it clear to me that had that been more serious I wouldn't have had the right to make a decision about procreation. It scared the hell out of me. But it mobilized me to asking myself what is it I want in life.

And, "I suddenly felt freezing cold, and I just felt--it was like I felt the presence of death. It was horrifying. I was in terror." Finally:

> I don't quite know what to call it. The nothingness perhaps . . . I can even trace it to a particular time . . . I had a bad enough accident to throw me into what I called then my cellar . . . I'd say it changed my life . . . I feel as though I have a much better sense of what the human condition is, and I feel

> as though I had no sense of what it was before . . . I guess what's called the mid-age crisis is one's real sense of mortality . . . And, of course, it's never left me. Or it sneaks up around me all the time, since then, but before then it wasn't there.

The woman described the significant reorientation of the crisis of generativity variously as a sense that she would die in time, that life is not for the future but for the present, and that one is responsible for the course of one's life. "If you truly face the possibility of dying," one of them said, "even if abstractly at that stage, plus some kind of lingering notion you're not living the life you want to live, at some point it comes together. It did for me." And, "I was leading my life in a hectic way, on the assumption that this, too, shall pass. Suddenly I said, wait, this is my life." Finally, with reference to her husband:

> Yes, between 35 and 40 is when I'd say I cut loose . . . I had to do it. Like deciding to give up smoking. It's not we deciding, because that doesn't work. Yeah, I think I cut loose somewhere along the line and said I had to take care of my own life. And sometimes I feel guilty about that. But I've done it.

The women described several more specific aspects of the reorientation that evolved during the stage of crisis of generativity. One of the most significant was a change in the quality of their professional ambitions, which no longer seemed as alluring as they once had, and which were no longer attached to an idealized goal such as the Nobel Prize, "I won't win the Nobel or Pulitzer Prize or the National Science Award. Nor do I want to work that hard . . . What are the sacrifices? You can't have it all, maybe. Maybe you don't get something for nothing. You have to put out. I don't want to be that one-sided. And looking back, I was one-sided with my dissertation. I made sacrifices in my relationships. Life is short . . . Time does go by." And, "In the most positive light it's defining success differently. Realizing you're not going to be a bank president because you're just not going to work that hard, for whatever."

Finally:

> In terms of aspirations, I've always wanted to be very good and leave at least a literature worth citing at some time in the future. I don't have illusions about having a major theory and that now (name of discipline) will never be the same because of it. My husband thinks the Nobel Prize is not a ridiculous as-

> piration. I tell him I think it requires talent I don't have, or more likely a commitment I don't have. Aspirations at that level mean you have do it almost exclusively. It's very hard to do while still trying to have a balanced life, and to feed other needs you have. It has to consume you to do it at that level. I don't think that will be the case. Work will always be extremely important and significant and a main part of my identity. But I don't think it'll have the exclusiveness in my identity it may have had before.

Two of the women described a more general sense of relative casualness in their ambitions, beginning in the crisis of generativity. "I still feel that sense of using my time and doing things with it. At the same time, I'm also enjoying the sense of slowing down. So I'm learning now to do something I haven't done before--to take it easier." And, "I can think over this research business, not just go from one thing to another in a state of high emergency . . . In the past it's taken this poverty mentality to push me. I've got to do this, and within such-and-such time. And I don't totally believe that anymore."

The women also tended to experience a new sense of equality in the relationship with the mentor. "So we were discussing issues that were relevant and maybe in the process coming to more of a sense of being equals as opposed to my being the child, in a way, in a professional sense, in that relationship. 'Cause I think he became less protective and more a friend." They were also likely to experience a new sense of autonomy as professionals. "I have a professional legitimacy now that gives me the license, but it also means the will. It's a sense in which you feel as though you can now stand on your own." One of the women felt a new sense of autonomy in her ability to survive economically, under any conditions. "I'll tell you this. If it all collapsed, if there were a true economic catastrophe, I could learn some practical skill, if I had to, and I could survive."

Nearly all the women expressed some change in the nature of their scholarly interests and for some this reflected a new humanitarian perspective. For example:

> Academia, you see, a lot of the problems with it is that many times you have to amplify what you do so much in order to see its worth. You have to really believe in the world of ideas. And rather than just enjoying the process of exploration you also occasionally ask yourself whether it's doing anybody else or the world any good. And so I have a feeling that I best fit in a place that allows me to be an academic studying, working

on, and maybe contributing to some real life issues. And I may more do that through consulting or through applied research, which I'm moving toward, than some of the very abstract research that I've done to make the career I've got.

The crisis of generativity was also apparently associated with a new sense of self-awareness. This was in part a sense of attunement to the inner life generally, "Twenty years ago I wasn't at all analytical about myself. I just, I don't know, I floated through my life until I was about 35, in a funny stage of sort of non-consciousness. And I figured that a job would always be there and somehow things would always work out." And, "So first you search for, you move out into external experience, I guess. My desire for broadening took the form of travel. I was sort of getting objective experience and saw a lot of people and saw a lot of things. But there wasn't a whole lot of internal change going on at that point. And I think that started coming later." The new awareness of self encompassed a new appreciation of inner relative strength and weaknesses. The woman who said she was "non-conscious" until age 35 also said, "I guess after 40 I began to think about the fact that I had strengths and limitations, too. And I'm concerned to find a job and keep a job that builds on my strengths and doesn't focus on my weaknesses. And twenty years ago I wasn't at all analytical about myself." Another woman said, in reference to a brief course of psychotherapy during the crisis of generativity, "He essentially made me believe I was stronger than I thought. And that what I saw as weaknesses through this whole transition period he saw as a kind of enormous strength. In that you coped, you survived, and you have self-insight. And so, stop expecting yourself to be superhuman."

Several of the women mentioned significant interactions with their parents during this stage, and one described such an interaction as an adolescent-like confrontation with her father that established a sense of equality between them:

I think a time comes where you look at your parents as one more adult, whom you happen to have a special relationship with. But the notion of their having peculiar wisdom or anything else gets cracked along the way. It's still important to please them, to have them accept you. That's important to work out. But you start negotiating what that means. With my father, we had a knock down, drag out fight, during the time I went through my . . . crisis . . . Essentially what I was saying to him was that if I violated every rule you've got, tell me you'll still love me . . . You do really start to renegotiate what the expectations are. What is involved in gaining each other's approval moves to an egalitarian decision rather than you conforming to something that was perpetuated from years before. And I think those breaks have to be made, and I think those breaks are often made by confrontation . . . It sounds like a late adulthood, but there's something akin to going through adolescence involved with it . . . It had . . . to do with the sense of, accept the fact that I made the decisions for my life.

A final, specific issue of concern during the crisis of generativity was the women's status as mother. The women in this study reported a sense of urgency in this stage about whether or not to have a child, or an additional child. Such a sense of urgency in deciding about motherhood, in the mid-thirties, is often attributed to a woman's sense of the approaching end of her childbearing years (Fabe and Wikler, 1979). The data of the present study, however, suggest that it is the increased sense of one's mortality, during the crisis of generativity, that lends a sense of urgency to decisions about procreation, as it does to decisions about the course of one's life generally. The following quotation refers to the desire for a first child; more generally, the women seemed to have a sense of urgency at this stage in resolving their identity as a mother, whether or not they already had, or expected to have, children.

I don't think I ever decided I did not want children. I always put it off, as though I had forever to make up my mind. You don't. The fact is I'm going to die sometime, and that's a fact of life. There's something about deciding you're going to start living now, not ten years from now. That things that are important to you you can't put off forever. You can't always wait until the next project's finished 'cause there'll always be a new project. At some point you got to stop messing around. Either you want to do it or you don't. It's clearer to me now than it was years ago . . . I was never very practical. For years I was dealing in the realm of--everything got so complicated, the meaning of life and this and that and the other thing. That the notion of being clear about the things you really want I never really faced . . . It's interesting that 35 is halfway through your lifespan. It's not conscious. I'm halfway through life, I'll have a crisis. But there is a time when you spend your life kind of preparing for what's ahead . . . At some stage you then have to say I no longer have my clear obsessions and hurdles to fol-

> low. I've now made it, what do I do now? You look around and you realize there are other things that have gone unexplored.

With reference to procreation, it is worth noting that three of the six women who had reached the latter part of the crisis of generativity had a relatively serious gynecological disorder at the turning point of age 33 or 38. This seems to reinforce the relationship between the crisis of generativity and the sense of oneself as a parent.

Much of the foregoing relates to Jaques' (1965) conception of the mid-life crisis. During the crisis of generativity, the shadow of death crossed the paths of these women. This brought with it a new internalization of identity, which encompassed a sense of the limitations of life and of achievement. Jung (1971) as well as Jaques viewed the mid-life crisis in reference to a sense of having lived a half of one's life; the data of this study also suggest that the biblical allotment of 70 years to human life may reflect, for women, a biological time clock. Jung's concept of the mid-life crisis is also relevant to the experience of the women in this study in another way. During the crisis of generativity, the women who had been oriented primarily toward professional achievement became concerned with the importance of their personal needs, and of human relationships generally.

In Erikson's terms, the existence of a crisis of generativity indicates that the issue of intimacy versus isolation has been fully resolved, making it possible for the issue of generativity versus stagnation to emerge. This process was well reflected in some of the women studied by a new sense of intimacy with the mentor--based on a feeling of equality--and a new sense of generativity as a fully independent scholar.

In his study of highly creative men, Jaques (1965) found that creativity began, or ended, or changed in quality at mid-life. With reference to the sample of women studied here, the scholarship of the achievement-oriented integrators changed in quality at mid-life. Similarly, one of the independence-oriented non-integrators shifted her professional focus from intellectual to artistic creativity. (It is pertinent, in this context, to note that the women business executives studied by Hennig and Jardim (1977) changed in the quality of their administrative capabilities after the mid-life crisis.) The family-oriented integrators began to commit themselves, at mid-life, to scholarship in their discipline, as did one of the independence-oriented non-integrators.

In the latter part of her crisis of generativity, one of the women in the subtype with a conventional career feared the loss of creative scholarly abilities, a threat which was an indication of the turmoil generated by the mid-life crisis. For others, often-mentioned instances of accident, illness, and surgery were other indications of the turmoil of this period. It may also be a factor in the epidemiological finding that the greater incidence of alcoholism occurs among individuals between the ages of 34 to 36 (Boyd, 1980).

At the time of the interviews, only three of the women in this study were beyond the crisis of generativity. Their experience at age 38 suggested that there is another period of mourning, or a turning point. For example, one woman said, in reference to work on her dissertation, "It was like I was taking the best part of myself and in a very systematic way I was destroying it, by doing this research . . . And I guess in the back of my mind, too, was the feeling that someday this part was going to be gone." And in reference to an experience at that time concerning both her mother and her dissertation, another woman said:

> All I'm sure of is the magic of (how the inspiration for a dissertation) came, POW!, with such conviction and clarity, in the middle of the deepest depression . . . Here was my mother and the whole house being kind of swept up and discarded, 'cause she was moving into a senior retirement home . . . I was lying next to her in the bed, feeling her, having a sense of her flesh, her body, near me and old. It was very sad . . . and I thought (the inspiration for the dissertation) was a miraculous experience. It was like it rose from the depths. It rose like this enormous, clear, bright bubble. And there it was. And it went on being very dark afterwards.

Referring to an operation that forced her to relinquish the prospect of motherhood, one woman said, "It was just a horrible experience with my body. And that kind of sobered me up, too, a little bit about this whole thing about babies and pregnancies. I think it must be, and is, very difficult."

In the stage of consolidation of generativity, the relative absence of idealization in images of self and other was reflected in a new sense of initiative in life and in a new desire to contribute to the welfare of others. For example:

> There is a side of me that reacts against the establishment, against the institution all the time . . . and you end up feeling imobilized. You end up kind of waiting to see what will happen. And sometimes this works. But other times I think, especially as I think about it now, it's better other times if you take the initiative. Because you get something more basic. You get a belief in yourself as an acting person who has some control over

her life.

And,"I'd like to try to do some kind of service work that would be something very direct and not be a job that I was paid for. Something I did just because somebody needs some kind of assistance."

After Generativity . . .

The data of this study do not extend beyond the start of the consolidation of generativity, but one can somewhat extrapolate from them to the rest of the life cycle. Both Erikson (1963) and Jaques (1965) posited one major life crisis after the crisis of generativity. Erikson called it the crisis of integrity versus despair, and Jaques the crisis at full maturity. With reference to the schema of development of self-other images of this study, this crisis can be regarded as involving the evolution of images of self and other, independent of reference to each other; the self as a separate human being and the other as a separate human being. Establishment of a sense of self, without reference to the other, would represent the birth of the self; death, or the loss of the self, would then follow the evolution of this sense of wholeness.

Erikson (1963) and Jaques (1965) have ascribed the last crisis of the life cycle to the age of about 65 to 70. This raises the question of the nature of personality development from age 38, the beginning of the consolidation of generativity, to age 65. Data of this study reveal turning points, at intervals of about five years, that bound the stages of development. The possibility that the stage of consolidation of generativity is some 25 years long is curious, and one would like to know more about this period of the life cycle.

The data of this study confirm the implicit assumption in stage theories of development, that at the appropriate age individuals generally contend with certain issues at various stages of life. Relative "success" or "failure" in development is reflected in the degree of identity diffusion, isolation, and stagnation in the experience of individuals. Development can also be assessed with reference to the assumption of adult roles. In this study, the independence-oriented non-integrators lagged a stage behind the two types of integrators in their commitment to a career and to a mate. These two perspectives of development may be relatively independent of each other, however, so that the independence-oriented non-integrators need not be regarded as less well-integrated personally than the two groups of integrators.

A significant indicator of a relative failure in development among individuals as highly educated as those in this study would be an end to creative productivity during the crisis of generativity. The one woman in this study who experienced a threat to continued achievement also experienced more extreme emotional turmoil during the crisis of generativity than any of the others. This finding is antithetical to that of Hennig and Jardim (1977). In comparing two groups of women business executives, Hennig and Jardim found that those who reached top-level management positions experienced a crisis at mid-life, whereas those who became locked into middle management positions did not experience a crisis at that period in their lives, although they became increasingly bitter about their lot in life thereafter. This difference suggests that both the presence of extreme turmoil and the absence of any obvious turmoil at mid-life may augur poorly for future development.

The findings of this study, with regard to stages of adult development, open up several avenues for future research. As with the types, one would like to apply the stages to different populations, and to both women and men. Further, because developmental crises seemed often to be reflected in medical and psychological difficulties for the women in this sample, one would also like to communicate the characteristics of the various stages to physicians and psychotherapists; a better understanding of adult development might contribute to more effective medical and psychotherapeutic treatment.

In general, further research would be useful to the fuller understanding of the process of adult development, the factors that contribute to its relative success or failure, and those that have bearing on intellectual and artistic creativity in adulthood.

REFERENCES

Bakan, D. The Duality of Human Existence. Chicago: Rand McNally, 1966.

Boyd, L. "The Grab Bag." San Francisco Sunday Examiner & Chronicle, June 29, 1980. In Sunday Punch Section, 8.

Bühler, C. "The Curve of Life as Studied in Biographies." Journal of Applied Psychology, 1935, 19, 405-409.

Erikson, E.H. Childhood and Society (2nd Ed.). New York: W.W. Norton, 1963.

Erikson, E.H. "Reflections on Dr. Borg's Life Cycle." Daedalus, Spring 1976, 105, 1-28.

Fabe, M. & Wikler, N. Up Against the Clock. New York: Random House, 1979.

Gould, R.L. "The Phases of Adult Life: A Study in Developmental Psychology." The American Journal of Psychiatry, 1972, 129 (5), 521-531.

Helson, R. & Mitchell, V. "Personality." In M.R. Rosenzweig and L.W. Porter (Eds.), Annual Review of Psychology (Vol. 29). Palo Alto: Annual Reviews, 1978.

Hennig, M. & Jardim, A. The Managerial Woman. Garden City, New York: Anchor Press, 1977.

Jaques, E. "Death and the Mid-life Crisis." International Journal of Psychoanalysis, 1965, 46, 502-514.

Jung, C. "The Stages of Life." In J. Campbell (Ed.), The Portable Jung. New York: Viking Press, 1971 (Originally published 1933).

Kohlberg, L. "Continuities in Childhood and Adult Moral Development Revisited." In P.R. Bates and K.W. Schaie (Eds.), Lifespan Developmental Psychology: Personality and Socialization. New York: Academic Press, 1973.

Levinson, D.J. The Seasons of a Man's Life. New York: Knopf, 1978.

Loevinger, J. "The Meaning and Measurement of Ego Development." American Psychologist, 1966, 21, 195-206.

Lowenthal, M., Thurner, M., & Chiriboga, D. Four Stages of Life. San Francisco: Jossey-Bass, 1975.

Press, A.K. "Our Radically Changing Society. Report on the Precentennial Conference, 'Perspectives on the Patterns of an Era.'" Radcliffe Quarterly, June 1978, 1-3; 28.

Stewart, W.A. "A Psychosocial Study of the Formation of the Early Adult Life Structure in Women." Doctoral dissertation, Columbia University, 1977. Dissertation Abstracts International, 1977, 38 (1-2), 381B-382B (University Microfilms No. 77-14, 849).

Vaillant, G.E. Adaptation to Life. Boston: Little, Brown, 1977.

van Dusen, R.A. & Sheldon, E.G. "The Changing Status of American Women: A Life Cycle Perspective." American Psychologist, 1976, 31 (2), 106-116.

Dying, Denying, and Willing the Obligatory

Edwin S. Shneidman

This paper is both an essay and a clinical report; primarily it is a case study which serves as an envelope to contain a set of concepts that are believed to be important in appreciating what human beings experience while they are dying from an illness. In addition, it is a brief "dictionary," presenting a glossary of (a relatively few) terms that I believe tc be essential in understanding and mollifying a thanatological situation.

These terms and phrases include the following: dying, death, an appropriate death, denying, and willing the obligatory.

Let us begin with a tautology which is also a truism: There is no greater threat to life than the threat to life, that is, the specter of death (or one's cessation).

The definition of "death" is constantly obfuscated by failing to distinguish between its two different operational meanings: _your_ death and _my_ death. Operationally speaking, it makes sense only for me to speak of _your_ death. I can observe it and I can feel it. The deepest feelings about your death are called my mourning. I observe that feeling in myself and in others and I call it grief. The essence of it is the sense of irretrievable loss. Its tragic distillation is encompassed in a poem, paradoxically entitled "Surprised by Joy" by William Wordsworth, written in 1815 in the memory of his dead four-year-old daughter. I welcome the opportunity to reproduce it here. (It merits untold re-readings.)

> Surprised by joy--impatient as the Wind
> I turned to share the transport--Oh! with whom
> But thee, deep buried in the silent tomb,
> That spot which no vicissitudes can find?
> Love, faithful love, recalled thee to my mind--
> But how could I forget thee? Through what power,
> Even for the least division of an hour,
> Had I been so beguiled as to be blind
> To my most grievous loss!--That thought's return
> Was the worst pang that sorrow ever bore,
> Save one, only one, when I stood forlorn,
> Knowing my heart's best treasure was no more;
> That neither present time, nor years unborn
> Could to my sight that heavenly face restore.

My death is something quite different. I can *never* experience my own death--for if I were experiencing anything, I would still be alive. However, I can certainly experience present feelings of apprehension, fear, dread, distress, indifference or even exultation at the idea, the fantasy, or the experience of my living through what I believe to be my dying period and of the prospect of my "being" dead, that is, no longer being at all. Fear of death is a quite understandable dread of nothingness or mystery. It is beyond impotence and beyond incapacity; it is psychologically difficult to comprehend naughtment or nullification. Melville put it in this frightening way: "Think of being reduced to a heap of offal, and all in one flash!" It is easier (albeit painful) to discuss another's death; I would much rather discuss *your* death--although the English historian Arnold Toynbee (1969) did raise the crucial question of whether a loving spouse should desire to survive the other spouse (and be left to mourn) or wish to predecease the other (and leave one's beloved with the burden of grief). It is a most painful question.

"Dying" is quite different. Dying, operationally defined, is being ill, with pain, and threatened, with horror, by the strong immanent possibility of "being" dead. Sometimes one believes one is dying and is mistaken; in those cases, one has "survived." In Sontag's essay, *Illness as Metaphor* (1978), she speaks persuasively about two worlds: the world of the well and the world of the ill (and how we each have a passport that permits us to move between). But she fails to recognize that third world, the world of the dying. Being ill, no matter how incapacitating or painful, does not have that often overwhelming sense of terror that seems to be an oft-present ingredient of the presentiment of dying.

There are not quite as many different scenarios of dying as there are people--but there are many. A dozen or two can be listed--and certainly we are now well beyond the point in our understanding when we need to speak of a half-dozen so-called "stages" of dying. Among the various stances in relation to the possibility of demise, we can distinguish: raging into the night (as the poet Dylan Thomas would have it); going to bed like a good child; viewing the entire process as a new and interesting experience--after all, one has never died before; being fearful and quaking in uncontrollable ways that exasperate both self and others; being regretful and rueful, almost nostalgic; being contemplative and somewhat resigned. And there is quiet surrender ("Come sweet death") and resignation; and there is terrorized capitulation; and there is desperate fighting for autonomy and control; and passive and dependent handing over of one's body to the doctors and technicians ("Take me and save me"). There is hopeful optimism that is discriminating and optimism that is denial--two attitudes that we must discuss much more, below. And there are many others--a large number of styles that reflect a vast number of different kinds of people.

"Denial" is not meant to mean that there is an absence of perception or complete disavowal of the event, but rather a failure to appreciate fully the significance or full implication of what is being perceived (Trunnel and Holt, 1974). Denial, in this psychological century, is traditionally thought of as a "mechanism of defense." It is a serious misconception to think of all mechanisms of defense as, in themselves, pathological or aberrant. Rather, they are the indispensable gyroscopes of the psycholgical life. Thus, it is a theoretical mistake to classify them as psychotic, neurotic, immature, and normal (Vaillant, 1977), inasmuch as almost any one of them, at one moment in time or another in an individual's life, might properly be placed at any one of these four levels of adaptation. The healthfulness or pathology of, for example, denial, depends on how it is used by an individual, under what circumstances, and in what relationship to the other mechanisms of survival that that individual employs. Specifically: To deny that one is dying at certain moments in one's living with a terminal disease is not necessarily, in itself, psychotic; on the contrary, it may be life-sustaining and simply sensible. *No* one wants to live with one's nose constantly stuck in the mud of life; sometimes it is healthy to be hopeful, even optimistic, and to deny the worst--even (or especially) in the face of seemingly intransigent facts. Hope is a buttress and an antidote to much that is dire and catastrophic in life.

That relationship between denial and hope merits special study (Arieti, 1979). Breznitz (1981), in his review of Arieti's book, *The Parnas* (1979), has this to say:

> Hope is different from denial. Rather than protecting oneself from the negative aspects of a terrible situation, a person can deliberately dwell upon the remaining positive elements, even if they are extremely limited. As things are developing from bad to worse, hope is becoming more restricted, but there is no need to ever give it up. . . . "Let hope grow in your heart, like roses in a garden; don't leave room only for the weeds of despair."
>
> Hope, unlike denial, need not be based on illusion and distortion of the present. It need not even use the vehicle of personal control over one's destiny. Modern psychology has yet to realize that one can be totally helpless, and yet hopeful. . . . Under the shadow of the darkest of all times, he reaches new spiritual heights. (p. 692)

Henry A. Murray--paraphrasing Otto Rank (1932)--in discussing Herman Melville's resignation to his fate, speaks of "a forthright willing of the obligatory" (1967). What I understand this to mean (in relation to death and dying) is that there is a great difference between an obligation and an obligatory. To have to visit one's commanding officer's home on a certain ceremonial occasion is an obligation; dying is an obligatory--there is _no_ choice. The key to _willing_ the obligatory lies in participating in one's own life, including one's pain and dying, with as much _grace_ (elegance, poise, self-possession, pride, purpose, good manners, good cheer) as one can.

Baldassare Castiglione, the sixteenth century Italian diplomat and man of letters, in his famous _The Book of the Courtier_ (1528), has given us, across the centuries, a guideline for this kind of grace. It is "that seasoning without which all the other properties and good qualities would be of little worth . . . avoiding the affectation in every way possible as though it were some very rough and dangerous reef . . . concealing all art and making whatever is done and said appear to be without effort and almost without any thought about it. Much grace comes of this: because everyone knows the difficulty of things that are rare and done well." (pp. 41, 43)--like dying with grace, especially when one is frightened and in pain.

And what of the pain of dying? By and large, so far as I can see, there is little or no actual pain in dying. Granted that there can be great suffering in disease, but dying is the end of disease and thus the end of misery. The principal pain in dying lies in the fears of the supposed pain of death. This is so because "death" has erroneously been given a "life of its own" as though it were an experience, or a state of being, or a transition to some horrendous mythological place. Nowadays, we can view dying more realistically as that relatively short period in which the individual reverts to being an essentially biological organism and withdraws (often in coma) to nurture itself in its last moments. In the gut-level wisdom of the body, these last moments are pain-free, governed by a still-active brain that is inured to almost everything but its own last few, fragmented feelings, and bent on trying to protect itself as well as possible from the very pain that it previously might have feared.

To "will the obligatory" in relation to death is to fall in line with the major immutable cycles of nature, especially human nature, and to understand not only that, as the poet said, "Life is grim, but not necessarily serious," but also that no one, absolutely no one, escapes being finite and mortal. And knowing this, then to accept it, to will it, and not to be in an unnecessary state of angst, or rebellion, or terror over it.

Murray (1959, 1981) wrote as follows:

> Facts of this order constitute the basis for the not uncommon experience among creative men as serving as a vehicle or mouthpiece of some supernatural or superpersonal imperative, of being an agent of evolution instead of a feverish egotistical little self. "This is the true joy in life," Bernard Shaw has written, "the being used for a purpose recognized by yourself as a mighty one." (pp. 42, 44).

There are connections between the idea of willing the obligatory and Ernest Hemingway's definition of courage as "grace under pressure." Willing the obligatory is not merely a passive act of capitulation to the inevitable, but rather a complicated act of perception, imagination, will, and behavior, in which you can seize the opportunity to use what is most heroic and sterling within yourself and do life's most difficult task as well as possible.

It is logical here to ask about the place of religion and faith. Here is an example in a letter written in a Nazi prison by a German pastor (Schneider, 1956) just before his execution, to his wife.

> Once again the chestnut tree is preaching a sermon to me. Its bare black branches reach out to me so promisingly bearing the small brown buds for next spring. I can see them close to the window and also in the top branches. They are already there even when the yellow falling foliage was still hiding them. Should we be so thankless and of so little faith that we deliberately overlook among the falling, withered leaves, the buds that here cling tenaciously to trunk and branches? Let us go on holding only ever more firmly and unequivocally to faith, live by it and act by it, because faith alone represents the victory over the prison of this world and its lethal power. (pp. 14-15).

That superb passage can serve as a spiritual Rorschach blot; each of us can project upon it whatever we wish to define as the cornerstone of our faith: Jesus, Jehovah, Confucius, Mohammed, Buddha, Krishna, Zeus, or faith in our own integrity as a finite human being. It is not that the person who eschews organized religion is bereft; it is that the person who lacks some stabilizing faith or pride--even (or especially) in one's self--is lost.

What one has to fight is hopelessness--even under torment, despite whatever calamities, however bleak the outlook. Hope is the keystone; faith and courage-with-pride are the two pillars on which it rests. These words--faith, courage, pride, hope--are easy to misinterpret. Each has to carry a great deal of weight.

It is also logical to ask about the place of philosophy and belief. Take the question posed by philosopher Stephen Pepper, "Can a Philosophy Make One Philosophical?" (1963)--that is, can one's thoughts make one calmer about dying. Pepper asserted that, in all of man's history there have been just a few comprehensive and adequate philosophies, which he called "world hypotheses." He commented, further, as follows:

> . . . An explicit philosophy is a guide greatly superior to a purely institutionalized ideology or creed. For even when not inadequate, the latter is rigid and dogmatic, whereas the former may be flexible and open to revision. (p. 127)

As a clinical thanatologist, I would go further and say that what seems to be important is not so much the content of any philosophy-of-life, religion or creed, but rather how firmly, easily, and comfortably that belief is held. When one is dying, the most important criterion of the usefulness of a belief-system or creed is not its truth value but the internal comfort that that belief-system gives to that person. This would seem to be so whether the person is creedishly devout, quietly agnostic, or querulously atheistic, as long as that person has (what may appear from someone else's view) the courage of his own confusions. In this sense, it is rather similar to your being comfortably in love with someone. The rational question, "What do you see in *that* person?," is not as important as your being able tranquilly (on whatever rational, or emotional, or unconscious grounds) to answer: "I like that person's company; it comforts me." If one can say with Martin Luther--but not necessarily in the context of Luther's beliefs--*Ich kann nichts anders* (I can do no other)--then you can be true to yourself and die as well as you can, given the tragically unnegotiable nature of the disease (which is killing you) and the general fragility of life (which is not in your favor).

Every once in a while a gifted student of human nature enunciates an especially felicitous concept: Freud's idea of dreams as wish fulfillment, Köhler's concept of insight, Tolman's cognitive maps, Maslow's peak experiences, or Murray's classifications of human needs. Avery Weisman's (1972) concept of "appropriate death" belongs, it seems to me, in such company. It is illuminating, elevating, just right, and on the humanitarian side of things. In essence, the basic notion--resting on the basic assumption that some deaths are better than others (just as some lives are better than others)--is that the beneficient thanatologist (physician, psychologist, nurse, clergyman) should do what he can, when interacting with a dying person, to help that person achieve a "good" death.

Weisman defines an appropriate death as "one in which there is a reduction of conflict, compatibility with the ego ideal, continuity of significant relationships, and consummation of prevailing wishes." (He says, "In short, an appropriate death is one which a person might choose for himself had he an option. It is not merely conclusive; it is consummatory"(p. 41).

I think of an appropriate death as the best possible death for that person (given that disease). It would be like an individually tailored glove for the (figurative) hand of that human being's personality, especially his (life-long) ways of dealing with stress, pain, duress, failure, and threat--all the negative things that dying might mean to him and against which he would need to defend or with which he would wish to cope. What an appropriate death is not is a store-bought, off-the-rack, wholesale plan of a small number of set stages into which every person is made to fit. The person should not be made to fit a plan; rather, the dying should be tailored to fit that person.

When we speak of a good death, we imply that it is appropriate not only for the decedent, but also for the principal survivors--a death they can "live with." The death is somehow consistent with the decedent's living image. While death itself is the ultimate violation, the nature of the death has not violated the image of the person who has died. In James Agee's evocative masterpiece, A Death in the Family (1957), Andrew tells Mary that Jay, her husband, died utterly unafraid. He was killed instantly; he was only briefly aware of the danger to him, and then it ended. Andrew says it this way: "Danger made him every inch of the man he was. And the next instant it was all over." His expression at the moment of death was "startled, resolute, and mad as hell. Not one trace of fear or pain." Mary is comforted to hear that her husband died without suffering and without weakness. Her mother's succinct judgment is: "Very appropriate."

Herman Hesse, who thought and wrote much about the meaning of death, has a particularly telling passage in one of the works of his early middle age, "Klein and Wagner" (1970):

> There was a spark floating in the darkness. He clung to it with all the ardor of his racked soul. It was a thought: useless to kill himself, to kill himself now; no point to exterminating himself, tearing himself limb from limb--it was useless. But it was good and redeeming to suffer, to ferment to ripeness amid tears and tortures, to be forged to completion amid blows and pangs. Then you had earned the right to die, and then dying was good, beautiful, and meaningful, the greatest blessing in the world, more blissful than any night of love; burned out and ut-

terly resigned to fall back into the womb, to be extinguished, redeemed, reborn. Such a death, such a ripe and good, noble death alone had meaning; it alone was salvation, it alone was homecoming. Longing cried in his heart. Where, where was the narrow, difficult path, where was the gateway? He was ready; with every quiver of his exhausted, agitated body, of his anguished mind, he yearned for it. (1970, p. 114)

The psychologically noteworthy aspects of this passage are the terms Hesse chooses to characterize an appropriate death: to ferment to ripeness; to be forged to completion; burned out and utterly resigned; good; noble; meaningful; salvation. To die at the right time and in the right way--those are the hallmarks of a sterling death.

We all recognize that after certain peaks in life's range, there are anticlimactic plateaus where life hangs heavy and time stands still. Shakespeare reminds us in *Julius Ceasar*. "There is a tide in the affairs of men. . . ." An appropriate death comes when one is ready for it. Avery Weisman (1966) quotes a doctor's comforting words to a dying patient: "I promise you that you will not die until you're prepared to die."

An appropriate death is appropriate to the individual's time of life, to his style of life, to his situation in life, to his mission (aspiration, goals, wishes) in life; and it is appropriate to the significant others in his life. Obviously, what is appropriate differs from person to person. One man's nemesis is another man's passion. Appropriateness has many dimensions, relating, at the least, to the state of one's health, competence, energy, prowess, zeal, hope, pain, and investment in his post-self.

A Case Example

Some little while ago--never mind how long exactly--an oncologist acquaintance contacted me to ask if I would see a patient and her husband primarily because, in spite of the fact that she had an intractable cancer, she would not admit that she was dying. Her denial was a source of concern to the husband--and to this physician. Would I please see her?

The patient was a 59-year-old comely female, obviously ill. We had, it seemed to me, instantaneous rapport. She was willing, even happy, to talk. I saw her seven times, a week apart--they had to drive in a fair distance for her visits with the physician and with me. Our last session was within the week of her death.

The patient was willing to see me, but initially had no great inner push to do so. After we began, she said that she "enjoyed" the sessions sufficiently to want to continue them, but the impetus came from the uneasiness, the restlessness, the anxiety of the husband and, equally, of her physician, attendant to her denial. The fact that she would not "admit that she was dying" was a source of visible perturbation on their part. Apparently, my assigned task in their eyes was to make her confess, own up, see the light, recognize what was really happening--then everything would be all right. Of course, I did not take the role of simply being their messenger, but, as it happened (with admittedly some activity on my part at some subtly critical points), there were some rather dramatic developments before the sessions were over.

There was an additional item of great concern to the husband. Theirs was a "mixed marriage"; specifically, he was Roman Catholic and she was Greek Orthodox. She had converted when they were married many years before, but now he and the grown children were in a panic to know in which religion she wished to be buried--it would be too awful for words if they unknowingly buried her in the "wrong" church. Because she took the position that she was simply ill (and there could be no talk of dying) he did not dare speak to her about these matters, certainly not funerals, especially hers. What was he to do? Could I please help him and get her to indicate her choice. From the family's view, the welfare of her very soul (not to mention their everlasting peace of mind) might depend on this.

I had her explicit permission to record the sessions, but due to some circumstances beyond my control--faulty tapes, faulty machines--I recorded only four sessions, the first and the last three. What is reproduced below--with my comments, indented--are verbatim sections from these tapes. Omissions are indicated by elision marks.

FIRST SESSION

S: Please tell me something about yourself.

T: Up until this illness, I never had a sick day in my life. I never was in the hospital except for having two children. I always had a lot of projects going, like the average housewife does, and I wasn't setting the world on fire, but I played cards once in a while and I cooked for the family and was always home when they were home and I did some needlepoint. I wasn't a television addict, although I watched it. Just a very average person. I enjoyed my family. I have a very good relationship with my family, my husband and my two children. My children are very, very devoted and just do *anything* they can.

I was quite young, 18, when I was married. I had a very, very,

very domineering mother. I'll say this to you, Doctor, because I feel I can talk to you. The older I get and the older my mother gets, I like her less--I love her, but I like her less.

S: I understand that.

T: She is a _very_ tough lady. Everything _must_ be her way. It's really only a man who can manage her. Takes a man to manage her. I have been _nothing_ to her all my life. She is like, like I am just a child, a kid, a whatever you want to call me. She is my boss, no matter the fact that I've reared two children who've made successes of their life, when I say they have gone to college which is nice, I feel.

I think my father must have had a very sad life. I don't think I ever really knew my father. And I often feel badly about that. My mother dominated him too. I can remember if she was angry at him, she would let it be known to me that I musn't talk to him either. My father died 32 years ago. The thing I remember the most is . . . he had leukemia. It hurts me to say it, it sticks in my throat but I have to be homest with you. And he said to me, he looked at me and he said, "I'm so afraid." And I just looked back at him and I didn't say anything. I couldn't say anything. I was, like, tongue-tied. I was in my 20's, and maybe I was just not as sharp as I should have been but I felt, Oh dear God, I want to say something, I want to comfort you, I wanna, I wanna help you, but I just looked at him, mute.

S: What would you have said if you had the voice to say it?

T: You mean if it were today?

S: If you could do it over again.

T: I would have talked to my father and I would have said, well, is it that you're afraid of dying, because many people are. But let's talk about it because everybody has to, or will, and would it help you to tell me why you said you were so afraid?

S: What do you think he would say?

T: I don't know.

S: Mrs. T., you're being seen by Dr. M. Why do you think he asked me to see you?

T: I think it was more my family that asked, that they felt I should see you than Dr. M. did. I think my family thinks that I am going into a shell; retreating--that sort of thing . . .

All we're doing now is waiting for the good cells to be rejuvenated. The bad cells were destroyed and the good ones at the same time during the radiation, and the bad ones are gone--they're destroyed, right? Now we're waiting for the good ones to regenerate themselves.

S: What has Dr. M. told you?

T: He hasn't really told me what he thinks of me now. I finished my radiation and they tell you to allow about 4 weeks or so, and then you start to feel better because you're very weak from radiation and I did start to feel better in about 4 weeks. Then all of a sudden I got this, if you want to call it, they don't call it a setback exactly, they call it what you expect with radiation. I got this, to the point where I couldn't eat. My food buds had been destroyed--I couldn't eat.

S: What is your family uptight about now?

T: Well, they feel very badly when they see me vomit, of course. They see, feel very badly to see how thin I am and how weak I am. I mean, I need help, you know, just to walk to your office. . . . To go back and say some more about myself. I was raised Greek Orthodox. My husband is Roman Catholic.

S: What did your mother think at any time when you were going to marry him?

T: There was big flak.

S: Whom did she want you to marry?

T: A doctor, a lawyer, Ph.D., or something. Greek Orthodox. She disliked my husband because she considered him definitely a foreigner.

S: Do you have any feelings of uneasiness or guilt that you're not Greek Orthodox today?

T: Yes.

S: Oh?

T: Well, when you're brought up to be one thing, as you get older, or as I get older, I should say, I sometimes wonder if there is any real big difference in all the religions whether they're the Jewish religion, the Catholic, the Protestants, they're all roads to one destination. And if they are, then why all this feeling of guilt or that you were bad because you let yourself stray. Does that make sense to you? If I'd have stayed Greek Orthodox, I wouldn't have strayed. I might tell you this, though. This I shouldn't skip. When we were married, we were married in the Catholic Church. Seven years after we were married, we did get married in the Orthodox Church. I always felt nervous about the children if it was the day to go to Mass or if it was a day to go to confirmation. I could never relax. You see, I could have handled that better if I had handled my mother better, but I didn't think of saying to my husband: Well, now look, since we were married in the Catholic Church and since this is confirmation day, I don't want to feel nervous about it, and this is the day we do so and thus, and you did agree to it and so let's relax about it. But you see, I was so used to kowtowing to my mother.

S: So you were caught between your husband and your mother.

T: I am a kind of person who, I think, I would have done a lot more things in life if she hadn't stifled me. I would've maybe explored the--and I don't want to say I have talents, 'cause I don't, although the family will say to me, you're very good with interior decorating, you know, one of those things. I think my mother held me back in being a better--I could have been a better person. . . .

S: How scared are you?

T: Of my illness?

S: If you wish.

T: Well, they told me that this radiation had seemed to help very much. I have put the illness, it would seem, in the back of my pocket, and I have been more concerned about getting this awful vomiting, diarrhea, and indigestion over with. That has absorbed me. I guess I say, Dear God, let me go to 70 or 80. You see, because I never had any illness. I never thought much about things like this.

I then spoke to the husband separately:

Mr. T: I feel that she's denying at this point, about how seriously ill she is. I mean, Dr. M. has told me that she's quite ill and it may only be a matter of a couple of weeks to a couple of months. And she doesn't seem to know, she doesn't act like she knows it. She talks about getting better, and I think the fact that she overcame a colostomy and chemotherapy and like that, and lasted this long, she thinks that this is going to go away too. She's told that the cells are going to regenerate and like that. As a matter of fact, I asked Dr. M. if I could bring my family in and we all sat in together.

S: Was she in on that meeting?

Mr. T: No.

S: What has Dr. M. told her?

Mr. T: Just that she has to muddle through this kind of thing, and that the extreme radiation that she experienced has killed the bad cells, and of course some of the good cells, and this is a side effect. They have to be regenerated, the cells have to be regenerated, and that's what she's hoping for. He knows she hasn't accepted it yet, and he's kind of letting it happen. He's told her nothing about that. He doesn't tell her, for instance, that when he tapped her last week, he found some fluid, which was positive, and she doesn't know any of that. I mean, I just thought that maybe it would be eased a little if she saw someone like you, and your name came up, and I said yeah, by all means, let's see you. I manage to live with it, but I'm fearful of what will happen as soon as she finds out, like I dreaded--I don't know how much went on with you today, but I almost dread going home with her in case she's gotten more out of you today than she's had up till now. Not that that's bad, I mean, you haven't, you didn't tell her anything? Like she said yesterday, "I don't know why I'm seeing him now."

S: You've used a very interesting word, denying. What do you think is bad about denying?

Mr. T: Nothing, that's why I think Dr. M. is letting her deny it.

S: Can you and the children live comfortably with that?

Mr T: Well, I guess I can, but, I only guess I can, but let me put it to you this way: My children think that she should be allowed to deny. I, on the other hand, am the kind of guy that feels if it were me, I would want to know about me.

S: What if it were she?

Mr. T: Well, if it's she, I mean, that's why we're here to see you.

After the first session, there were two sessions that were not recorded. Some interesting things occurred during those sessions.

The second meeting was occupied almost entirely with her anamnestic recall, largely about her overbearing mother, and more details, all on the positive side, about her husband and her children. In our third meeting she spoke of something seemingly innocuous--like taking a university extension course or planting a garden--and she asked my advice about it. Should she do those things? I shifted the content of her question and said that a good general rule of life was to do _important_ things when one _didn't_ have to, so that one's judgments were not contaminated by a sense of pressure or urgency. She asked, "Like what?" I said, like getting married, getting divorced, buying or selling a house and then I added--for this was the reason for making this point--like making arrangements for one's funeral. To this last she said, "Oh, do you think so?" I said,"Yes, of course," and then, in an act that is decidedly unusual for me in a pschotherapy setting, I took my paid-up mortuary card out of my wallet (which I had taken pains to find and put in my wallet with the specific hope that this kind of occasion would occur) and I showed it to her. "It's a good idea," I said, "to make these arrangements when you don't have to, when you're not desperate, when you still have health, like you." I remember her smiling and I also remember wondering inwardly whether or not we were now silent partners in a collusion that was, in a way that did not need to be made explicit, painfully clear to both of us.

The not-entirely-surprising development in the following session was her straightforward announcement, at the very beginning of her hour, that she and her husband had that very week purchased two cemetery lots. The choice of cemetery and mortuary set the seal on the religious ceremony she wanted at her funeral. Her family knew exactly what to do; and she herself had turned a corner.

FOURTH SESSION

She began the next (fourth) session as follows:

T: I want to ask, can you gauge, I guess I'm just going to have to be blunt and say, when a person will die by the symptoms that they are showing outwardly by getting more weak, losing more weight, can things like that say to you, well, it's going to be about two weeks or it's going to be about three weeks? It could be months or a few weeks.

S: Do you feel you have changed much in the last couple of weeks?

T: In energy level, yes. I don't go downstairs anymore.

S: You seem almost impatient.

T: That describes it. 'Cause I always like to get things done once I decided to do it. But I shouldn't want to act like I'm dying, like I wanted to die soon?

S: No, you have to act exactly how you feel.

T: Although some days when I (coughs), when I don't feel good, I think oh, it wouldn't be so bad to just get this over with, you know. Like when one . . . two nights ago, I had a very bad night, I was up all night, I was vomiting and I had indigestion or what they say isn't indigestion but it feels like it, and I was just miserable and finally when I got to sleep, I slept till 4 o'clock the next day. I just wish I could talk like my husband does, and I'm sure he isn't doing it just to please me, 'cause he's a very frank and pragmatic person, but he says, honey, there's nothing to it, you just, just stop and then I remembered you saying once the brain stops, that's it. And then there's nothing to fear--there's nothing. . . .

S: There's no pain.

T: As the brain stops. I have a pain here where the colostomy used to be.

S: There's no pain to death.

T: Well, there's no pain to death, as you go out. It's what happens before, the pain of the illness. That's the part that worries me. Nothing will happen?

S: Nothing that you need to fear will happen. You will simply stop being, and your brain will stop functioning and then you may have an adventure that you have never had before and none of us has experienced. There is nothing to tell us that it should be fearsome.

T: Sometimes I feel I'm all straightened out and then other times I feel like I'm all mixed up. . . . My family is top drawer. Oh, I'm most appreciative, I'm grateful, and I thank my husband 100 times a day. (Crying) Yesterday, or maybe 2 days ago it was, when I slept till 4 o'clock, and I was completely out, they kept coming up to check on me. And my daughter came over at one o'clock to give me a bath, and when I was sleeping, and she finally went home and she came back at 7:30 that night and gave me the bath and you know, that was pretty darn good. . . . Right now, if I were to describe myself to you, I would say that I'm in a state of mix-up. I'm not quite sure, you know, one week I say darn it, I'm not gonna let this get me, I'll just be strong and admirable, so people will say--not so they'll say, but so they could say--well, she was courageous. And then other weeks, other days, I'm despairing. And I think, oh God, let me get this over with.

S: Do you show that despair or verbalize it?

T: My husband says he doesn't think I verbalize very much. Like the other night we got talking and he said, you know, you don't talk very much, you keep everything in. Pretty much. Not always. But quite a bit.

S: Do you have some concern about what other people will say about you?

T: You want to be thought of as having been courageous and sort of tough. Like, "She went out in style." . . . I guess it would just be nicer than all shrieking and yelling and that kind of thing. When my children were born, I had instructions from my mother how to behave.

S: Are you looking to me for instructions as to how to handle what may be ahead of you?

T: Now that you mention it, I wouldn't mind.

S: We've moved a long way in the last month, when we couldn't even mention certain topics.

T: No, I want to mention death and dying. I want to get this as much out mentioning it as I can. It's true, I couldn't have mentioned death and dying a couple of months ago.

S: Say again what you think permitted you to be able to talk with this amount of openness and candor; how did that happen?

T: Well, I guess it's fortified by the knowledge that you were here to give me an answer or back me up or, knowing I had you in my, what do they say where the baseball players go?

S: In your dugout, in your corner?

T: Yes. I think that's what made me able to do it and I decided to just say the words. I had, it seems like, rapport with you when we first met. It's because you concentrate on the mind.

S: On what's going on in your head.

T: Yes. So I feel that I can say death, and dying, and cemeteries, and, and things that I couldn't say before.

S: Do you feel safe in here?

T: Yes. Very. Very. I would think that now I'm a person who could have used you, let's just say bluntly like that, when I was about 25. It would have changed my whole life.

FIFTH SESSION

S: In the last couple of weeks, you've made some changes in your life. Say something about those, would you?

T: Well, going to the cemetery and making a decision on that.

S: You'd put that off for some years, hadn't you?

T: Yes, all my life.

S: How did that come about; how do you think you were able to do that?

T: Well, you put the seed of thought in my head and made me realize that maybe it was important now. And then my husband said, let's do it tomorrow. And that's how it got done so fast.

S: How is it you didn't resist it as you had resisted it before?

T: Because I'm wondering if I'm on my way out.

S: Now you've never said that before.

T: It was hard for me to say it, it stuck in my throat. But I had to answer your question. (Cries) I wonder if they, they-- Dr. M., his team, my family, those people--if they know that I'm not long for this world and so they want me to get, get my ducks in a row. Things all lined up and put in order. This summer I was jovial and smiling and kidding and happy and feeling good and all, and it's just been since October that all this happened. And now that Dr. M. and my family wanted me to see you, I just have a feeling that you are preparing me for something.

S: Like what, dear?

T: That I'm going to die and it may be very soon. Maybe you don't know but maybe they know. So they wanted you to do the preparation. I can't say that you know, because I don't know that you know, but maybe some of the group knows.

S: How does that make you feel toward me?

T: Oh, most certainly no animosity or no . . . I just think it's a hard job for you.

And I . . . every once in a while when I have been trying to find some hope for myself, I say, well it's still possible if you can gain some weight, that maybe you can, you can gain some weight; maybe you can still fight this battle. (Cries) Every once in a while I get sort of sarcastic with myself and I say, well, what the hell, everybody has to go, so (crying) I would have just like to enjoy it a little longer and then other times I say, well, maybe I will. Maybe if I can eat and get heavier. I look like an old witch running through the hills in England, you know.

S: This is a place where you can talk about your fears, your angers, your hates, your yearnings, all of those things.

T: I want to get to know my granddaughters better and longer, do more things with them, take them to the circus, take them to the ballet, go to the zoo with them, go to a library with them. When my daughters, or granddaughters were born, those daughters asked me to write a letter and seal it and were going to give it to them on their 21st birthdays and then, for instance, I said, don't ever forget the wonders of a library and then, and, and having compassion for people and not looking down your nose at them, and, and . . . and giving of yourself, things like that. I won't be . . . (crying) . . . I won't be around to maybe talk to them along those lines and have a little fun with them. Now I think they'll never know me (crying throughout). Unless, you know, a couple more years of this (unintelligible) . . . I hope it helps. I alternately think maybe I'll have a little more time and then I alternately think maybe I won't. You can't imagine my husband. You cannot imagine. Everybody talks about him and they don't even know the little things that happen when we're in the house alone. I mean if I get up at night, you know, if I'm just up to use the bathroom, the commode, you know, if, am I sick or am I all right, do I need something? He's just been everything, he's taken over the complete house, I mean he, not only that, but he'll say, good morning beauty, you know. What a good fellow. And anticipate if the pillows need to go this way or this way or up or down. I mean, I could talk for hours about him. And if he's downstairs and he thinks he hears me wanting him, even if I don't, he comes galloping up: Did you call or something? And he's just wonderful. Unless you're a very philosophical person and have shrugged your shoulders in your youth and say heck, I know it's going to happen so I don't even think about it. I think it takes a lot of talking about it to get used to it. You know, I have had a funny feeling all my life. My father was 61 or so when he died and I always had the feeling I was going to die at the age he died. When I think about it, which I would try not to, and I would put it right out of my mind. That haunts me sometimes, too. (long pause) He was 61 too. I was 30 when he died and he was 31 when I was born.

SIXTH SESSION

S: I see you have a notebook. Do you have an agenda?

T: I have one thing, one major thing to say.

S: Please.

T: I want to know how one person such as I copes with the thought of death and dying with perhaps a short time, without panicking and without making it awful for their family.

S: My, you've moved a long way, haven't you? What has permitted you to talk in this way, a way in which you couldn't even bear to think as recently as a month ago?

T: You.

S: In what way?

T: Well, just your, something about you, your demeanor, your confidence-building properties, if you will. Just you. Or else, you have a certain talent that maybe others don't have, for allowing a person to bring that out . . . I think I'll fall into a pit of snakes.

S: What, of despair?

T: No, when one dies. You know, in Catholic school they teach you if you're not good, you'll, you'll fall into a pit of snakes or you'll go into purgatory or all that stuff, that fire and brimstone.

S: I don't believe that at all, and I don't believe it for you. I'm not your priest and this is not a confessional. I don't believe in the notion of a pit of snakes. It sounds very superstitious to me.

T: I think how I had so much living left to do. I've always felt more vigorous than my age. I always, I would never have gone out without nail polish and some makeup, and you know, a pair of earrings or whatever. Now, I'm just too weak to bother. I feel very weak. I just feel very depressed, like I, all I want to do is lay in bed, really. You know, I look at the trees and they are starting to bloom and I think oh, I won't see such and such a tree, I won't be here when it's bloomimg. (Cries) Katharine Hepburn said, "Why worry about something that's inevitable?" With my husband, I tell him I'm going to talk about death now where I couldn't have said that to him maybe 6 months ago.

S: What's his response to that?

T: He says, that's good. That's what I told you. He's a very pragmatic person. And he said he has never feared death because he felt he had a good life and he enjoyed life. He enjoyed his family and his work and his pleasures. So he said I'm ready anytime.

S: In that, there's a great compliment to you, isn't there?

T: To use the vernacular, Doctor, he has always been crazy about me. It's always been a romance, not just a marriage. There's never been an anniversary that he's forgotten. You know the play--the movie and the play--Streetcar Named Desire? Well, in my youth, in my 20's, when he was courting me, I got mad, angry and I called him Stanley Kowalski. And then you know I was sorry about it the next ten minutes, but I did do it and he knew I was hurt. And the next day he sent me a telegram with some endearing phrase on it, signed Stanley. I still have it and it's yellowed. . . . Give me a thought to think on this week.

S: That your therapist called you a beautiful, gutsy lady.

T: Well, I appreciate that. But I mean something a little more than that might give me some solace.

S: Well, I'll give you another thought that goes along with that. You have led a life that most people in the world would envy. You, you have found a man in the world you've gotten along with, you have, you have wonderful children. You have been a decent citizen of the world. You can't do more than that.

T: That I should think of death and dying in relation to the good life I've had.

S: Yes.

T: And that's it.

S: If you want a thought for the week.

T: And to try not to fear it because it's something we all face.

SEVENTH (AND LAST) SESSION

S: What is happening?

T: Well, this week I wrote a few letters to be mailed later (crying) to my dearest friends whose dear friendship has meant to me over the years. This is to a special group, not just everybody I know. Trying to do this in a satisfying way.

S: How tender.

T: What each one's certain personality meant, or ways, or however you want to put it, because you have many friends and many different temperaments and not every friend is the same. About a dozen.

S: Do you happen to have any such letter with you?

T: I can next week. I don't want them mailed till right afterward. . . . And I looked out today and I thought how beautiful it was and (crying), I hated it. . . . I intend to write three short ones there, but all I'll say is (crying) Dear Tommy, we've said it all. Love again, Joanne. Because we have said it all, all our lives. So it will only be something like that. And to the children, the same way. Maybe two sentences. . . . I still feel that I need more. Is there anything you can, other than about death and dying, other than to look back on the good life? I still feel--oh, that I maybe haven't accomplished much in, in, in conquering that area, or maybe you never conquer it. Maybe you just always keep trying. . . . I gave them their baby books when they were pregnant at a shower and that meant more to them than any gift that they got at the shower. They sat on my bed and I gave them my rings. Even my engagement and wedding rings, see. . . . I'm not very good company around the house. I feel badly about that (crying). Yes, I really do. I just, just look at me, maybe an ad for a pretty dress and I'll think oh, that would be nice for the summer and then I think where I'll be in the summer. Probably . . . maybe . . . I just don't want to be dour and let everybody down. The thought of death is terror for me. Does it terrify you? . . . I don't do much crying at home. Actually, Tommy puts me to bed, puts a cold compress on my eyes, that's when I do my crying. I asked him if he had cried lately, I said I never see your eyes red. I never see you look like you've cried and you take your walks and you kind of get it out of your system. He said, the night I knew--the day I knew you had the operation to reverse the colostomy and it was a long operation and Dr. M. came out and he looked so tired and so defeated and so disappointed because he hadn't been able to get it all and then Tommy knew I was gonna have radiation and he, I guess he thought then that, you know, there was just a slim chance, and he said that day (crying) he went out and had a long, long cry. But since then, he apparently hasn't. He's, he anticipates every move I make, he's always busy, if you know what I mean. Maybe he does shed a few tears that are gone by the morning, because I go to bed anywhere between 8 and 10. But right now he has himself under very good control. He knew that they were going to try everything but that the chances were slim. . . . And he said, well, we have good children, they won't let me down. Or maybe I'll go fast. The price of a happy marriage--one has to be left as the mourner. Well, it's like some people say, well, I don't want to get married, I don't want to get committed to any-

> thing. Then I won't be, then I won't be in danger of feeling badly. Nothing is free. . . . So I must just concentrate on the good aspects of what I've had. I meant it in the way, in the sense of trying to just--to say the words death and dying, which is hard; to keep thinking of the good that we had. That's the most good I can do. . . . Do some people wish they'd never been born?

* * * * * *

There are no fixed stages in the extended dying process.For each individual it is an idiosyncratic journey, just as that life has been. But it can be a period of heightened psychodynamic drama during which rather dramatic changes in behavior occur, based on shifts and readjustments of insight, self-regard, needs, relationships to others, and coping stratagems (mechanisms of defense). The pressures to "do something" are perhaps greater in the dying interval than during any other period of comparable length in one's life. This is realistically so because, at that time, it is "now or never." But there is also pressure for freedom from pain and freedom from the thoughts of naughtment. That is what, among other factors, keeps denial going.

In this case, there was basic personality strength, in the context of a rather good and supporting marriage and devoted children (even taking into account a relationship with an overbearing mother) that reasserted itself after an episode of understandably wishing that the growing cancer weren't so. And curiously (but not atypically), she, the dying person, had gone beyond her period of denying and was able to verbalize her feelings about dying and death to herself but was loath to speak of them to her loved ones because she felt that _they_ were not yet ready to hear her talk about these topics--a condition that we might call mutual defense.

In the end, denial behind her, she moved rather gracefully toward her death, appropriate for herself and her loved ones, willing her own obligatory. She understood and accepted that the cancer was doing its lethal work and that her earthly life was coming to its end. Her triumph was that she could be willingly and gracefully sanguine about this irremediable fatal matter.

An interesting post-mortem clinical question is whether this process would have happened with this person in any event or whether the clinical thantologist played an indispensable role in catalyzing these changes. It is not possible to say, but who would want to turn away the effusive statements of gratitude from her physician, husband, and children?

REFERENCES

Agee, J. *A Death in the Family*. New York: McDowell, Obolensky, 1957.

Arieti, S. *The Parnas*. New York: Basic Books, 1979.

Becker, E. *Denial of Death*. New York: The Free Press, 1973.

Breznitz, S. "Denial of Evil: Review of S. Arieti's *The Parnas*." *Contemporary Psychology*, 1981, *26*, 692-693.

Castiglione, B. *Il Cortegiano*. (The Book of the Courtier.) (C.S. Singleton, Trans.) Garden City, N.J.: Anchor Books, 1959. (Originally published 1528.)

Hesse, H. "Klein and Wagner." In *Klingsor's Last Summer*. New York: Noonday Press, 1970.

Murray, H.A. "Preparations for the Scaffold of a Comprehensive System." In S. Koch (Ed.), *Psychology: A Study of a Science*. New York: McGraw-Hill, 1959; reprinted in E.S. Shneidman (Ed.), *Endeavors in Psychology: Selections from the Personology of H.A. Murray*. New York: Harper and Row, 1981.

Murray, H.A. "Dead to the World: The Passions of Herman Melville." In E.S. Shneidman (Ed.), *Essays in Self-Destruction*. New York: Science House, 1967.

Pepper, S. "Can a Philosophy Make One Philosophical?" In E.S. Shneidman (Ed.), *Essays in Self-Destruction*. New York: Science House, 1967.

Rank, O. *Art and the Artist*. New York: Knopf, 1932.

Schneider, P. "Letter to his Wife, November 7, 1937." In H. Gollwitzer and others (Eds.), *Dying We Live*. New York: Pantheon Books, 1956.

Sontag, S. *Illness as Metaphor*. New York: Farrar, Straus, and Giroux, 1978.

Toynbee, A. *Man's Concern with Death*. New York: McGraw-Hill, 1969.

Trunnel, E. & Holt, W. "The Concept of Denial or Disavowal." *Journal of the American Psychiatric Association*, 1974, *22*, 769-784.

Vaillant, G. *Adaptation to Life*. Boston: Little Brown, 1977.

Weisman, A.D. *On Dying and Denying*. New York: Behavioral Publications, 1972.

Psychology and Humanism

M. Brewster Smith

Nevitt Sanford has run a large part of the life course in front of me as a kind of quasi-elder brother, an exemplar whose path has crossed mine repeatedly and whom I am accustomed to looking across and up to as a pathfinding psychologist. When I found my way to Henry Murray's Harvard Psychological Clinic in the fall of 1940, Nevitt's reputation still clung to the yellow clapboard building with "wisteria on the outside, hysteria on the inside," where he had participated in Murray's (1938) *Explorations* that had been a primary lure in bringing me to Harvard. Back at Harvard's new Department of Social Relations after the war, I read the ponderous galleys of *The Authoritarian Personality* (Adorno, Frenkel-Brunswik, Levinson, and Sanford, 1950), with great intellectual excitement. Its fusion of psychoanalytic and social-psychological theory and method in empirical research on central left-liberal social and political issues was a close fit to my own commitments, so much so that I have been repeatedly concerned with the vicissitudes of research on authoritarianism and social character in the three decades that have since elapsed (for example, Smith, 1978d, 1980).

A little later, I had a hand in bringing Nevitt to Vassar to rescue a faltering collegiate mental health program--where, of course, he produced the major research classic on college education from a personalistic standpoint (Sanford, 1962). Nevitt was available to Vassar because of his honorable role at Berkeley as nonsigner of the famous loyalty oath, a *cause celebre* of liberal academe that I came to assimilate to my personal past when years later I joined the Berkeley family. I followed in some of Nevitt's paths in SPSSI (the Society for the Psychological Study of Social Issues), an organization with which we both identified strongly. And when in recent years I played an administrative role at the Santa Cruz campus of the University of California, I helped to arrange for Nevitt to come with an action research team to study some of our organizational problems (the study unfortunately collapsed in the face of the kind of political mishap to which such risky research is always vulner-

----

This essay was originally presented as the Psi Chi Distinguished Lecture at the meetings of the American Psychological Association, Los Angeles, August 26, 1981. A somewhat different version has already been published (Smith, 1982a).

able).

In all of these connections and in many others as a colleague in psychology, I have come to know and cherish Nevitt as a prime contributor to Henry Murray's tradition of a humanly rich psychology of personality--a psychology of personality also conceived as embedded in its social context. Further, he has exemplified for me and for many others how psychological science can be developed in interdisciplinary company and applied to the enrichment and advancement of people--a risky and often subversive activity, though it is far from un-American!

So it is very appropriate that I adapt this paper to honor Nevitt's role in humanizing psychology. A veteran of many battles over psychological and social issues that his commitments have entailed, Nevitt carries his scars with grace. In the nature of things, these battles do not lead to final victories--or, happily, to final defeats either. If we enter the fray without the illusion that final victory is possible, that Utopia lies just around the corner, there is no occasion for disillusionment. To many of us, Nevitt represents the ideal type of "Happy Warrior," a committed and engaged, wise and astute psychologist, blessed with elegant style in word and action and a sense of humor, sometimes wry, sometimes ribald, that helps him and us to maintain perspective. May he flourish, and may his breed not become extinct!

Psychology and Humanism

The object of this essay is to reclaim "humanistic psychology" from the movement so labelled, so as once again, in Nevitt's spirit, to push _psychology_ to become more humanistic. During the dozen years that I have been teaching psychology at Santa Cruz, I have felt an increasingly urgent need to distinguish humanism in psychology from the humanistic movement. Santa Cruz is not very far from Big Sur and Esalen, the erstwhile Mecca of the humanistic psychology movement. I arrived there in 1970 near the apogee of the humanistic movement. There was just no way that I could go about doing psychology following my own conceptions and preferences and forget about "humanistic psychology." In fact, the greater number of undergraduates who flocked into the psychology major wanted what they thought was humanistic psychology, and did _not_ want what they thought was scientific psychology (which was what most of the regular faculty wanted to teach them). Mostly they assumed an inherent opposition between humanistic and scientific psychology. The discordance between student desires and expectations, on the one hand, and faculty values and intentions, on the other, presented me with a special problem, since one major part of my parentage as a psychologist, as a student of Henry Murray and Gordon Allport, left me regarding my enduring commitments to psychology as a science (according to my changing view of what is proper science for human psychology). Although I could not regard myself as a proponent of hardnosed mainstream scientific psychology in the style of American behaviorism or more generally of the positivistic tradition (an earlier part of my heritage), I could also not be at all happy with the irrationalist and anti-scientific affinities of the humanistic psychology movement. If I accepted the humanistic label for myself, I found myself thrown in with strange bedfellows! My continuing ambivalence is reflected in the fact that not long ago I joined APA Division 32 (Humanistic Psychology), but I have stayed out of AHP (the Association for Humanistic Psychology).

The 1980's find the humanistic psychology movement in decline. So it may be good time to take stock, and, I hope, to reclaim the humanistic label for better purposes. This essay is part of my campaign to recapture the flag of humanism in psychology.

Deficiencies of the Humanistic Movement in Psychology

To make some of the sources of my discomfort and discontent with the humanistic movement more concrete, let me pick some illustrative bones with humanistic psychology as it reached me through my undergraduate students, and one major bone as I encountered it in discussions with the movement's leaders.

The students tended to be entranced by the gimmicky techniques and concepts that the movement fostered with little self-criticism (Farson, 1978). Most of the students wanted to become therapists--indeed, on the strength of a weekend workshop or so, a number of them thought that they already _were_ therapists--and they wanted authoritative, easy answers and dramatically clear models. They confused demonstrations and testimonials with evidence. They wanted to be "true believers." Symbolic of my complaint on this score was the fact that when I reached some of the students who had aspirations for graduate school as seniors in a course on "History and Systems of Psychology," one of my minor but serious objectives had to be to get them to respond to the stimulus "Gestalt psychology" not with Fritz Perls--or at least, not only with him--but with Wertheimer, Köhler, and Koffka!

A more fundamental conceptual defect that seemed to me almost universal in my students' versions of humanistic psychology was their simple identification of humanism with the most superficial, bland optimism--"positive" rather than "negative" thinking. Shades of Mary Baker Eddy and Norman Vincent Peale! Of course, they had reason to make that identification. If one accepts the schematized classification of assumptions about human nature according to the prototypes put forth by Hobbes, Locke, and Rousseau, and identifies (among our near contemporaries) Freud with the Hobbesian stress on innate evil predispositions and Skinner with the Lockean empiricist assumption of malleability under environmental programming, then Rousseau's romantic view of the intrinsic goodness of human nature was surely carried forward by _some_ of the humanistic leaders. It is implied in Maslow's and Rogers' conceptions of self-actualization that provided an ideology for the "human potential" movement. (See Smith, 1973.)

Still, what can you do when students regularly respond to a comprehensive exam question on "Why do humanistic psychologists often look with favor on the contribution of Carl Jung?" by saying, mainly, "Because he had a positive, optimistic view of human nature?" Optimism is taken as an unquestioned good, and as _the_ defining criterion of humanistic psychology, so that alleged humanistic theorists are seen as optimistic regardless of how bad the fit. Optimism does not at all fit Jung, who surely transcends the optimism-pessimism dichotomy, nor, of course, does it fit Rollo May's existentialist strand of humanistic psychology with its special resonance to tragic aspects of the human condition. It does fit a recurrent American weakness for the Pollyanna perspective, which may understandably be activated in times like now that make it hard for the young to sustain rational hope--hard for their elders, too!

The Leadership of the Humanistic Psychology Movement

My bone to pick with the leadership of the humanistic psychology movement comes from my participation in a 1975 conference on theory in humanistic psychology organized by Rollo May and Fred Massarik (Gilbert, 1975). The transcendental, "transpersonal" preoccupations of many of the participants --among them, Arthur Deikmen, Stan Grof, Willis Harman, Stanley Krippner, Claudio Naranjo, Jonas Salk, and Huston Smith--captured much of the conference discussion, tending to eclipse the more wordly orientations of such participants as Gregory Bateson, Kenneth Benne, and Frank Severin. (I don't expect the surviving participants to accept this crude dichotomy!) I sensed much essentially religious yearning, which makes me suspicious of the movement's openness to extra sensory perception and its commitments to Eastern religion (not, mind you, its _interest in_ Eastern religion, from which psychology has much to learn).

Putting matters tactfully, I was recorded as saying in summary comments at the end of the conference:

> I have been struck by the extent to which we have been preoccupied with the esoteric, with the outer boundaries, with the growing edges, rather to the detriment of our consideration of the humanistic psychology of everyday life here on . . . earth. I do think there's a job there. Academic, conventional psychology has been inept and needs help in dealing with it. For us to be of help may require some balance in our concern with placing our metapsychology in a cosmic framework and our fascination with the esoteric edges. Carl (Rogers') remarks last night suggest that when one is looking at the humanistic psychology of everyday life, some of the polarities such as freedom and determinism begin to vanish in syntheses. I think, for example, that one could interpret what Carl was saying as a determinist account of how one engenders freedom. This is indeed what a scientifically conceived humanistic psychology of concrete everyday life could contribute. . . . I question whether some of our concern with reattaining a cosmic subordination of man to a greater universal scheme may not be more interpretable in terms of our fright at the isolation of man in the rather terrifying present situation. (Smith, in Gilbert, 1975, pp. 54-55)

In a word, it seemed to me that much of the leadership of the humanistic psychology movement was running away from the human in search of the supernatural and divine.

Illustrative of this trend, which seems to me so opposed to a time-honored meaning of humanism, was the total neglect at the conference of one of the stellar figures in mid-century psychological humanism (though not humanistic psychology): Erich Fromm. Fromm's long and productive life has only recently come to an end, and I think he should be among the heroes of a proper humanistic psychology. His integration of nondoctrinaire Marxist and psychoanalytic thought in responsible ethical commentary and social criticism represents at its best the kind of humanism that is captured in the title of one of his earliest and finest books, *Man for Himself* (1947), which we ought to rephrase as human beings for *themselves*. There was also total neglect of the more academically focused humanism of Henry Murray (1981; Smith, 1982). And Nevitt Sanford, whose version of humanism encompasses the concerns of both Fromm and Murray, was conspicuously absent.

The humanistic current represented by these major figures has Renaissance roots in writers like Shakespeare and Montaigne who celebrated the wonders of earthly human life, and it can be traced through one of the major strands of existential humanistic writing from Nietzsche to Sartre to Camus. Human dignity inheres in taking responsibility for one's life and living it zestfully. Because of human mortality and human insufficiency, the aspiration to do so has as aspect of inherent tragedy. In this tradition, the sense of tragedy goes with the worth and deeper meaning of being human.

To a considerable extent, as I've said, the humanistic movement fostered a bland optimism that is antithetical to the tragic. But its transcendental tendencies also linked it with another strand of existential-humanistic thought, one that might be evoked by the classical names of Pascal and Kierkegaard, and the lesser recent name of Ernest Becker (1973). This tradition saw human insufficiency as more saliently irremediable, and via various detours found its answer in religious faith. In this view of the human situation, people who aspire to make their own choices, to stand on their own feet, and to assert their own value--their own values, are presumptuous, inauthentic, and unredeemed.

I am elaborating on this particular bone that I have to pick with official humanistic psychology, because suddenly it has become relevant to value controversies in the public domain. The tradition of Erich Fromm, Henry Murray, and Nevitt Sanford, and of Shakespeare, Montaigne, Nietzsche, Sartre, and Camus is obviously that of _secular humanism_--the aptly baptized enemy of "prime time preachers" like Jerry Falwell (see Hadden and Swann, 1981). Most psychologists do not belong to the self-ascribed "moral majority," and we are mostly in such inadequate communication with the minority of people who think of themselves that way that the emergence of "secular humanism" as a bad thing comes as a big surprise. Unprepared as we may be, we Secular Humanists have to step forward now to accept the label with pride! We have to promulgate secular humanism as a Good, not an Evil!

Please do not misunderstand me: I do not want to impose a restrictive version of "secular humanism" upon humanistic psychology. Even if I wanted to,I couldn't! Rather, I am calling attention to the small and insufficient degree to which this important humanistic tradition, which is generally compatible with a scientific psychology, has been represented in the humanistic psychology movement. The polarity of Montaigne versus Pascal, Nietzsche versus Kierkegaard, Fromm versus Becker reflects dialectical complexities of the human condition which will continue to resist simple solution--and which, from either pole, make the Pollyanna bias of the human potential movement seem shallow and inadequate.

The Recent History of Humanistic Psychology

At this point, some perspective on recent history may be helpful. It is well known, of course, that humanistic psychology emerged as a movement at the old Saybrook Conference of 1964, "which brought together some 20 or 25 of the leading figures in psychology and the humanistic disciplines. Gardner Murphy was there, so was Harry Murray, Jacques Barzun, Rene DuBos, George Kelly, Abe Maslow, Gordon Allport, and Charlotte Buhler." (May, in Gilbert, 1975, p. 4). Carl Rogers, and Rollo May, whom I've been quoting, were also there. To continue with the quotation: "That conference developed out of the groundswell of protest against the theory of man of behaviorism on the one side and orthodox psychoanalysis on the other. That is why we are often called the Third Force. There was a feeling on all sides among different psychologists that neither of these two versions of psychology dealt with human beings as human. Nor did they deal with real problems of life. They left great numbers of people feeling alienated and empty. At the conference we discussed what the chief elements of humanistic psychology would be." (May, in Gilbert, 1975, p.4)

Note that at the inception of the humanistic psychology movement, the creators of American personality psychology--Allport, Murray, Murphy, and Kelly--took part, as well as the leaders of humanistic psychology in the next generation: Rogers, Maslow, and May, and some proper humanists, too! The older generation of personality psychologists were ready to join in a "Third Force," but they had not cast off anchor from scientific aspirations. Rather, they were dissatisfied with the main tendency of the psychological science of the time, and wanted to correct it.

What happened in sequel could not have been predicted. Almost immediately, the idea of humanistic psychology got swept up in the counter-cultural movement of the 1960's, with its irrationalist, transcendental, antinominal, and drug-oriented features. The older academic leaders dropped out of the movement, some in dismay. Esalen emerged and thrived. The "culture of seekership" seemed momentarily to be "greening" America (Reich, 1970; Kanter, 1972; Smith, 1978a). In humanistic psychology, the now-dominating counter cultural features led to its further alienation from scientific and academic psychology. By the end of the 1970's, humanistic psychology had become quite isolated from the academic mainstream--and it had also lost much of the thrust of excitement that had come from its participation in the counter-culture, now scattered and spent though leaving enduring marks. It is this alienated, isolated movement that mainly speaks for humanistic psychology today. It is time for a change!

The situation in psychology today is very different from what is was when the "Third Force" embarked on its unplanned trajectory in the early

1960's. Hardnosed scientific psychology has changed. Cognitive psychology, advanced by the same sort of toughminded scientists, has superseded behaviorism. Thought, consciousness, even mind have become respectable in scientific psychology. The fashionable computer metaphor of information processing is obviously a large advance from a humanistic perspective, in comparison with the telephone switchboard that lurked behind the cruder mechanism of S-R behaviorism. Psychoanalysis, on its part, is now out of fashion inside and outside of psychology. But it has also benefitted indirectly from the impact of information science in its clearer understanding of the difference between "real" physical energy and wholly metaphorical psychic energy--with many theorists entirely giving up psychic energy as misleading (Holt, 1972; Schafer, 1976). A new focus on selfhood has emerged (Kohut, 1971). Altogether, the less popular psychoanalysis of today is far less dogmatic and physicalistic, much more open to humanistic concerns. In the meantime, the eclipse of personality psychology--as exemplified in the erstwhile extreme situationism of Mischel (1968)--has been followed by a Phoenix-like rebirth. A vigorous psychology of personality is again in view. (See Epstein, 1979, 1980; Tomkins, 1980.) So the grounds that led the "Third Force" to secede have been modified substantially in the course of two decades.

Yet this hopeful characterization overlooks enormous difficulties that remain in the way of realizing the objectives of the founders of humanistic psychology, as expressed in my quotation from Rollo May. Cognitive psychology with its flow-charts is still preoccupied with details of unsynthesized models that are far from comprehending human self-awareness. Information-processing psychology substantially remains a promise rather than a fully realized achievement and as yet it has not begun to encompass the life of affect and human values. Psychoanalysis remains heavily sectarian. As for the psychology of personality, though it is once more legitimate, it lacks consensual models, and for purposes of teaching, it remains stuck in the eclecticism of the proliferating editions of Hall and Lindzey (1978). In this situation, there is still a challenging role for psychologists who regard themselves as humanists, and who want to make the science and profession of psychology more humanistic. What, in the present psychological scene, might we intelligibly mean by a humanistic approach? I offer a personal vision, hoping that it may have some consensual appeal.

A Vision of a Humanistic Approach

The first part of my vision is a matter of context. I agree with Sigmund Koch (1976) that the ambition to create a single coherent science of psychology, whether Newtonian or Einsteinian, has been a disastrous will-o'-the-wisp. It has led us away from humanly and scientifically significant problems, rather than toward them. In making the point that we would do better to think of an array of loosely linked psychological studies, Koch likes to assume the role of iconoclast. Erstwhile behaviorists cannot stand him, and he takes pleasure in offending humanistic psychologists, too (Koch, 1971). But Howard Kendler (1981), who still shows attachment to his origins in the neo-behaviorism of Spence, arrives at much the same judgment. To me, abandoning the goal of creating <u>the</u> science of psychology is only liberating, freeing us from vulnerable pretense and needless self-castigation.

Among the psychological studies, some are very close to biology and physiology, and unquestionably belong to the natural sciences. Others border on the humanities, and just as clearly require interpretive methods if they are to be pursued intelligently at all. According to this view, which I am urging, there is no more reason to expect a monolithic, coherent, and encompassing humanistic psychology than there is to call unrealistically for such a unified psychological science. There is room for both reductionist and holistic approaches. Like the psychological studies generally, humanistic psychology can afford to be open and undogmatic in regard to subject matter and method, much in the spirit of William James near the origins of our discipline. It cannot afford to be otherwise! (Surely one of the bitterest lessons to be learned from the history of psychology is the high cost of its dogmatic exclusions in the name of science, whether in the introspectionism of Titchener or the behaviorism of Watson--to name two of our more disastrous dogmatists.) There should be less occasion for humanistic psychologists to regard themselves as an embattled "Third Force" in such an open and tolerant conception of the larger field.

So much for a context that should be conducive to the release of creativity. It need not imply chaotic formlessness or lack of direction. Given the present lay of the land in the psychological studies, I have several suggestions in regard to foci for humanistic emphasis.

In the first place, a humanistic psychology has special responsibility to keep windows open on actual human experience. In the past, the special window afforded by the helping relationship of psychotherapy has played an enormous role in providing the basis for such understanding as we have attained of human psychology. Imperfect, unreliable, distorting, yes, but indispensible. As concern with therapy becomes more technical, we will continue to need psychologists of broad sympathy and curiosity to tell us about ourselves as we and the world change.

Another window, that provided by the arts and letters, has been much less used by psychologists. Humanistic psychologists have mostly not been humanists! The loss is ours. Henry Murray (1981) is the outstanding exception. I have in mind not only artistic and literary products as sources of insight into contemporary and historical human experience, but also the literature of criticism and interpretation that has been concerned with psychological issues. A human psychology that is uninformed about the cultural crises of modernity as these are revealed in contemporary arts and letters risks superficiality and irrelevance.

Of course these distinctively humanistic windows are not the only or even necessarily the main sources of knowledge for the aspects of psychology that are humanistic in the sense of aspiring to contribute to human self-understanding. For too long, our methods have played an inappropriate role in defining psychology. Methods should follow from questions, goals, and contexts, in humanistic psychology as in psycholgical studies generally.

The Consciousness of Self

Among the questions and goals that presently seem to me central to the humanistic side of psychology are those involved in attaining a better understanding of the reflexive, self-referential aspects of human consciousness--to revert to William James' (1890) chapter heading, "The Consciousness of Self." In another essay (Smith, 1985) I have struggled to carry forward one more step my earlier efforts (Smith, 1978b, 1980) to bring evolutionary, historical, cross-cultural, and developmental research and scholarship to bear on the emergence and nature of selfhood. I argue for the centrality in the very constitution of selfhood of culturally provided systems of metaphor of the kind recently analyzed by Lakoff and Johnson (1980). The conception I just voiced that a humanistic psychology should "contribute to human self-understanding" presupposes self-referential reflectiveness, and assumes that self-understanding has consequences that can enhance human freedom--maybe dignity too!

There are many paths to a better understanding of self-reference in consciousness. Thus, Hofstadter's (1979) _Gödel, Escher, Bach_ is a first-rate contribution to humanistic psychology. Its playful but serious extrapolation from a theory of Artificial Intelligence focuses on the logico-mathematical problems involved in self-reference in a way that is most refreshing for a psychological reader. Human self-reference--more generally, human consciousness--involves cultural symbol systems, through which people in each culture maintain a meaningful, coherent, and livable interpretation of self and world. It follows that the aspects of psychological studies that deal with phenomena affected by how we construe our selves, how we construe one another and the world--and that includes most of personality and social psychology--have to attend to the cultural and historical context, if they are to be faithful to their scientific task. So personality and social psychology are in an odd position among the disciplines, There is a hackneyed distinction, first promulgated by Dilthey, between the natural sciences built around the enterprise of causal explanation, and the human or mental or cultural studies built around meaningful interpretation and understanding--put another way, the distinction between concern with causes and with reasons. It seems to me increasingly clear that personality and social psychology have no choice but to face <u>both</u> ways, to choose <u>both</u> strategies. (See Smith, 1978c.) That our self-<u>interpretations</u> do make a causal difference, and can be referred to causal antecedents, is manifestly the case, as the large recent literature on locus of control and attributional processes amply documents (for example, Baum and Singer, 1980). The applied areas linked to personality and social psychology--clinical, counseling, industrial, and the like--are inextricably committed to the causal framework, since their practitioners trade in bringing about desired changes; and (except for the strong counter-current of behavior modification with its investments in the former world-view of positivism) the applied areas are mostly committed by their human focus to strategies of interpretation as well.

Psychology has only begun to work through the implications of this view of its task insofar as it concerns human persons. Gergen (1973, 1982) launched a major controversy in social psychology about its essentially historical nature--a controversy that has still to see its full fruition. As for the psychology of personality, it has yet to be reviewed from a culturally and historically sophisticated perspective (Smith, 1985), but it seems obvious (to me) that some of the rather sterile arguments between, say, Freudian theory and role theory of personality look quite different from a perspective that regards the content and perhaps even the organizing framework of selfhood as open to cultural difference and historic change. As interactionist personality psychology arises from the ashes of situationism, I hope it will show more sophistication about these matters than was apparent in the relatively culture-bound past enshrined in Hall and Lindzey (1978).

The Study of Life-Span Human Development

I bring to a close this personal shopping list of current and needed developments to advance the humanistic aspect of the psychological studies by calling your attention to the relevance of a major contemporary current that is still gaining momentum: the study of life-span human development (see Lerner and Busch-Rossnagel, 1981). In a number of respects, this interdisciplinary movement in which psychologists have played a central part is contributing in novel ways and sensibly to humanistic science. Its concern with the whole life course regains an essential ingredient of the holistic perspective in the study of lives as engaged by Murray and Sanford. It sees human lives as undergoing individual development and aging while embedded in the society with which they interact and participating in historical social change. Its distinctive methodological ideal--so-called cohort-sequential longitudinal design--is concerned with teasing apart inferences about the effects of being born into history at a particular time, the effects of having lived so many years, and those assignable to something peculiar to the time when any data under consideration were collected--the familiar cohort, age, and period effects. So it is much concerned with people's role in history, both as doers and as done to. As the movement has developed, it has called into question earlier assumptions about the stability of people's psychological characteristics, and about the determinative impact of early experience: perhaps incidental features of the movement that nevertheless align it with the sense promoted by humanists in psychology that people can and should do something about their lives (Brim and Kagan, 1980; Lerner and Busch-Rossnagel, 1981).

I began this consideration of psychology and humanism with complaints about the humanistic psychology movement, concerning its predilection for a blandly optimistic view of human nature, and its insufficient regard for the "secular humanism" so well represented by Nevitt Sanford, Henry Murray, and Erich Fromm--and I should now like to add Isidor Chein (1972), another recent major loss to psychology. I saw the movement as having been deflected after its founding by the leading personality psychologists of the '60's. Now, I claimed, the movement is running out of steam, and it is propitious to try to capture the banner of Humanistic Psychology for new endeavors that can find their place in a more open and tolerant, less dogmatically restrictive family of psychological studies.

I stressed in particular the essentially humanistic problem of understanding and formulating the nature and implications of the reflexiveness of human self-consciousness. The implications for personality psychology as it is reborn seem important to me. The enthusiastic new perspective of life-span human development is sensitively attuned to the two-way street of people's participation in society and history. It could provide a new frame for studies of the formative symbolic ingredients of selfhood that I have especially been urging.

REFERENCES

Adorno, T.W., Frenkel-Brunswik, E., Levinson, D.J., & Sanford, R.N. *The Authoritarian Personality*. New York: Harper and Row, 1950.

Baum, A. & Singer, J.E. (Eds.). *Advances in Evironmental Psychology: Applications of Personal Control*. Hillsdale, New Jersey: Erlbaum, 1980.

Becker, E. *The Denial of Death*. New York: Free Press, 1973.

Brim, O.G., Jr. & Kagan, J. (Eds). *Constancy and Change in Human Development*. Cambridge: Harvard University Press, 1980.

Chein, I. *The Science of Behavior and the Image of Man*. New York: Basic Books, 1972.

Epstein, S. "The Stability of Behavior: I. On Predicting Most of the People Most of the Time." *Journal of Personality and Social Psychology*, 1979, *37*, 1097-1126.

Epstein, S. "The Stability of Behavior: II. Implications for Psychological Research." *American Psychologist*, 1980, *35*, 790-806.

Farson, R. "The Technology of Humanism." *Journal of Humanistic Psychology*, 1978, *18* (2), 5-35.

Fromm, E. *Man For Himself: An Inquiry Into the Psychology of Ethics*. New York: Rinehart, 1947.

Gergen, K. "Social Psychology as History." *Journal of Personality and Social Psychology*, 1973, *26*, 309-320.

Gergen, K. *Toward Transformation in Social Knowledge*. New York: Springer-Verlag, 1982.

Hadden, J.K. & Swann, C.E. *Prime Time Teachers: The Rising Power of Televangelism*. Reading, Massachusetts: Addison-Wesley, 1981.

Hall, C. & Lindzey, G. *Theories of Personality* (3rd Edition). New York: Wiley, 1978.

Hofstadter, D.R. *Gödel, Escher, Bach: An External Golden Braid*. New York: Basic Books, 1979.

Holt, R.R. "Freud's Mechanistic and Humanistic Images of Man." In R.R. Holt and E. Peterfreund (Eds.), *Psychoanalysis and Contemporary Science*, 1972, *1*, 3-24.

James, W. "The Consciousness of Self." In *Principles of Psychology* (Vol. 1), New York: Holt, 1980.

Kanter, R.M. *Commitment and Community*. Cambridge, Massachusetts: Harvard University Press, 1972.

Kendler, H.H. *Psychology: A Science in Conflict*. New York: Oxford University Press, 1981.

Koch, S. "The Image of Man Implicit in Encounter Group Therapy." *Journal of Humanistic Psychology*, 1971, *11* (2), 109-128.

Koch, S. "Language Communities, Search Cells, and the Psychological Studies." In J.K. Cole and W.J. Arnold (Eds.), Nebraska Symposium on Motivation. Lincoln, Nebraska: University of Nebraska Press, 1976.

Kohut, H. The Analysis of the Self. New York: International Universities Press, 1971.

Lakoff, G. & Johnson, M. Metaphors We Live By. Chicago: University of Chicago Press, 1980.

Lerner, R.M.& Busch-Rossnagel, N. (Eds.). Individuals as Producers of their Development: A Life-Span Perspective. New York: Academic Press, 1981.

Mischel, W. Personality and Assessment. New York: Wiley, 1968.

Murray, H.A. Explorations in Personality. New York: Oxford University Press, 1938.

Murray, H.A. & Shneidman, E.S. (Eds.). Endeavors in Psychology. New York: Harper and Row, 1981.

Reich, C.A. The Greening of America. New York: Random House, 1970.

Sanford, N. (Ed.). The American College: A Psychological and Social Interpretation of the Higher Learning. New York: Wiley, 1962.

Schafer, R. A New Language for Psychoanalysis. New Haven, Conn.: Yale University Press, 1976.

Smith, M.B. "On Self-Actualization: A Transambivalent Examination of a Focal Problem in Maslow's Psychology." Journal of Humanistic Psychology, 1973, 13 (2), 17-33.

Smith, M.B. "Encounter Groups and Humanistic Psychology." In K.W. Back (Ed.), In Search of Community: Encounter Groups and Social Change. Denver, Colorado: Westview Press, 1978a.

Smith, M.B. "Perspectives on Selfhood." American Psychologist, 1978b, 33, 1053-1063.

Smith, M.B. "Humanism and Behaviorism in Psychology: Theory and Practice." Journal of Humanistic Psychology, 1978c, 18 (1), 27-36.

Smith, M.B. "Landmarks in the Literature: The Psychology of Prejudice. (Retrospective Review Essay on T.W. Adorno and others, The Authoritarian Personality, and G.W. Allport, The Nature of Prejudice)." New York University Education Quarterly, 1978d, 9 (No. 2), 29-32.

Smith, M.B. "Attitudes, Values, and Selfhood." In H.E. Howe, Jr., and M.M. Page (Eds.), Nebraska Symposium on Motivation. Lincoln, Nebraska: University of Nebraska Press, 1980.

Smith, M.B. "Psychology and Humanism." Journal of Humanistic Psychology, 1982a, 22 (2), 44-55.

Smith, M.B. "Psychology Encompasses a Wide Range of Concerns, Including Human Values." In "Symposium on Aspects of the Personological System of Henry A. Murray." Personality and Social Psychology Bulletin, 1982b, 8, 619-623.

Smith, M.B. "The Metaphorical Basis of Selfhood." In A. Marsella, G. DeVos, and F. Hsu (Eds.), _Culture and Self_. New York" Methuen (Tavistock Publication), 1985.

Tomkins, S. "The Rise, Fall, and Resurrection of the Study of Personality." Paper presented at the meetings of the American Psychological Association, Montreal, September, 1980.

Bibliography of Nevitt Sanford

PERSONALITY THEORY AND HUMAN PROBLEMS

"Psychological Work at the Norfolk Prison Colony." _Psychological Exchange_, 1935.

"Some Leads for Research in Adolescent Development." _Proceedings, Biennial Meeting, Society for Research in Child Development_. Washington, D.C.: Society for Research in Child Development, 1936.

"The Effects of Abstinence From Food Upon Imaginal Processes: A Preliminary Experiment." _Journal of Psychology_, 1936, _2_, 129-136.

"The Effects of Abstinence From Food Upon Imaginal Processes: A Further Experiment." _Journal of Psychology_, 1937, _3_, 145-159.

"Observation of Experiments and Post-Experimental Interviews." In H.A. Murray (Ed.), _Explorations in Personality_. New York: Oxford University Press, 1938.

"An Experiment to Test the Validity of the Rorschach Test." (with M. Adkins and E. Cobb) _Psychological Bulletin_, 1939, _36_, 662 (abstract).

"The Analysis of Qualitative Records in Longitudinal Studies of Child Development." _Proceedings, Biennial Meeting, Society for Research in Child Development_. Washington, D.C.: Society for Research in Child Development, 1940.

"Some Quantitative Results From the Analysis of Children's Stories." _Psychological Bulletin_, 1941, _8_, 749 (abstract).

The Thematic Apperception Test: A Manual of Directions for Scoring and Interpretation. (with R.W. White) Cambridge: Harvard University, Harvard Psychological Clinic, 1941.

"Some Correlates of the Harding Morale Scale." _Psychological Bulletin_, 1942, _39_, 614 (abstract).

"American Conscience and the Coming Peace." _Journal of Abnormal and Social Psychology_, 1943, _38_, 158-165.

"A Psychoanalytic Study of Three Types of Criminals." _Journal of Criminal Psychopathology_, 1943, _5_, 57-59.

"Personality Correlates of Morale: Evidence From Individual Cases." _Journal of Personality_, 1943, _12_, No.3, 207-227.

"Personality Patterns in School Children." In R. Barker, J. Kounin and E. Wright (Eds.), _Child Behavior and Development_, New York:McGraw-Hill,1943.

Physique, Personality and Scholarship. (with M. Adkins, D. Miller, and E. Cobb) Monograph of the Society for Research in Child Development, 1943, 8, No. 1.

"Psychological Approaches to the Young Delinquent." Journal of Consulting Psychology, 1943, 7, 223-229.

"Scales for the Measurement of War Optimism: I. Military Optimism; II. Optimism on Consequences of the War." (with H.S. Conrad) Journal of Psychology, 1943, 16, 285-316.

"Some Personality Correlates of Morale." (with H.S. Conrad) Journal of Abnormal and Social Psychology, 1943, 38, 3-20.

"Some Specific War Attitudes of the College Students." (with H.S. Conrad) Journal of Psychology, 1944, 17, 153-185.

"On Being a Father." In Irwin Child (Ed.), Psychology for the Returning Service Men. London: Penguin, 1945.

"Age as a Factor in the Recall of Interrupted Tasks." Psychological Review, 1946, 53, 234-240.

"Optimism and Religion." American Psychologist, 1946, 1, 451 (abstract).

"Psychological Determinants of Optimism Regarding Consequences of the War." (with H.S. Conrad and K. Franck) Journal of Psychology, 1946, 22, 207-235.

"Recommended Graduate Training Programs in Clinical Psychology." (with E. Hilgard, L. Kelley, B. Luckey, T. Shaffer, and D. Shakow) American Psychologist, 1947, 2, 539-558.

"Clinical Training Facilities." Report of the Committee on Training in Clinical Psychology." (with E. Hilgard, L. Kelly, B. Luckey, L. Shaffer, and D. Shakow) American Psychologist, 1948, 3, 315-318.

"Physical and Physiological Correlates of Personality Structure." In C. Kluckhohn and H.A. Murray (Eds.), Personality in Nature, Society, and Culture. New York: Knopf, 1948.

"Psychotherapy and Counseling." Journal of Consulting Psychology, 1948, 12, 65-67.

"Relapse Into Old Habits." In G. Murphy (Ed.), Human Nature and Enduring Peace. New York: Holt, 1948.

"The Interview." In the Office of Strategic Services Assesment Staff (Ed.), The Assesment of Man. New York: Rinehart, 1948.

"What Are the Conditions of Self-Defensive Forgetting?" (with J.J. Risser) Journal of Personality, 1948, 17, 244-260.

"Preface." In B. Aron, Manual for Scoring the Thematic Apperception Test. Berkeley: Willis Berg, 1950.

"Masculinity-Femininity in the Structure of Personality." Proceedings, International Congress of Psychology, Stockholm, 1951.

"Clinical Methods: Psychotherapy." Annual Review of Psychology. Stanford, CA: Annual Reviews, 1953, 4, 317-342.

"The Interview in Personality Appraisal." Proceedings of the Invitational Conference on Testing Problems. Educational Testing Service, Princeton, N.J., 1953. (Also in A. Anastasi (Ed.), Testing Problems in Perspective. Washington, D.C.: American Council on Education, 1966.)

"Family Impact on Personality: The Point of View of a Psychoanalyst." In J.E. Hulett and R. Stagner (Eds.), Problems in Social Psychology. Urbana, Illinois: University of Illinois Press, 1954.

"Introduction: Symposium on Social Variables in Personality Determination." Montreal: Proceedings of the International Congress of Psychology, 1954.

"The Dynamics of Identification." Psychological Review, 1955, 62, 106-118.

"Clinical and Actuarial Prediction in a Setting of Action Research." Proceedings of the 1955 Invitational Conference on Testing Problems. Princeton: Educational Testing Service, 1956.

"Psychotherapy and the American Public." In M.E. Krout (Ed.), Psychology, Psychiatry, and the Public Interest. Minneapolis: University of Minnesota Press, 1956.

"Surface and Depth in the Individual Personality." Psychological Review, 1956, 63, 349-359.

"What Should One Tell?" Newsletter of the Society for the Psychological Study of Social Issues, May 1956.

"Freud and American Psychology." Sociological Review (British), 1957, 6, 49-66.

"Mental Illness and Health: The Point of View of Child Development." Proceedings, 1957 Mental Health Forum. New York: Mental Health Council,

"The New Social Science and Its Critics." The Humanist, 1957, 2, 83-93.

"Foreword." In M. Deutsch (Ed.), Role of the Social Sciences in Desegregation. New York: Anti-Defamation League, 1958.

"Foreword." In E. Maccoby, T. Newcomb, and E. Hartley (Eds.), Readings in Social Psychology. New York: Holt, 1958.

"Discussion of Papers: T.S. Szasz, A Critical Analysis of Some Aspects of the Libido Theory, and E. Pumpian-Mindlin, Propositions Concerning Energetic-Economic Aspects of Libido Theory." In L. Bellak (Ed.), Conceptual and Methodological Problems in Psychoanalysis. Annals of the New York Academy of Science, 1959, 76, 990-996.

"The Development of the Healthy Personality in the Society of Today." In Modern Mental Health Concepts and Their Application in Public Health Education. Berkeley: University of California, School of Public Health, 1959.

"Notes on the Recognition of Excellence." In A. Yarmolinsky (Ed.), The Recognition of Excellence. Washington: Stern Family Fund, 1960.

"Creativity and Conformity." In D.W. MacKinnon (Ed.), The Creative Person. Berkeley: University of California, Institute of Personality Assessment and Research, 1961.

"Research Problems Relating to Measuring Personality Change in Psychotherapy." In H. Strupp and L. Luborsky (Eds.), Second Conference on Research in Psychotherapy. Washington: American Psychological Association, 1962.

"What is a Normal Personality?" In J. Katz, P. Nochlin, and R. Stover, (Eds.), Writers on Ethics. New York: Van Nostrand, 1962.

"The Freeing and Acting Out of Impulse in Late Adolescence: Evidence From Two Cases." In R.W. White (Ed.), The Study of Lives: Essays on Personality in Honor of Henry A. Murray. New York: Atherton, 1963.

"Ego Processes in Learning." In N. Lambert and others (Eds.), The Protection and Promotion of Mental Health in Schools. Washington: Public Health Service Publication #1226, Mental Health Monograph #5, U.S. Department of Health, Education and Welfare, 1964.

"Individual Conflict and Organizational Interaction." In R.L. Kahn and Elise Boulding (Eds.), Power and Conflict in Organizations. New York: Basic Books, 1964.

"Personality: Its Place in Psychology." In S. Koch (Ed.), Psychology: A Study of a Science. New York: McGraw-Hill, 1964.

"Preface." In R. Blum and E. Blum, The Utopiates: An Epidemiological Study of Drug Use. New York: Atherton, 1964.

"The Alcohol Problem." Menninger Quarterly, 1964, 18, No.4, 12-21.

"Changing Drinking Patterns Among American Youth." Bulletin of the Society of Medical Friends of Wine, 1965, 7.

"Social Science and Social Reform," Journal of Social Issues, 1965, 21, 54-70.

"The Prevention of Mental Illness." In B.B. Wolman (Ed.),Handbook of Clinical Psychology. New York: McGraw-Hill, 1965.

"Will Psychologists Study Human Problems?" American Psychologist, 1965, 20, 192-202.

"Conceptions of Alcoholism." In S. Cahn (Ed.), Treatment Methods and Milieus in Social Work With Alcoholics. Berkeley: Social Welfare Extension, University of California, 1966.

"Psychiatry Viewed From the Outside: The Challenge of the Next Ten Years." American Journal of Psychiatry, 1966, 123, 519-522.

"Psychological and Developmental Aspects of the Adolescent Years as They Apply to the Use of Alcohol." In H.B. Bruyn (Ed.), Alcohol and College Youth. Berkeley: American College Health Association, 1966.

Self and Society: Social Change and Individual Development. New York: Atherton Press, 1966.

"The Study of Human Problems as an Approach to Greater Knowledge About Man." In J. Fishman (Ed.), Expanding Horizons of Knowledge About Man: A Symposium. New York: Ferkauf Graduate School of Humanities and Social Sciences, Yeshiva University, 1966.

"Cognition and Personality Development." In E.M. Bower and W. Hollister (Eds.), Behavioral Science Frontiers in Education. New York: McGraw-Hill, 1967.

"The Development of Social Responsibility." American Journal of Orthopsychiatry, 1967, 37, 22-29.

"The Influence of Social-Personality Theory on Research in Smoking Behavior: Overview." In S.V. Zagona (Ed.), Studies and Issues in Smoking Behavior. Tucson, Arizona: The University of Arizona Press, 1967.

"The Public Image of Business: Up or Down? The Educator's Views." In Proceedings of the 10th Executives' Symposium. Moraga, California: St. Mary's College, 1967.

"Drinking and Personality." In J. Katz (Ed.), No Time for Youth. San Francisco: Jossey-Bass, 1968.

"I Know How It Is Done But I Just Can't Do It: Discussion of Rollo May's Paper." In R.B. McLeod (Ed.), William James: Unfinished Business. Washington: American Psychological Association, 1968.

"Personality and Patterns of Alcohol Consumption." Journal of Consulting and Clinical Psychology, 1968, 32, 13-17.

"The Activists' Corner: On Human Problems and the University." Journal of Social Issues, July 1968, 24:3, 165-172. (with D. Krech)

"The Activists' Corner: On the Training of Clinicians to Society and Problem-Oriented Generalists." Journal of Social Issues, 1969, 25, 247-255. (with D. Krech)

"The Activists' Corner: On Activism as Engagement and Experience." Journal of Social Issues, 1969, 25, 155-164. (with D. Krech)

"The Activists' Corner: On the Question of Training in Social Psychology." Journal of Social Issues, 1969, 25, 189-197. (with R. Carlson)

"Community Actions and the Prevention of Alcoholism." In D. Adelson and B. Kalis (Eds.), Community Psychology and Mental Health. San Francisco: Chandler Publishing Company, 1970.

Issues in Personality Theory. San Francisco: Jossey-Bass, 1970.

"The Decline of Individualism." Public Health Reports, 1970, 85, 213-219.

"Whatever Happened to Action Research?" Journal of Social Issues, 1970, 26, No.4, 3-23.

"Foreword." In C. Leuba, A Road to Creativity. North Quincy, Massachusetts: Christopher, 1971.

"Is the Concept of Prevention Necessary or Useful?" In S. Golann and C. Eisdorfer (Eds.), _Handbook of Community Psychology_. New York: Appleton-Century-Crofts, 1972.

"Accountability for Planned Change: The Professional as a Change Agent." In Ruth Heflin (Ed.), _Proceedings of the Sixth Annual Meeting of the Association of Administrators of Home Economics_. Manhattan, Kansas: Kansas State University, 1973.

"A Perspective From Outside Anthropology." In E.A. Hoebel and R.L. Currier (Eds.), _American Social and Cultural Anthropology, Past and Future: Proceedings of the Conference at Spring Hill_, 1977.

"Foreword." In E. Koile, _Listening as a Way of Becoming_. Waco, Texas: Regency Books, 1977.

"The Founding of the Institute of Personality Assessment and Research." In H. Gough and D. MacKinnon (Eds.), _History and Present Status of Personality Assessment_. Berkeley: University of California, Institute of Personality Assessment and Research, 1977.

"The Founding of the Institute of Personality Assessment and Research," "Origins of Personality Assessment at the Harvard Psychological Clinic." In H. Gough and D. Mackinnon (Eds.), _History and Present Status of Personality Assessment_. Berkeley: University of California, Institute of Personality Assessment and Research, 1977.

"The Loss and Rediscovery of Moral Character." In G.J. DiRenzo (Ed.), _We The People: American Character and Social Change_. Westport, Connecticut: Greenwood Press, 1977.

AUTHORITARIAN PERSONALITY AND SOCIAL DESTRUCTIVENESS

"A Scale for the Measurement of Anti-Semitism." (with D. Levinson) _Journal of Psychology_, 1944, _17_, 339-370.

"Some Personality Factors in Anti-Semitism." (with E. Frenkel-Brunswik) _Journal of Psychology_, 1945, _20_, 271-291.

"Dominance Versus Autocracy and the Democratic Character." _Childhood Education_, 1946, _23_, 109-115.

"Identification With the Enemy: A Case Study of an American Quisling." _Journal of Personality_. 1946, _15_, 53-58.

"Should There Be a Quota System for Minority Groups?" (with D. Levinson) _Educational Forum_, January 1946, 217-235.

"The Anti-Democratic Individual." (with E. Frenkel-Brunswik and D. Levinson) In T. Newcomb and E. Harley (Eds.), _Readings in Social Psychology_. New York: Holt, 1947.

"The Measurement of Implicit Anti-Democratic Trends." *American Psychologist*, 1947, *2*, 412 (abstract).

"Ethnocentrism in Relation to Some Religious Attitudes and Practices." (with D. Levinson) *American Psychologist*, 1948, *3*, 350-351 (abstract).

The Authoritarian Personality. (with T.W. Adorno, E. Frenkel-Brunswik, and D. Levinson) New York: Harper, 1950.

"Individual and Social Change in a Community Under Pressure: The Oath Controversy." *Journal of Social Issues*, 1953, *9*, 25-42.

"Recent Developments in Connection With the Investigation of the Authoritarian Personality." *Sociological Review* (British), 1954, *1*, 11-33.

"A New Instrument for Studying Authoritarianism in Personality." (with M. Freedman and H. Webster) *Journal of Psychology*, 1955, *40*, 73-84.

"Some Psychodynamic Correlates of Authoritarianism in Women." (with M. Freedman and H. Webster) *American Psychologist*, 1955, *10*, 341 (abstract).

"A Study of Authoritarianism and Psychopathology." (with M. Freedman and H. Webster) *Journal of Psychology*, 1956, *41*, 315-322.

"The Approach of the Authoritarian Personality." In J.S. McCary (Ed.), *The Psychology of Personality*. New York: Logos Press, 1956.

"Toward a Critical Social Science: A Comment on the My Lai Massacre." (with E. Opton, Jr.) *Transaction*, 1970, *7*, 4-7.

"Collective Destructiveness and Dehumanization." *International Journal of Group Tensions*, 1971, *1*, 26-41.

Sanctions for Evil: Sources of Social Destructiveness. (Ed.), San Francisco: Jossey-Bass, 1971 (with C. Comstock).

"The Dynamics of Prejudice." In P. Watson (Ed.), *The Psychology of Racism*. London: Penguin, 1971.

"Collective Destructiveness: Sources and Remedies." In G. Usdin (Ed.), *Perspectives on Violence*. New York: Brunner/Mazel, 1972.

"Nevitt Sanford on Authoritarianism." *Psychology Today*, 1972, *6*, No.6, 96-98, 140-143.

"The Authoritarian Personality in Contemporary Perspective." In J. Knutson (Ed.), *Handbook of Political Psychology*. San Francisco: Jossey Bass, 1973.

HIGHER EDUCATION AND ADULT DEVELOPMENT

"We Study the Alumnae." *Vassar Alumnae Magazine*, December 1954, *39*.

"Research Programs in College Health, Report of the Chairman of Committee 15." *Proceedings of the Fourth National Conference on Health in Colleges*. New York: American College Health Association, 1955.

"Personality Development During the College Years." (with D. Brown, M. Freedman, and H. Webster) Journal of Social Issues, 1956, 12, 1-71.

"Personality Development During the College Years." Personnel-o-Gram. Washington: Proceedings of 1956 Annual Convention of American College Personnel Association, 1956.

"Impact of a Woman's College Upon Its Students." In A. Traxler (Ed.), Long-Range Planning for Education. Washington: American Council on Education, 1957.

"Impulse-Expression as a Variable in Personality." (with M. Freedman and H. Webster) Psychological Monographs, 1957, 71, 1-21.

"Is College Education Wasted on Women?" Ladies' Home Journal, May 1957.

"Report on the Vassar Research." In The American College Student. Washington: Proceedings of the 1957 Meeting of the Policies and Program Committee, American Council on Education, 1957.

"The Uncertain Senior." Journal of National Association of Women's Deans and Counselors, 1957, 21, 9-15.

"Changing Sex Roles, Socialization and Education." Human Development Bulletin. Chicago: Committee on Human Development, University of Chicago, 1958.

Social Science and Higher Education: A Comprehensive Bibliography. Boston: Researchers' Technical Bureau, 1958.

"The Mellon Research Program Today." Vassar Alumnae Magazine, October 1958, 43.

"The Professor Looks at the Student." In R. Cooper (Ed.), The Two Ends of the Log. Minneapolis: University of Minnesota Press, 1958.

"Knowledge of Students Through the Social Studies." In N. Brown (Ed.), Spotlight on the College Student. Washington: American Council on Education, 1959.

"Motivation of High Achievers." In O.D. David (Ed.), The Education of Woman: Signs for the Future. Washington: American Council on Education, 1959.

"A Psychologist Speculates About New Perspectives in Education for Citizenship." In F. Patterson (Ed.), The Adolescent Citizen. Glencoe, Illinois: The Free Press, 1960.

"Recent Social Change and Its Impact on Higher Education." Educational Record, 1960, 41, 335-338.

"The Development of Maturity of Personality in College." In T.R. McConnell (Ed.), Selection and Educational Differentiation. Berkeley: Field Service Center and Center for the Study of Higher Education, University of California, 1960.

"Theories of Higher Education and the Experimental College." In S. Harris (Ed.), Higher Education in the United States. Cambridge: Harvard University Press, 1960.

"Recent Research on the American College Student." In N. Brown (Ed.), Orientation to College Learning. Washington: American Council on Education, 1961.

"Education for Individual Development." Conference of Directors of College and University Counseling Services. Lincoln, Nebraska: Counseling Center, University of Nebraska, 1962.

"Ends and Means in Higher Education." In G.K. Smith (Ed.), Current Issues in Higher Education, 1962. Washington: American Association of Higher Education, 1962.

"General Education and the Theory of Personality Development." Proceedings of the Symposium on Undergraduate Development. Brunswik, Maine: Bowdoin College, 1962.

"Implications of Personality Studies for Curriculum and Personnel Planning." In R. Sutherland (Ed.), Personality Development on the College Campus. Austin, Texas: The Hogg Foundation, University of Texas, 1962.

The American College: A Psychological and Social Interpretation of the Higher Learning. New York: John Wiley, 1962.

"The Successful College." NEA Journal, November 1961.

"Today's Students Look at Themselves, Their Society, and Their Profession." Professional Imperatives: Report of 17th Annual TEPS Conference. New York: National Education Association, 1962.

"Discussion--Chaos in College Admissions." Changing Times, August 1963, 17, No.8, 17-20.

"Education and the Preservation of Freedom." In Proceedings of the 20th Annual Utah Conference on Higher Education. Cedar City, Utah: College of Southern Utah, 1963.

"Factors Related to the Effectiveness of Student Interaction With the College Social System." Proceedings of Conference on Higher Education and Mental Health. Gainesville, Florida: Student Health Service, University of Florida, 1963.

"Higher Education as a Social Problem." American Review, 1963, 3, 92.

"Measuring the Success of a College." In K. Wilson (Ed.), Research Related to College Admissions. Atlanta: Southern Regional Education Board, 1963.

"One Cheer for Excellence." The Intellectual Climate of the Liberal Arts College, Proceedings of the Claremont Conference of the Western Association of Schools and Colleges. Oakland, California: Western Association of Schools and Colleges, 1963.

"A New Approach to Liberal Education." Saturday Review, January 18, 1964, 62-64.

College and Character: A Briefer Version of "The American College." New York: John Wiley, 1964.

"College Students and Public Concern." Vassar Alumnae Magazine, Summer, 1964, 49.

"The College Our Times Require." Proceedings of the Asilomar Conference of San Francisco State University. San Francisco: San Francisco State University, 1964.

"Causes of the Student Revolution." (with J. Katz) Saturday Review, December 18, 1965, 48, No.51, 64-66.

"General Education and Personality Theory." Teachers' College Record, 1965, 66, 721-732.

"Morals on the Campus." NEA Journal, 1965, 54, 20.

"Students and the University's Purpose." President's Bulletin Board. Nashville, Tennessee: Division of Higher Education, Board of Education, The Methodist Church, 1965.

"The Human Problems Institute and General Education." Daedalus, 1965, 94, 642-662. (Reprinted in J. Kagan (Ed.), Creativity and Learning. Boston: Houghton-Mifflin, 1967.)

"Freedom and Authority in Higher Education." (with J. Katz) Comparative Education (British), March 1967, 3, No.2, 101-106.

"Needed: A Clearer Definition of Sex Roles." Women's Education, 1966, 5, 2.

"Sex and Drinking Among College Students: Prospects for a New Ethic." Old Oregon, 1966.

"Social Change and the College Student." In W.A. Geier (Ed.), Today's Student and His University. Nashville, Tennessee: Board of Education, The Methodist Church, 1966.

"The Size of the University and Its Implications." In W.A. Geier (Ed.), Today's Student and His University. Nashville, Tennessee: Board of Education, The Methodist Church, 1966.

"The Development of Social Responsibility Through the College Expxerience." In E.J. McGrath (Ed.), The Liberal Arts College's Respsonsibility for the Individual Student. New York: Institute for Higher Education, Teachers College, Columbia, 1966.

"The Great University in the Great Society." Proceedings of New York State Teachers' Association Higher Education Conference. Albany, New York: New York State Teachers Association, 1966.

"The New Student Power and Needed Reforms." (with J. Katz) Phi Delta Kappan, 1966, 47, 397-401.

"The Turbulent Years." (with J. Katz) Stanford Today, Winter, 1966, 7-11.

"Universal Higher Education: Implications for Education and for Adjustment of Curricula to Individual Students." In E.J. McGrath (Ed.),

Universal Higher Education. New York: McGraw-Hill, 1966.

"Innovation in Higher Education: Attacking the Issues." In W. Hamlin (Ed.), *Dimensions of Change in Higher Education*. Yellow Springs, Ohio: Union for Research and Experimentation in Higher Education, Antioch College, 1967.

"New Directions in Educating for Creativity." In P. Heist (Ed.), *Education for Creativity*. Berkeley: University of California Center for Research and Development in Higher Education, 1967.

"On Filling a Role and Being a Man." In K. Smith (Ed.), *In Search of Leaders: Current Issues in Higher Education*. Washington: American Association for Higher Education, 1967.

"The College Student of Today and Tomorrow." *Journal of the Association of Deans and Administrators of Student Affairs*, 1967, *5*, 221-228.

"The Generation Gap." *California Monthly*, 1967, *57*, 28-37.

"The Students We Teach Today." *The Journal of the Canadian Association of Student Personnel Services*, 1967, *1*, 8-16.

Where Colleges Fail: A Study of the Student as a Person. San Francisco: Jossey-Bass, 1967.

"A Failure of Authority." *Journal of the Canadian Council of Associations of University Student Personnel Services*, 1968, 3-15.

"College Seniors and Social Responsibility." NEA Journal, 1968, *57*, 52-54.

"Counseling: Emerging Role in Higher Education." In E. Garduk (Ed.), *New Dimensions of Student Personnel Work*. Washington: Howard University Press, 1968.

"Education for Individual Development." *American Journal of Orthopsychiatry*, 1968, *38*, 858-868.

Education for Individual Development. Washington: U.S. Office of Education, 1968.

"Education in 1968." In E. Underwood and J.D. Jordon (Eds.), *Crisis: Addresses Delivered at the Spring Symposium*. Mars Hill, North Carolina: Mars Hill College, 1968.

"Foreword." In W.B. Martin, *Alternative to Irrelevance*. Nashville, Tennessee: Abingdon Press, 1968.

"Preface." In R. Evans, *Resistance to Innovation in Higher Education*. San Francisco: Jossey-Bass, 1968.

"Personality Development and Creativity in the Soviet Union." In P. Heist (Ed.), *The Creative College Student*. San Francisco: Jossey-Bass, 1968.

"The Aims of College Education." In C.W. Havice (Ed.), *Campus Values*. New York: Scribner's, 1968.

"The College Student of 1980." In A.C. Eurich (Ed.), *Campus 1980: The Shape of the Future of American Higher Education*. New York: Dell, 1968.

"The University and the Life of the Student: The Next 100 Years." In J. Walsh (Ed.), The University in a Developing World Society. Notre Dame, Indiana: University of Notre Dame Press, 1968.

"What Is an Excellent Liberal Arts College?" In S.S. Letter (Ed.), New Prospects for the Small Liberal Arts College. New York: Teachers College Press, 1968.

"Making College More Educational and Less Custodial." Denver: Proceedings of the 1st Annual Meeting of the American Association of Presidents of Independent Colleges, 1969.

"Research With Students as Action and Education." American Psychologist, 1969, 24, 544-546.

Search for Relevance (with J. Axelrod, M. Freedman, W. Hatch, and J. Katz). San Francisco: Jossey-Bass, 1969.

"Students in University Government." In The De Young Lectures. Normal, Illinois: Illinois State University, 1969.

"Loss of Talent." In F.F. Har eroad (Ed.), Issues of the Seventies: Student Needs, Society's Concerns and Institutional Responses. San Francisco: Jossey-Bass, 1970.

"The Campus Crisis in Authority." Educational Record, Spring, 1970, 112-115.

"The Concept of Regional Centers for Ethnic Studies." Journal of the Association of Governing Boards of Colleges and Universities, 1970.

"The Contribution of Higher Education to the Life of Society." In R. Niblett (Ed.), Higher Education: Demand and Response, London: Tavistock, 1969; San Francisco: Jossey-Bass, 1970.

"Academic Culture and the Teacher's Development." Soundings , Winter, 1971-72, 357-371.

"Foreword." In A. Cohen and F. Brawner, Confronting Identity: The Community College Instructor. Englewood Cliffs, New Jersey: Prentice-Hall, 1971.

"Humanizing Education Beyond the High School." In K.C. Edson (Ed.), New Directions in Higher Education: Proceedings of the Nothern California Educational Conference. Iowa City, Iowa: ACT Publications, 1971.

"Science and Social Development." Education, 1971, 92, 1-8.

"The New Values and Faculty Response." In E. McGrath and R. Stine (Eds.), Prospects for Renewal. San Francisco: Jossey-Bass, 1972.

And a Time to Integrate. Lubbock, Texas: Texas Technical University Complex, 1973.

"The Faculty Member Yesterday and Today." (with M. Freedman) In M. Freedman (Ed.), Facilitating Faculty Development. New Directions in Higher Education, 1, 1-15. San Francisco: Jossey-Bass, 1973.

"The Role of Athletics in Student Development." (with K. Borgstrom and M. Lozoff). In J. Katz (Ed.), Services for Students. New Directions for Higher Education, 1973, 1 ,No.3, 51-68.

"Epilogue: Psychological Stress in the Campus Community." In B. Bloom (Ed.), Psychological Stress in the Campus Community. New York: Behavioral Publications, 1975.

"Graduate Education, Then and Now." In J. Katz and R. Hartnett (Eds.), Scholars in the Making: The Development of Graduate and Professional Students. Cambridge, Massachusetts: Ballinger Press, 1976. Also in the American Psychologist, 1976, 31, 756-764.

"The College Student in a Turbulent Society." In R. L. Simmons (Ed.), Proceedings of Annual Meeting of the Association of College Unions International, 1977.

College and Character: Revised Edition. (Ed.), (with J. Axelrod) Orinda, California: Montaigne, 1979.

Learning After College. Orinda, California: Montaigne, 1980.

"A Model for Action Research." In P. Reason and J. Rowan (Eds.), Human Inquiry: A Sourcebook of New Paradigm Research. New York: Wiley, 1981.

"The Approach of the American College." American Journal of Education, 1981, 90, 99-102.

"Foreword." In A. Chickering (Ed.), The Modern American College. San Francisco: Jossey-Bass, 1981.

"Personology (as Well as the Personolgist) Is Shaped by Many and Varied Sources." Personality and Social Psychology Bulletin, 1982, 8, 605-608.

The Authoritarian Personality: Abridged Edition. New York: Norton, 1982 (with D.J. Levinson).

"Foreword." In J.M. Whiteley, Character Development in College Students. Schenectady, New York: Character Research Press, 1982.

"Some Introductory Notes." In S. Riess (Ed.), The Oral History of Mary Cover Jones. Berkeley: University of California Regional Oral History Office, 1982.

"Social Psychology: Its Place in Personology." American Psychologist, 1982, 37, 896-903.

"Gordon Allport and I." Personality Forum, 1983, 1.

"This Week's Citation Classic (The Authoritarian Personality)." Current Contents, 1984, 16, 16.

"What Have We Learned About Personality?" In S. Koch and D. Leary (Eds.), A Century of Psychology as Science. New York: McGraw-Hill, 1985.

"Some Recollections of the Free Speech Movement." Journal of Counseling and Development, 1985, 64, 14-18.

Index

S

T

V

W

Z